REMEMBERING
AWAKE

How to Love and Play Creation with Y/our Soul

JULIE FOSTER, MD

Pen & Publish
Saint Louis, Missouri

Published by Pen & Publish, LLC, USA

Saint Louis, Missouri
(314) 827-6567
www.PenandPublish.com
info@PenandPublish.com

Print ISBN: 978-1-956897-51-7
ebook ISBN: 978-1-956897-52-4
Library of Congress Control Number: 2024945226

Cover and interior mandala illustrations by Gail Alexander (gail-alexander.com).

This book is dedicated to our soul.

We are timeless beings playing creation in at least 144,000 dimensions, and we have forgotten how magical we are.

When we agreed to have consciousness in this dimension, we agreed to do so with a profound case of amnesia.

We are beings who create our realities with the vibration of unconditional love.

We are in a period of cosmic grace where the veil of fear responsible for our amnesia is evaporating as we have begun to understand that fear is just another vibration of love.

I hope this book helps you greet the remembering of just how magnificent your fractal of our soul is with a little more ease and grace than I did when I awakened.

I hope that every fractal of our soul in all timelines eventually remembers that we are constantly in a symphony of creation that is always beautiful.

However, when the symphony of our soul is in the harmony of singularity, there are no words to describe the bliss of this loving cohesion.

In this muted state of surrender, your beautiful mind will be able to start to comprehend how much it is loved and thus soften into a state of vulnerability where your energetic field feels safe enough to love open your heart so that the connection to the glorious oneness of our soul is never lost.

I love you all and am profoundly grateful for the awe-inspiring note you are playing in our symphony.

Thank you for the brilliance and courage you grace our soul with.

It is an honor to play the game of Earth with your brilliant spectrum of loving light.

Contents

FOREWORD
Jenniffer Weigel

We have a choice in how we show up in the world. If you've picked up this book, I would guess you are choosing to dive into your path as a healer. And luckily for you, Dr. Julie Foster has moved at lightning speed to embrace her gifts, combining her traditional role as medical doctor with her expanding multidimensional healing abilities.

To know Julie is to love her zest for a spiritual life, and her deep desire to activate her God particle within. As a teacher in my Spiritual Social Club online community, I have watched her move mountains (and birth universes) to the benefit of all who attend her classes. I tell her she is a Tesla, while oftentimes the rest of us feel like a stick shift trying to get into third gear. To watch her absorb the latest technologies and bring them to the foreground of our group has been both inspiring and impressive. I can imagine her as a child, being voted "Most Likely to Succeed" with her tenacity and thirst for knowledge. I learned a long time ago that you can't give what you don't have, and Julie is filling her toolbox with knowledge to get you where you need to be as you lug around your "human suit" in our 3D existence. She has found new ways to heal herself, so she can help you do the same.

For the past twenty-five years, I have been inhaling all things "spiritual" in an attempt to raise my frequency as I moved from my job as a journalist, to a spiritual author and teacher. I see in Julie the same hunger for information. Luckily for her, the downloads are coming in quickly and effectively. More people are being called to understand the tasks of the lightworker. I often explain this as a new pilot trying to learn how to fly a plane, despite having never seen the cockpit. While this is a big responsibility, we can't rise to the challenges unless we show up for Earth School to do the hard work. This means healing the inner child, other "lifetimes" (some would say "sametimes," as time and space are an illusion in this linear world), and checking for any bruises we have not addressed.

Julie shares with you the different modalities that helped her crack wide open into the multiverse that awaits all of us who are willing to understand our story, and rewrite it from a place of empowerment. Do you want to be a victim to your world, or are you able to understand that we are all connected with the ability to heal our wounds by taking ownership of the process? Every bruise that is pushed in your life is an opportunity to heal and grow. What Julie calls "ouchies" that come from others' behaviors are reminders of what you are needing to love and heal within yourself. They are you, and we are all one. This unified thinking is hard for many to understand, but it is the only way we can truly heal.

The best spiritual healers are those who have been there, done that, got the T-shirt. We know we can't help you if we don't know how hard the journey can be. You've got to feel it to heal it. And the energies are moving so fast these days, it's like our smart phones that constantly need updates; our operating systems are not what they used to be, and we need to be flexible if we want to keep up. I call it "tending to your healing hygiene"; you have to get schooled on using your toolbox, and set your intention to raise up our vibrations.

When reading Julie's book, if you feel some of the material is complex (and believe me, this happens with a lot of spiritual texts we crack open for enlightenment), know that your energy field is being expanded just by having it in your hands. Julie's intention is enough to raise your frequency. That alone is a miracle of how quickly we are evolving.

I also recommend using this book as an oracle, asking the divine, "What do I need to focus on today?" and then seeing what page you are inspired to open. Lightworkers have a responsibility to ingest as much knowledge as they can and start activating the information during this great awakening. This is not an ego boost, but a required call to action in this moment in time. You chose to incarnate now to get our consciousness "over the hump" and help us love into the higher dimensions.

Life can be full of love and "gigglegasms" as Julie calls them, but it starts by getting your hands dirty while you dig out the weeds in your garden. So, I invite you to show up for your soul's expansion. If you decide to set the intention to be part of this journey, you will never have a day without learning or growing.

Jenniffer Weigel is the author of several books, including *Stay Tuned* and *I'm Spiritual, Dammit!* She is also the creator of the Spiritual Social Club and host of *The Jen Weigel Show.*

Introduction

I am blessed so I can be a blessing. This phrase has become my mantra for the past year, but looking back, it has also been the story of my life. My journey in this lifetime began in a small town in Massachusetts in the '70s. As a female born in 1970, I was able to wear my favorite T-shirt at about the age of ten that said, "Anything boys can do, girls can do better." Before this time, the ludicrous idea that a girl could be better than a boy at anything was not allowed. I was allowed to play sports and had a Little League coach who played me more than the boys because I was better than them. I had teachers who put me in charge of the class when they used the restroom or had to leave the classroom for other reasons. In high school, I had teachers and a guidance counselor who helped me pick the right college and ensured I went to a private four-year school for free by helping me get the required scholarships. I was admitted into medical school thanks to my college professors, coaches, and dean, along with the doctor who interviewed me for medical school, who appreciated where I had come from and said, "I like people like you." The efforts of these beautiful souls that ensured I ended up where I was meant to be has been a great blessing because I have loved helping people heal over the almost thirty years I have been graced with being an MD.

These were all blessings. My father was born in Canada and his earliest language was French. He did not get to go to high school because he was required to work after eighth grade. He grew up in an abusive household and was unable to understand that there might be a better way to raise your children than through threats and violence. My mother was skilled in being the docile wife who never questioned the rule of the man of the house. My childhood was a blessing. By the age of four, I knew the reality that my parents lived in was not the one meant for me to be boxed in during this lifetime. I knew they both had limitations in their toolbox of wisdom that kept them from knowing what love could be, and this allowed me to be open to receiving advice and love from other sources outside my family. Understanding that the way they played gender rules was ridiculous helped me to choose what being a woman in this time meant to me. It also helped me want to love the wounded "male" and "female" energies of all humans so that we remember that we have no gender as our higher selves and are only the note of love we are meant to play for all. This openness has been one of the essential parts of my journey of remembering awake.

What does "remembering awake" mean? To me, it is knowing in your gut that there is no such thing as time—all vibrations are from the energy of Source, which is love—and that we are one soul. Awake is the place you become in the felt sense when your mind accepts and embraces and becomes the one energy everything is made of. (The felt sense is a place where you remember and know without doubt that we are one soul that came from one source of creation, but you cannot describe this because the beauty and magnificence of us as one combined entity can only be experienced, not described.) Awake is remembering, knowing, and loving all 144,000 dimensions of "your" consciousness and all the energy that surrounds you in those dimensions. Awake is knowing you are made of light that is connected to all energy. Awake is the vibration of your body in the frequency of creation, which, at this time, I describe as acceptance with the undertone of unconditional love. Remembering is understanding that you just have to remember that you are the energy of awake. There are no lessons to be learned or time to be passed, just opportunities to remember how sacred the energy of our soul is and how much joy can be discovered in playing one soul. The opportunities to play open will grace you when you are open to an energetic exchange with the light that is standing in front of you and wearing a human suit.

It is time for all of us to love open the boxes that we call family, work, friends, beliefs, highest/lowest, good/bad. By permanently dissolving these boxes, we can find new ways to love. I hope this book, based on a collection of blogs our soul wrote between 2022 and 2024, helps guide you to remember awake.

1

Playing Awake with Nature

The importance of receiving

Energy can neither be created nor destroyed, so we must receive it to share it.

After a wonderful healing session, a patient hugged me goodbye with gratitude for being taught how to love himself. I told him that I had shown him how to love himself, and now he was to show others how to do so.

He asked, "Doc, are you running a Ponzi scheme?"

I giggled. "Yes, I am; get to work."

Will you be part of my Ponzi scheme, please?

One of the most complex challenges for many humans is receiving loving energy. This is a paradox because many of us are always searching for someone to love us, but when gifted with the chance to receive, we feel like we are not worthy. Sometimes, we have been brainwashed into the vibration that receiving is for the weak and refuse or dismiss the love that is constantly being offered to us. Please understand that if you are one of these people with a hard time receiving, you are denying someone the chance to share their unique version of love with you. You are slowing the spread of the one consciousness that we will all find bliss in one day by missing an opportunity to understand another at the soul level. Trust me, these are moments you do not want to miss. You are also depriving others of learning how to express the unique note of love they are creating for the symphony that will evolve our amazing soul.

I am a healer. Many healers have great difficulty receiving, and most are unaware of or deny this fact. I learned this valuable lesson of the importance of receiving in January 2022 when I had COVID-19. With this bout of COVID-19, many of my friends called to share their love with me and to tell me to get better, and as each one did, my stomach hurt. I went within to ask why it hurt my stomach when someone tried to share love with me. The answer I felt was that I would need to love them perfectly in return, and this created fear and anxiety within me. This ridiculous reaction made me realize I had been brainwashed into a concept that is so often taught in this dimension: Love is conditional, and you are not worthy of love. Thus, I was blocking the reception of the love they were trying to grace me with.

Thankfully, I had an intuitive insight in which I realized that by not allowing myself to *receive* love, I would be unable to *share* love. I am a healer, and a healer channels love to offer a vibration of its essence to help others heal, so I decided that I was done with not receiving the love that others had to offer me. To heal others, I needed to be able to receive the love myself.

The COVID-19 symptoms were stomach-based. In this wounded part of my solar plexus, I discovered a limiting belief box of the vibration of "not enough." This box was created with and full of energies we have collected throughout time that tell us we are not worthy of love. It is time for us to love these boxes open. So, while lying in bed, trying to rest and heal myself of the symptoms COVID-19 was gracing me with, I asked for—and willingly chose to receive—celestial help that loved open and dissolved the "not enough" boxes within me. I have been able to receive the love of others since this time. As all healers know, there is no greater gift than helping another to find light and love and watching it open them to discovering how amazing their unique love is.

Thus, thanks to the help from the other side of the veil and the help of the loving energy of the souls on this side of the veil, who I am graced to call my friends, I incorporated the vibration of receiving that day. I healed one of my solar plexus wounds that told me I was "not enough." From that day on, I have made it a point to receive when others are willing to grace me with their love.

Healers I have received from

Below, I've listed some of the amazing healers who I have received from and the boxes that they have helped dissolve in me. I want to thank them and let you all know the energetic transformations of the gifts they have shared with me.

- My Rolfer, Robin Graber. Every time I allow her to touch me, she removes old trauma from my body through the love she pours into my fascia. She heals the trapped energy of the fearful thoughts I have chosen to give energy to in this dimension and others.
- Patti Dettori, my biodynamically gifted massage therapist. She has taken me on journeys to other dimensions of my consciousness to access healing and wisdom. She has also stitched the broken energy connections in my meridian systems back into coherence with her loving heart and hands.
- Eva Marquez[1] has guided me with her loving insights and helped me remember and incorporate the vastness of my soul in this dimension.
- Lori Rhodes.[2] If you have not tried biofield tuning, you should. Lori helped me reincorporate energies from a birth trauma (I had no idea I had a birth trauma) and the parts of my energetic field I had left with the energy of my abusive father. These energies may have been from trying to heal him at a young age, or they could be the fear and frustration I allowed him to trigger in me. My childhood taught me to disappear. Lori helped me reclaim the energy I had left in other realms when I chose to leave this dimension and travel to a kinder and safer one.
- Gretchen Oehler Hogg[3] took me on a soul journey that gave me a hologram room to explore the energies of the multiverses, a healing table to lie on to rest and restore, and a counsel to converse with when I needed guidance. In the holodeck travel, I remembered how to connect with all of humanity and beyond. My counsel lovingly

reminded me I came to this dimension to teach love. I go to the healing table I created that day to heal whenever I feel called.

- Heather Sprigg.[4] This angel of light gave me messages and guidance about who I am and what purpose I am meant to fulfill in this lifetime. She graced me with a vision that drove me to love myself more so I could love you all with more bandwidth. Heather, you have helped me open my heart so it can connect to more of the 144,000 dimensions of my consciousness and love our soul with more wisdom, patience, and compassion in all of them.

- Erika A. Olivas[5] is an emotion code healer and so much more, and she has helped me release trapped emotions and heal ancestral lines. Also, when we play together, you all benefit from the love we create by blending earth and sky.

- Angela Muñoz[6] is a powerful, imaginative, multidimensional friend and healer who plays with me in multiple dimensions as we heal each other in ways we cannot understand and where we (you are there also) create new energies for humanity. We created an angelic energy together once. Thank you, Angela.

- Dr. Sue Morter[7] has helped me explore the potential of my gifts and taught me how to share them with greater ease. She has guided me into exploring and remembering my gifts in so many ways—and with so much patience. Our soul should be eternally grateful for her essence in this dimension. Her BodyAwake Yoga, monthly healing meditations, the JourneyAwake trip to Egypt, and the classes I have taken with her have transmuted so many of my boxes and, in doing so, made me realize that when we love ourselves open, we birth loving consciousness for all to heal with.

- Jenniffer Weigel.[8] Thank you, Jen, for your Spiritual Social Club. You are light healing the planet and beyond through the safe space you have created where so many can remember their gifts without fear and through the powerful healers you connect with your loving vibrations. Thank you for believing in me enough to let me share my version of how to heal with love in your Spiritual Social Club events and for the countless gigglegasms we have had. If you play with Jen, you will laugh hard enough that you may get a little pee in your pants and some peanut butter whiskey up your nose.

- Abigail Zoe Martin, thank you for being the angel of powerful light you are and for using your strength, wisdom, and love to gift the planet with a place to showcase the possibilities we all have within if we love ourselves enough to find them. Thank you for believing in me and introducing me to the lights of so many beautiful versions of our soul all over the world.

- Gail Alexander[9] has opened me to new realms with her powerful mandalas. She has held space for me to embody with conviction the gifts that I am meant to share in this dimension. She has been a wonderful friend to validate experiences I have had that are hard to imagine possible in this 3D realm.

- Pat Longo[10] is a very loving soul with an incredibly healing vibration. She also has a heart that is so loving that it indescribably connects with your heart. Through her heart, I have seen how she sees my soul. Have you ever been blessed with seeing how magnificent you are through the eyes and kindness of another? Pat emits this wonderful gift and gives me the confidence to be the powerful crystal of loving light I intend to be in this realm. Thank you, Pat.

- Flo Magdalena[11] helped me realize that when we step into our light in this dimension, we are emitting and sharing it in all dimensions. She validated that I do not ground like others, and it is because I was not meant to and that I am a pain in the ass (I mean, a joyous rebel) that will not be limited by "you can't do that" in more than one dimension.

- Therese Rowley. In a past-life regression reading, she helped me understand that the lifetimes we call "evil and dark" offer the opportunity to create and share new and powerful versions of love. She also helped me relax into opening and receiving—without fear—all the loving wisdom the universe has to offer me.

- John Loffreda. I have called John at least a few times to help validate that the new reality I have chosen to live in over the last four years is, in fact, real. He has validated my gifts and my ability to channel many entities. He also helped me giggle this gift into acceptance by asking me if I stored Jeshua, Mary Magdalene, Shiva, Raphael, and Buddha in a kangaroo pouch and whipped them out to play with when they are needed.

These are just a few of the healers I have allowed myself to be vulnerable enough to receive from so that I can truly fulfill my purpose, which is to share the love I have within with whomever crosses my path and chooses to receive it. The light we emit flows into the Earth and ethers of this and all dimensions so that it can be embodied by all versions of our loving soul whenever they are ready for it. These healers have allowed energy flow from Source to move through them so that it can move with greater ease through me. They have all helped dissolve my pain body so I can be more effective at sharing pure Source energy with my patients. When we receive, we heal, and our capacity to vibrate in love expands. So will you receive today so that y/our pain body can heal and we can all vibrate in our beautiful, unique vibrational note of love to create a symphony of love that heals the multiverse? Most of the amazing souls I mentioned above do remote healing. Please play in the vibration of receiving today. I love you all. We got this.

The river of love we all flow in

When the river of unconditional love within you flows unhindered, you will feel Source's awe, humility, and creative potential.

Wouldn't it be nice if when you met another soul, you had nothing to offer but the space and wisdom of the universe within you to listen and know what energies were meant to be exchanged between your souls that day? One of my most persistent fears is being in judgment. As humans, we are taught to compare ourselves to all of those around us. When we judge, we lose the capacity to be in oneness. When I have been in judgment in the past, I have lost the ability to allow Source to flow through me to offer a vibration for another to heal with, resulting in a patient saying, "Doc, where is your juju today?" When we do not sense we are in oneness, we feel pain. However, we live in a dimension of duality, and there may be times when our judgment may be beneficial for ourselves and the one we judge. If we open our hearts and thus are in the flow of the river of Source, our judgment comes from love. If we are flowing in the navigational tool of duality that we call our "mind," our judgment may come from fear.

Let me explain. At times, someone else's loving judgment has given me epiphanies that have opened doors to new ways to play Earth that I would not have seen without their judgment. As a resident, I was discussing a topic I cannot remember with Marnie, a slightly older and energetically wiser resident. I had a strong opinion about the side I was choosing to believe I thought I was "right." Marnie gave me new ideas that argued for the side I felt was "wrong," and I then changed my belief and put my energy into the "wrong" side being "right." She then said, "You are so black and white."

I was a twenty-six-year-old who had never really been able to be present in the "now." I was always completing the tasks at hand to get to the next step in my life. I lived that way until my first child was born when I was thirty. But this idea of living in gray by slowing down and allowing a more encompassing spectrum of energies to be felt and incorporated into my field changed how I processed information from that day on. When residing in "gray," it is impossible to choose black or white. I see gray as the dimension of our consciousness that is the soup that all the thoughts of our soul and all other more intelligent energies of God or Source (like trees or rocks—these energies are old and wise because they have no Ego) have. This gray soup is where we can create in the singularity of our one heart rather than the duality of our mind. (My definition of *God* is all energy ever created, and that energy exists as loving peace.)

Imagine how wise and complete you can know you are when you allow yourself to become a channel—river—of our collective thought and interact with all around you through this all-encompassing wisdom. I have only seen this river flowing through one soul so far. I saw it as a river of silver mirrors that reflect who you are and the potential of what you/ we can create. The mirrors reflect the loving consciousness of creation in which we all participate through what we think. The soul it was flowing through played in that river often, and I saw her gift as the reminder of the potential we all have within us to be mirrors of loving light for each other. If you are flowing in this river and judge, you are judging from love, and the words you exchange with another may help them love open if they choose to hear your words through the river of light that flows within them. Sometimes in the past when I have judged, it has been beneficial for me and another version of my soul to allow the energy of judgment to be part of the intricate web of Source that flows through all of us that is connecting us and helping us love open to each other in ways we cannot understand much of the time. Even when judgment has come from fear in another or in me, it has been an opportunity to bring love in to transmute a box inside where fear has cemented me to that step of my path. Upon release from that box, I can open and flow to another bend in the river of loving light I am meant to embody in this dimension.

So consider asking your mind to jump in and become one with the wise reflective mirrors of the river of our collective consciousness today when you greet another. Listen and maybe even become the compilation of thoughts and emotions that underlie the words of your conversations. Open and become the essence of the collective thoughts of our beautiful soul, and then reflect that light on the version of our soul standing in front of you or, better yet, the energy of the version gathered around you in all directions and all dimensions. Remember that the dimension just above the river of our collective thoughts is the golden dimension of acceptance of all energy as love. It's the place where we become one with the energetic vibration we know as peace. It is a place where all the energies we have ever been or will be are equally valued, and thus all worthy of love.

Your entelechy/star seed/God particle/tree of life

Entelechy is a word I learned from Jean Houston.[12] I took her Unlock Your Quantum Powers class in 2022. In philosophy, *entelechy* is the concept of something (or someone) realizing its (or their) potential. She explains entelechy as an acorn that can become a unique oak tree. Using this analogy, we begin to surrender into understanding in the felt sense all of the possibilities our soul and humans are capable of manifesting, which were with us at our conception both as a soul and a human. Our entelechy represents our cosmic connection and wisdom as they sprout and grow our unique roots and branches (connections to our past and future). The bumps and bruises we have picked up on our journeys shape the uniquely crooked extensions of the energy field we call our tree. We all have intricate knots in our tree that are the unique wisdom our soul has collected for the cosmos.

By tapping into the entelechy, or star seed, within us and using it as a guide and a friend, we can grow in any direction and into anything we imagine. However, just as a tree needs water and minerals from the earth's amazing soil, our roots need to be able to secure and nourish us through open, unobstructed pathways for our growth. If we get stuck on a particular energy, such a rumination loop of the same thought over and over, our tree does not grow. Likewise, our branches will be enticed into stretching open to new places when seeking nourishment from the sun, Source, and other souls that we have the privilege of crossing paths with and being present enough to absorb and exchange the spark of life created when energies merge.

As you read this book, please understand that all experiences you get to integrate into the growth of your entelechy are a blessing. All the emotions we experience in a human suit nourish us. Some may cause rapid growth of our trees. And some may cause beautiful, intricate knots that deserve our honor and respect because they symbolize times our soul perceived suffering so that we would better understand the yin and yang of energy exchange. With this understanding, we can play the game of creation with more grace and ease and expand our capacity to create.

For our tree to stretch to new heights, our branches need to be flexible, or they will break when we weather storms. If you feel your tree has broken branches, this is fine. Branches need to break for a new branch to grow in the new direction that your soul was craving to explore. Our roots and leaves can nourish the branches only if our tree is healthy and open, not hindered by blocked energy pathways from stuck emotions we are not processing because of fear, denial, lack of insight, or anger. When we have a healthy energy tree, our entelechy will be accessible. Our entelechy's intelligence and connection to universal consciousness will help us root and branch out, uninhibited by the extremely limited human belief system we have been brainwashed into accepting as reality. Accessing your entelechy by remembering who you truly are will remove the restrictions of human capability that we have been taught exist. When we are clear of these restrictions, we can then really start our journey into the connected and purposeful life that our souls and humans crave. Your entelechy/star seed/God particle is Source within you. How will you care for your tree today? How will you let someone else help you care for your tree? How will you help another care for their tree?

When I wrote about our entelechy as a blog in 2022, I had just taken my first in-person energy class and was glad to meet Susan Nelson, who wrote this poem in 2010 and shared it with the class.

Tree

I hug mother earth
Grounded by her richness
My arms reach out to the heavens
Dancing in the wind
I offer my canopy as sanctuary
Sheltering and nourishing
I have writhed in the storms, scarred and aging
Remaining grounded in mother earth

As I stretch toward the heavens
The tree and I are one
Claiming our place in the sun

This poem helped me incorporate the powerful image of a tree into how we can all heal. To me, hugging Mother Earth and grounding in her richness means you can exchange energy with her in such a way that your roots absorb her patience, wisdom, energy, power, and compassion as she absorbs and uses your emotions to create new energy. When my arms reach out to the heavens and dance in the wind, my energy branches are connected to Source, my "future" self, everyone and everything my path will connect with, and the energy of casting aside current and past beliefs and being free of the prisons of limitation that belief can trap us in. When we make room to bend and absorb without judgment or the restriction of old limitations of possibility, we can create things we never imagined because we are creating from a collective energy and "mind." Offering my canopy as a sanctuary means I will cherish all the energy I am part of and become vulnerable enough to love open and hold space for all beings so they can remember how to find the love and wisdom inside them. In sheltering and nourishing ourselves and others, we create the healing essence of a cosmic womb that can birth new energy to nourish and heal humanity and the rest of our cosmic soul.

The storms you've weathered have left you with scars that remind you of the compassion you have gained by understanding why another may be suffering. Realizing the experience of aging is a beautiful gift, as every step of our journey can give birth to new insights and wisdom. When we remain grounded, our roots can mend all we have ever been and touched. Stretching toward the heavens gives us the creative inspiration and strength to be the unconditional love of Source, the energy we all heal, grow, and create with. As you heal yourself, all that your branches and roots have ever connected with will heal. So, through this book, it is my hope you rediscover your entelechy/star seed/God particle and the beautiful, unique energy tree of our soul that you are and become one with it. Claim your essential place as part of the collective loving light of the universe, for your light is a cherished and precious gift to all.

Here is another tree quote from a friend.

"I am rooted to the earth, and I can sway with
all that comes my way." —Daniela Borgia

Your elements

Several healing arts, including Chinese philosophy, believe our human suits
and Earth environment are composed of five elements: fire, water, earth,
wood, and air/metal. I believe we can transmute our pain by acknowledg-
ing it, combining with it, and allowing it to flow through the five elements
within us.

Your pain is power, connection, and wisdom. It is time to stop ignoring, burying, or saving it for another day and instead embrace, love, and
incorporate the experience it blessed you with into the transmutative energy
of essence you are made of. When you love your pain instead of fearing
it or walling it off with alcohol, exercise, sex, or any other addiction, a
new world of power, connection, and creativity will reveal itself. Thomas
Cleary's translations of the Daoist books *The Immortal Sisters* and *The Secret
of the Golden Flower* discuss the alchemy of the five elements as they relate
to the healing art of acupuncture.[13, 14] The wisdom from which the art of
acupuncture is created guides us to embody peace and health by creating
a "now" where our elements are in balance. Conversely, we create diseases
when they are not balanced.

We become Source when we embrace and allow the power of these
five elements to combine in mutual respect and harmony. The way I understand the elements, water represents our soul, and fire is the tool that
is our human mind/Ego and the emotions this energy generates. Earth
is our beautiful planet, wood is the strength and confidence we feel when
we are connected and nourished by Earth's wisdom and heart, and air or
metal is the energy that connects us to Source. These elements need and
desire union with each other more than we may ever understand. When
we guide them into balance, your union with this beautiful symbiosis of
the diverse energies you have within you can create new soul energy and
vibrations for Source. You may feel this balance as the sparkling light of
joy, humility, peace, or of feeling blessed.

The spectrum of your emotions is your fire element (aka the wounds
and despair of a separated human Ego). When you recognize and allow
yourself to feel the beautiful fires burning within you and immerse yourself

in them with gratitude, you open a pathway for your soul to combine with them. You can even see our fires as fireworks or the explosions of your powerful emotions to be viewed with awe and wonder. Your beautiful, watery soul does not understand the dark and light of emotions as you perceive them. Your soul wishes to comfort and caress all of them. Your water/soul sees your fire as rocks in the river; it has been graced with the blessing to flow around, through, and by those rocks so that it can experience the thrill of combining new energies to taste, touch, feel, hear, and see with. The soul's purpose is to experience energy and gather it to be used for creation. There is no judgment of your fire from your soul or Source. Only your human judges its emotions. Your soul sees your fires as information for Source and an opportunity to show your human what unconditional love is.

So, allow your fire element to be loved and appreciated by your water element. Allow these two elements to combine in a perfectly symbiotic sphere of yin and yang. Allow this symbiotic energy sphere to heal you with the loving energy created when these two elements merge as one infinite loop of playful experience. By the way, I also see my stuck emotions/fires as knots in my tree, and I like to imagine the water of my soul pouring in through my head or out in all directions from the core of my body.

Next, imagine gifting this energy ball to the Earth and releasing it into her heart, womb, or ley lines. The Earth wishes to understand the experience that our souls have while in a human suit in this 3D realm of duality. She wishes to incorporate the energy you are blessed with creating through the alchemy of your fire and water, and she desires you to feed her with this new energy and the new song you have created by allowing this fusion. I find it helpful to picture the earth you have created through the blend of your fire and water. Picture that earth draining down your legs into a sacred and timeless connection with the heart, wisdom, patience, and timeless compassion of the entity we call Earth. Connect your root chakra, chakras in your hands and feet, or even your whole hara line into the Earth's heart, or crawl inside and lie in her loving womb. While you're connected to her essence, open and receive the wisdom she has been waiting to give you. Become one with the peace of the Earth's stillness and be guided in the alchemy of the transmuting of your fear, which has been expressing itself in the form of anger, frustration, anxiety, depression, etc. Please don't ever forget to thank the keepers of the Earth who have been supporting her energy since the dawn of creation. They allow this dimension to exist and provide a pathway for you to become one with this magnificent loving and healing energy.

As you sit in gratitude for a glimpse at this wise stillness, the Earth will begin to transform you. She will take the energy you feed her and create new energy in the form of the wood element. She will gift you with strong tree roots that connect with her and thus nourish your energy in this dimension. If you open your heart and mind and allow yourself to be held by this loving, patient, compassionate, timeless energy, your tree will grow strong and proud of its power and uniqueness. When you nourish your tree enough such that you love it unconditionally, the sun inside your belly will shine. Your tree will then produce your metal or air element. This element radiates from your core and shines through your branches. You will feel and know peace when you are connected to Source through your branches and the Earth through your roots. Within this peace, we can expand into all our lifetimes, all universes, and all "time." We become Source/God/the tree of life and are able to remember we are the light of all the essence of the cosmos, emitting itself into the human suit and experiences we are choosing to create. We remember that "home" is cosmic unified consciousness, and we can know, coexist with, and embody this indescribable vibration at any time by choosing to allow the elements of this dimension to flow in perfect harmony.

I want to offer another version of the alchemy of the elements that I discovered in the poetry of *The Immortal Sisters*. Your water is north, your fire is south, your wood is east, your metal is west, and earth is your center. This is another way of understanding this dimension; our Source can be perceived as Earth and thus is our center. The Earth becomes a central sun. In this scenario, the elements are perceived to represent the four directions. When we unify these energies, we are guided into remembering that we are Source, and we access the felt sense of that truth in our core.

I invite you to try another way to play with the five elements. This was revealed to me during a BodyAwake Yoga session with Dr. Sue Morter. I saw the water of my soul flowing out through my core into the tree we call fascia. Through the fascia, the water flowed into all 144,000 dimensions of my consciousness, combined with the fires of emotions that reside in the time I call the essence of my/our soul. At the end of the fascia were all the "earths," or other realms of duality that "I AM"/we are. Then, from those "earths," I received the wood, or wisdom, of our consciousness, and brought it back into my central sun to share with this and all dimensions.

You can use the infinity symbol, the ankh, triangles, or whatever other geometric guide your mind feels like exploring as a conduit for this energy to travel on. To me, our fascia is a spiderweb of our collective consciousness through which we can travel, share, receive, communicate, and evolve. Playing transmutation through the elements with it is a game I will be exploring in the future. I invite you to develop your way of playing five elements.

How will you nourish y/our tree today? Which knot in your tree have you not yet appreciated and allowed the fire it is made of to be alchemized by the loving water of y/our soul? When you have alchemized a knot, please honor your mind and soul for gathering emotions for our soul to incorporate into its collective wisdom and compassion. Will you allow your soul/water element to caress with and alchemize your fires into energy to feed the beautiful entity we call Earth? This union is something both have been longing for. Will you help them join hands, rejoice, and weep in the joy of being allowed to combine again so the Earth can feed you with her love and help you find strength, purpose, and peace? Will you receive and incorporate the energy of wood into your being and breathe open the sun inside you so that you can remember you are Source in a dimension of duality?

Your songbird

It is time for you to take a deep breath, pause time, and marvel at the beauty of the unique songs you are creating every day.

The "I" Ego is blamed for creating an isolated world where we are separate from each other and thus suffer. Many have suggested that you shed your "I" Ego entirely so that you may become one with Source when you meditate. In his book *Metahuman*, Deepak Chopra suggests we can be the singing bird and the bird observing the singing bird simultaneously.[15] We choose consciousness in the form of a human body because it allows us to gather the energy of the powerful range of deep emotions that the "I" Ego attached to the human suit experiences. Transmuting our emotions creates beautiful energy songs that expand our unified consciousness/God/Source.

The "I" of the human suit you perceive yourself to be is necessary to transmute emotion, which is the vibration of creation in this dimension. The "we/one" (the perfectly melded symbiosis of the human mind and soul/our soul) absorbs all the notes you create without judgment but with fascination, wonder, encouragement, and awe. The "we/one" is the consciousness that cherishes sharing all the beautiful yin and yang notes you create with Source. It is time for us to be in the moment and be present to witness all the beautiful music we are creating for our collective consciousness by being the brain/mind of the songbird and the heart that witnesses with humility and unconditionally loves all the notes the songbird creates. It is time to realize that in this dimension of duality, we get to be the bird/creator and the spectator who gets lost in the magnificence of the spectrum of vibrations that, when unified, compose the glorious harmony that is the symphony of our collective soul.

The freedom you will feel in being the spectator who lives without judgment will not disappoint. Enjoy and be honored by how strong, intelligent, and loving your songbird can be as it gathers the experiences of this human suit and transmutes them into wisdom and compassion for our collective soul. We can use that wisdom and compassion to create a world where our souls—in any suit they choose to emit—will greet each other with a soul seed to soul seed (open heart to open heart) recognition that will end all violence. You will also gain a new appreciation of how beautiful you are and how precious every note you create on your journey of the privilege of this lifetime is. You may even see how many others are inspired and brightened by your uniquely majestic songs. Will you embrace duality and be the isolated creator within and simultaneously the totality of y/our soul that surrounds and supports you with more love than you can imagine possible and watch yourself create beautiful music today?

White caps

We experience an ocean of emotions so that we can create.

I recently gained a new perspective on the beauty of the oceans that grace the planet with life while on a cruise. As I watched the ocean form white caps with its opposing wave forces and then saw the white caps dissolve back into the expansive, solitary body of water our oceans inhabit, I realized the ocean is trying to teach us how to flow with our emotional outbursts.

We are all fantastic creator beings who choose to focus and experience a conscious existence in this dimension to experience the energy associated with the power of emotion in a 3D reality. Our emotions are nothing other than the force of an ocean wave. They can be small and gentle or tsunami-like. When we encounter another soul in the vast ocean of Earth, we can align and create a wave together, at peace, and thus create a calm sea. Or we can create a white cap through opposition. We differ from the ocean because we get stuck in the white cap and forget to dissolve back into the birthright of our unity.

The ocean is wise and understands that opposing forces are essential to create life. Without white caps, the ocean would not churn and bring plankton to the surface. Without plankton, there would be no ocean food source. However, the ocean also understands that when the energy of the white cap is no longer needed, its molecules of water will come back into unity until called on again to serve the purpose of the whole by creating another life-sustaining energetic explosion.

What if you tried to see your painful or uncomfortable emotions as life-sustaining white caps? What if the souls you encounter that cause your creative juices to rise were the souls you were most grateful to play with in this 3D realm because they remind you of your importance in the game of creation that we are all playing? What if you could be so grateful for the white caps in your life that you saw the peace and connection underneath them and could instantly transmute the power of opposition back into the peace of unity?

I invite you today to embody the wisdom of the ocean. Flow with others as a wave, be a sea of calm, and be grateful for the white caps you create with others to sustain the Earth in its energetic dance of creation. Remember we are all one soul playing in flow with one another for the benefit of all. I love you all. Thank you for playing with the power of 3D emotions in this realm with me/us.

The eye of the storm

Even a category 5 hurricane has a calm eye in the center.

Many of us have felt the hurricane of energies meant to make us uncomfortable enough to remember who we are and why we choose to have consciousness in this dimension. These energetic explosions are not easy for anyone. I am inviting you to take a deep breath and realize that you are generating this hurricane from within yourself for your benefit.

In this dimension, we perceive reality through a movie we create from within. Our movies are filled with struggle and strife with ourselves and others so that we can be uncomfortable enough to embrace change and become one with the divinity within us that is the eye of our storm. Accept that the powerful storms you generate are your Ego's interpretation of energy in the realm of duality mixing with your soul's wisdom and understanding of emotion. The calm eye of the storm is created when you open your heart and love the storm you are generating with the version of your soul you are creating the storm with (the human you don't agree with and perceive as separate from you). When you love the storm, you can understand how to flow in singularity in a dimension of duality.

Why are we generating such a great hurricane? Because it's not easy to uproot and detach from the perceived safety of the limiting belief systems that we have been brainwashed into vibrating with and manifesting reality through. For most of us, it takes the energy of a hurricane to release these limitations and open the veils into the realms of endless possibility and creativity. These storms and shifts in our energies cause many to question their sanity and experience their life's most significant identity crisis.

Collectively, we are going through a spiritual enlightenment that many perceive as the most significant storm in human history. It is not. These storms have happened many times before, and we have collectively grown from previous energies similar to this one. When you are in one of your daily storms, I invite you to retract your senses and explore deep within yourself to find the eye of calm within you so you can sense love, light, and connection beyond this dimension. The storm around you is all the distractions of the human realm that you have created for your benefit. The eye is the divine love within you that finds peace in your storm. When you become the eye within by breathing through your heart, belly, in between, or both combined, you will find an eye created from love and peace that is incomprehensible to the human mind. You will sense that every energy created is inside you, loving and cheering on y/our soul's evolution.

Y/our eye is the true self you have been searching for. It is where you create the storm that pushes you to remember, embody, and project into your reality the beautiful celestial being you are. It is where you are connected to everything and nothing, as there is no separation from all energies ever created. It is where you find peace—where you may least expect it.

Once you find your eye and surrender your Ego to its wisdom, calm, peace, and ONE soul/energy perspective, you can expand it. You can love your eye enough to make it take up your whole aura. You can love your eye enough that it can penetrate others' storms and give them a glimpse of the inner peace possible for them if they find their eye. If you need help finding your own eye, ask a local or remote healer to guide you on this step of your journey of self-discovery. Trust that you will be guided to the healer who resonates most closely with your current frequency to help you. It is time for all of us to feel the peace in embodying and loving the divine self within ourselves and others.

The portals to other realities and timelines for some of the people closest to me have been ripped open these past few years. This opening is causing a dark night of the soul for many. The shift in realities that many are going through is bringing old fear and doubt into their awareness. These emotions are never comfortable, but please understand they are coming from within you and causing a perceived storm around you to lead you into deep healing. It is time to stop fighting the energy we are creating for our benefit. It is time to put down our swords, stones, and sticks and erase this barbaric, outdated way of playing the game of life. The pride of the Ego is trying to find a way to destroy the storm, but instead of fighting it, we need to let our hearts open and incorporate these amazing awakening thundering energies into our toolboxes of communication by loving them into the harmonious frequency of the divine eye that lies within us. Life in the dimension of the Earth was created to experience all emotions, but it is more fun and blissful when we play it while embodying the frequencies of light, love, and peace found within us through our calm eye. For within that eye lies the oneness of all, and residing in this ONE, we can find a peace that we have never dreamed possible. Our eye is where the peaceful vibration that is God (all energy combined) can be known and shared and where we can connect and heal with the "eyes" we see through in all the dimensions that our consciousness inhabits. Y/our eye is where we find and accept our shared divinity.

It is time for all of us to heal ourselves and each other in a timeframe we never thought possible. When we access the divinity within, there is no time; there is just love. Will you surrender to the ONE blissfully connected divine eye within you today? Will you love yourself and others in its frequency of peace for the collective? Will you join me in the bliss of knowing there is the most loving collective consciousness inside of you, and it's just waiting for you to contribute to it uniquely and let its light shine out of you? Please love yourself enough to ask the storm you are currently creating to melt into y/our eye and heal today. You are so supported and loved and never alone in this process. If you need help, ask, and you shall always receive guidance on how to remember that you can walk through any storm when you know you are the "I AM" within.

The wisdom of a flower

In the spring in Nevada, for a very short time, the different flowers on the trail I ride my bike on regularly, take turns making the landscape beautiful and filling me with joy, wonder, and gratitude.

They don't have to think about when it is their turn to show their beauty to sustain their species; they just do. They also bloom in the wide range of temperatures and the changing moisture of the northern Nevada spring. Why is it that sometimes, as a human, we use our mind—which was meant to expand our creativity and connection—to keep us from blossoming? The mind may tell us things like, "You are not smart or courageous enough to accomplish that," so we cower and miss a chance to blossom. Why do we allow these missed opportunities to happen? How does a flower have more tenacity than we do at times?

It is time to start thinking differently. It is time for us to tell our minds to work with us instead of against us. It is time for us to start understanding why it is so hard for us to feel comfort in blossoming when it is our divine privilege and purpose to do so. When you feel like you are not enough of something, I encourage you to take five to ten deep breaths, see what feeling or past trauma may be generating that thought, and gently release it with love. Tell that feeling or thought, "You may no longer control me and keep me from my divine beauty and purpose." You may have to do this with several feelings and past traumas, but the more you do it, the easier it gets, and the more you want to blossom—not just once a year but as often as possible.

When you blossom, you connect with others because the light emanating from within will be impossible for others not to want to connect with. And just like the flower has to bloom for its species to sustain itself, your bloom will heal the human species and help it thrive through the love and passion you will contribute to the whole. Unlike flowers, we can blossom anytime and as often as we want. When will you bloom next? How frequently will you choose to show the beauty within you to others? Who will you inspire when you dare to clear the uncomfortable emotions that keep you from being the unique gift you were meant to be to the vibration we call humanity and, in doing so, all other vibrations of our consciousness?

Here is another way to ask you to open and share the loving essence of your flower with all. The vibration of the atoms that solidify your human suit determines the energy bandwidth of the reality you emit. We were all created from love. When the atoms of your energy field are vibrating in love, your energy field is open and endless, and you are one with universal consciousness. When you are in fear, your energy field is constricted, boxed, and self-imprisoned, and the wavelengths of energy that shape your reality are very limited. Think of your energetic field as a flower. When a flower is open, it shares its beauty and joy with all, lighting the path of all that feel it. When it is constricted, its wondrous essence is hidden within a shield of protection, and the only reality the flower can see and create with is the one made of the darkness and isolation within. When one discovers the ability to find the extremely powerful light that is the totality of y/our love in the middle of this darkness and isolation, an inner sun is rediscovered. However, many souls in human suits have forgotten they are beautiful stars and thus need to be reminded of this by finding an external light to guide them on their path of rediscovering the sun within.

Think of something you love and feel how the flower of your heart melts, opens, and radiates that love outward to be unconsciously shared with grace and ease. When you radiate this light, others can sense it and often gather around you to taste, smell, touch, see, and feel the beauty of your unique petals and stamens of light. Imagine how they will incorporate it and what will be birthed by spreading the pollen that is the vibration of your love. Imagine that the open flower of your heart is so relaxing that it is capable of guiding another's heart to ripen and open. Imagine how fun it would be if humanity could be a field of open, unique flowers so grateful to be unified and blossoming together that they dissolve and connect without trying into the sway of the symphony of universal love. In this harmonious vibrational field of blooming universal love, we will remember we are one soul that decided to have consciousness in this realm of duality to play creation in the state of awe experienced when we find reverence in the magnificence of every flower we are graced to witness in our lifetime. Please be patient with some flowers, as they have not yet bloomed and are offering you an opportunity to be present and witness the grandeur of their blooming process.

So, how will you express your flower in the game of Earth today? Will you allow love to radiate from your center and melt open to share your beauty and wisdom with others? Or will you shield it in fear? Will you sense the darkness of another and close your petals in fear to protect yourself? Or will you choose to let more love flow from your heart and stay open and become a sun of loving light that opens another magnificent flower that forgot it was here to share the fragrant light within it? Will you see another and share the flowers that are beautiful reflections of our souls to create a new, unique flower for others to marvel at?

Our souls have been shielding their magnificence in fear for too long. I ask that you melt open the flower of your heart to share it with humanity today. We are here to share our beauty and create from the unbelievable amount of humility we will feel when our soul freely shares its love with itself. Will you shine open today? Will you please share your flower of loving light with all? It is time to play the game of creation in a field of love that emits from the booming hearts of humanity united in the sparkling opening fragrance of love that all of our stars were simultaneously created from.

2

Exploring Ego

Ego

We choose consciousness in this dimension to experience the dance of Ego.

We are one soul in higher dimensions. We get bored of this bliss and are creator beings, so we come to this 3D realm to experience separation. We land and ask to forget our oneness so that our creative abilities expand. We ask to experience all the heavy and the light emotions in a 3D body with senses to collect the powerful vibrations of those emotions so that we can create and may become wiser, more compassionate, kinder, and more loving. We forget that we are in a game of creation called the Earth dance. Each step we take in this dance through the lens of separation is a gift of the energetic experience that we choose to collect for our one soul to create with.

How does the "I" Ego gift us the illusion of our soul's separateness? It does so through judgment. We are incessant judgers. We judge behavior, beliefs, dance step choices, clothing, hair, moods, etc. We do this without any effort most of the time. It is a paradox of beauty and great sadness. We experience the vibration of separateness from our one soul through judgment, which is needed to experience all emotions in this realm. But the price of judgment is that we forsake the bliss of knowing we are God because we lose the capacity to vibrate in our collective frequency of unconditional love.

So, how can we play this amazing game of duality with less pain and suffering? Thank judgment (Maya, Satan, and all other gods of duality) for helping you play the game of Earth in separation every time you judge. Thank the game for allowing you to be the most magnificent creator. Honor yourself for collecting ouchy emotions in so many dimensions of our consciousness, and then release the illusion of judgment as soon as possible. Instead of looking into the soul or experience you are currently judging through a lens of separateness, look at it through the lens of love and oneness. Remember, all judgment is a way for you/us to learn another way to love and collect energies we could not collect without the illusion of separateness. Love yourself when you are in self-judgment. Love those judging you for playing the game of Earth the way it was meant to be played. Remember, the sooner we release the judgment illusion, the more fun the game of Earth is.

We came to this dimension to dance in separation through Ego to create a magical symphony of harmony. Thank your "I" Ego for the duality it graces you with daily. In this gratitude and love for your Ego, ask it to remember it is a beautiful and necessary part of creation. Your Ego contributes energy to our collective soul with the bliss of connection found through the surrender of its gifts and wisdom to our collective soul. Will you remember the joy of surrendering your unique Ego note to our collective soul today? I promise if you do, you will not regret it. Our soul can play this game of life with a lot more vitality and passion if we dance in and out of duality with grace and ease. Look at the energies you are graced with, experiencing today in awe of the power of both the separateness (the creation of your unique note of our soul while feeling you are separate from it), and surrender of the energy we call "I" Ego (surrendering yourself to the knowledge that there is one soul here and that we find bliss when we share our unique note with the totality of our symphony) that is essential for the game of duality we call Earth.

Pride

The word *pride* can be a double-edged sword. At one time, I was trying to convince a beautiful, loving soul that within her marriage, her opinion mattered, her voice deserved to be heard, and her desires were valid. She responded that the Bible says that pride is a sin. This belief was her way of justifying and rationalizing the submission of her light to another in a way that dimmed it instead of brightening it. One of the definitions of *pride* in *Webster's* is "self-respect." Should self-respect be considered a sin? Should we even be giving the word *sin* any energetic power in the first place? We all have moments that have not aligned with the vibration of love. These moments are the grace of being human, not the energy attached to the word *sin*. Please offer the love you have within you to transmute the vibration of the word *sin* into the vibration of acceptance of the word *experience*.

So, back to pride. We are in an energetic transformation in this dimension right now that is magnificent beyond words. That magnificence emanates from you. I want you to know that your light is needed to create this new loving world that manifests from the hearts of the amazing souls inhabiting this planet. If you lack self-respect, your light will always be beautiful but hidden, and you will be too shy to embrace its true power and potential. This fear of your magic keeps this planet spinning in pain and "darkness." I invite you today to start the never-ending path to loving the fear of your magnificence out of existence.

How is this done? You chose to fully participate with surrender to a journey within yourself of unwinding all the false beliefs you have accumulated in your many dimensions about how you will never be enough. *Know for a fact you are always enough, and you are always achieving or remembering the perfection of your note with each step of your journey.* There may be moments that don't feel good when you get lost in the heavier emotions that cause pain. These are still perfect. They allow you to collect new pathways to loving yourself through humility and surrender.

Who do you surrender to? That is your choice. You may call that energy God, the divine, the creator, Source, Buddha, Christ, friend, or your divine light. It does not matter what you call it as long as you know it is with you, loving you always, and would not exist without you. This energy wants you to remember you have never been alone, to rediscover that you are magic, and to have the confidence to embody and emit that magic while connected to our soul so the symphony we create is allowed to witness and combine with your beauty.

The shifts in my abilities to perceive and embody the vibrations of our collective loving consciousness in such a way I can then offer pathways for others to heal with these frequencies have been so rapid in the last year that about every four to six weeks, I have been embodying the emotion of fear. I have often said, "Who am I?" concerning the change from who I perceived "I" was to the "I" energy that radiated from me now. However, a wise, fantastic friend recently told me, "Julie, the person you think you were was not you. You are now just discovering who you are." This insight helped so much. We are all constantly discovering who we are. We are all constantly evolving. I invite you to surrender to this self-discovery with compassion and patience because the continuous birth of a connected soul is a sacred event that should not be rushed or criticized but witnessed with fascination.

So, will you step into the discovery of how magical you are with me today by allowing the vibration of pride to flow through you and align all of your cells with your special note? I can't wait to hear what you have to offer me and our soul with your magical vibration. Please love yourself enough to play your note for me. Please respect yourself enough to understand the offering of the note you have within to share with all of us is one we cannot thrive without.

How can we use "pride" or "Ego" to brighten our light? The societal, energetically ingrained belief box that we should not love ourselves and put our wants and needs first at times can harm everyone and everything we exchange our energetic essence with. Without love and compassion for ourselves, we will always lack the ability to love and have compassion for another. In order to emit and exchange a vibration of energy at its true resonance, your energetic field must be in that resonance. You can never manifest unconditional love sustainably if you cannot sustain it for yourself. The good news is unconditional love can be extremely impactful, even if only in small amounts of "time," because love is the frequency of our essence that opens the doors for our global society to thrive and resonate in a peaceful symphony again.

I want to elaborate on the charged word *Ego*. I think all humans have a dichotomous Ego. We have the "I" Ego that sees itself as separate from the whole and is influenced by the pain bodies and shadow figures that are part of our energy fields until we choose to love these barbed-wire fences that entangle our minds in prisons created by the illusion of fear. We are freed and become one with all and in flow by remembering that these prisons of entanglement in stuck emotions are the steps of our journeys that we have been blessed with.

Within us, there is also a "we" Ego, birthed from the symbiosis of our mind, soul, and collective soul. This Ego vibrates in the resonance of unconditional love and finds its joy-filled identity in service to the one energy we were all created from. When we identify as the mind or "I" of our human Ego, our energy resonates in duality, and we participate in a separating realm of proving we are smarter, richer, prettier, stronger, etc., than everyone around us with the false belief that doing this is a good thing. It is a lonely world when an individual feels the need to stand above others and thus is never connected with anyone. Most of our current belief systems brainwash us into believing that we thrive in the 3D realms through this vibration of the "I" Ego. However, the "I" Ego keeps us from falling in love with and having compassion for who we are now because that person is never "enough" of anything. The "I" Ego keeps us from understanding our birthright to embody and create unconditional love by keeping us isolated in a prison of fear. In this state of fear, we forget that we are at peace when we are the energy of an open and vulnerable heart flowing and connecting to others in an endless sea of unconditional love. The "I" Ego is attached to the energetic "wounds" of all time (which occur when we enter realms of duality for the benefit of collecting energetic "wounds"). It thus prevents us from understanding how perfect we are, just as we are right now. The "I" Ego navigates in the illusion that there is a "right and wrong" and thrives in the frequency of judgment. Thus, it's limited in its ability to open and connect in love.

The "we" Ego is the one we need to allow pride to strengthen and grow as large as possible. The "we" Ego is the tool we use to create and sustain unconditional love. The "we" Ego can dissolve the illusion of our limiting belief system and create anything imaginable because it is everyone and everything. The "we" Ego shows you bliss and peace by lovingly guiding your "I" into softening and melting until it understands it has never been alone and has always been loved and appreciated for *all* the energies it has collected for our one soul. It's those energies that help us expand in our capacity to find new ways to love and play the creation game with. The "we" Ego drives our planet and beyond to thrive by performing the unique and necessary tasks and services it was created for.

So, how do we access the "we" Ego instead of the "I" Ego? It can be just as simple as recognizing all behaviors and beliefs that create division and separation and choosing to no longer fuel them with your attention. We have been taught to wear a cloak woven from our perceived deficiencies that separates us from others. This cloak is composed of fear, anger, judgment, etc. When we feel a physical body symptom like muscle spasms, palpitations, or stomach upset, an underlying separating emotional energy is causing that symptom. The body is a miracle in this way. It will reveal to you when you are straying from the bliss of connection with the "we" Ego to the isolation of the "I" Ego by causing discomfort. When you get a physical symptom, I recommend you go within and find the uncomfortable emotion behind it and say to that energy, "You may no longer control me. You may not keep me from embodying the unconditional love I am made of, and I release you with love, light, and one thousand blessings to your next highest good." Or just hug the part of your body in pain until the ouch dissolves. In doing so, understand that you just reclaimed a piece of y/our loving energy from an energetic prison back into the energy you travel the cosmos in by using the magnificent power of your caring heart to transmute it back into the love of our collective soul. Believe it or not, when you unravel your energetic emotional tangles, issues like hot flashes, palpitations, plantar fasciitis, and more disappear.

As we shed the cloak of isolation that is the "I" Ego, we gain access to the "we" Ego. Our "we" Ego thrives on connection, lifts others, creates joy and laughter, has compassion and tenderness that brings tears to one's eyes, and does not know there is a vibration that would consider acts of service as derogatory. It thrives on knowing it can fully enjoy the soul standing before it for its current vibrational state without any reservations or judgments. It marvels at all the steps of the journeys our souls are taking. It is also connected to Source and is content at all times. The "we" Ego knows your purpose, and it is not afraid of performing it or being hindered or wounded by the emotions or actions of others because it understands that "others" are part of it. It is the Ego of the entelechy the universe gave you to create love with.

Another way to start to shed your cloak/pain body/shadow figures is to consider being OK with the step of the journey that your human and soul are on NOW. See the step as necessary for you or someone else—quite a bit of our journey is for the benefit of "others." Even our "errant" behaviors and emotions are for our growth and the growth of others. At the end of each day, ask, "What did I do today that made me feel more love and connection or that made me feel more isolated and lost?" Be grateful for the opportunities that cross your path in an attempt to awaken you through perceived pain. The interactions that grab the attention of your "I" Ego through perceived discomfort offer you a pathway to discovering your "we" Ego and remembering you are at all times the kindheartedness and love of a divine parent. You can receive and embody that love to transmute and shed the cloak of perceived separation from the whole that has kept you in the "I" Ego. Be the divine parent who loves you so much that there is no judgment for your steps—there is just love, support, and appreciation of the wonderful child's journey.

Our unified soul is part of all our human suits and is inside of us. It watches our "humans" suffer from all the self-flagellation we insist on because of the limiting beliefs we allow to continue to run our operating systems. It is time to say a gentle or stern no to being limited and release the rumination loops of what no longer serves us. Wouldn't it be fun if the light of your soul could penetrate and shine through every crevice of the energetic field that you call yourself in this dimension? Wouldn't it be fun to know in the felt energetic sense the totality of "you" without the "I" Ego veiling you from the vastness and bliss of the light, love, wisdom, and guidance of the "we"? We all have a lot of playing with new ways to love ahead of us to make this planet more loving and peaceful. It is time to embrace the power of the unlimited supply of love we were given and have access to at all times. It's time to get the play done through the bliss of connection we can access with our "we" Ego. Love can heal anything. It is time we remember this and start by loving and healing ourselves so we can offer guidance to heal and love others. How will you love yourself or another today? How will you change your negative perception of Ego today? Can you unconditionally love someone who is frustrating you today because they are playing duality in an "I" Ego state instead of a "we" Ego state? Can you play in the "we" Ego state so often that your "I" Ego symbioses with your "we" Ego?

Power

In her book *Sunlight on Water*, Flo Magdalena talks about dissolving your "edges."[1] When diving into the freedom of dissolving into light, dancing on the water, and becoming one with all, the last part of me that would dissolve is the energy of fear of power. I realized that my/our "power" comes from surrendering to the light and the love of unified consciousness. This "power" is the energy of love and peace our souls were created with. We remember and embody this energy when we love ourselves open enough to be the ocean of creative, loving consciousness instead of being the drop of water or grain of sand that the human mind was created to play the game of polarity in.

One of the reasons we fear our power in this dimension is because we immerse ourselves in the realm of duality. We identify and pick a side to play on in the illusion of duality. In this tug-of-war with "dark" and "light," we pull hard against the half of our soul on the other side of the rope. When playing tug-of-war, we identify with the energy of the polarity that we cling to with the other humans who also identify with that side. We do not realize we are tearing our soul in half when we play tug-of-war because we forget that the souls we perceive as separate and "wrong" on the other side of the rope are actually part of our one soul. We will be at peace when we stop pulling and wanting what we feel is "right" to win. We need to put down the rope, walk to the center of the division, and open our hearts in hopes of finding a river that connects the hearts of all on both sides of the rope. Through surrender into the flow of this river of connection, we remember that we are all made of the same endless ocean of light. When we embody the peace we find in the flow of this remembered connection to our whole, we may never want to play tug-of-war to be "right" again. We may play it to create through duality. Still, the tugging will only occur to appreciate the many different viewpoints and realities of experience that our soul has collected to expand the loving wisdom of unified consciousness. Many of us temporarily can find access to this blissful remembrance of our wholeness, but we do not embody it with the totality we are capable of.

I invite you to dissolve into the light around you with greater frequency. Set the intention of melting open and merging with the wisdom and love of the collective consciousness found in all the "light" that surrounds you (other people, animals, elements of earth, other beings, and the other dimensions of our unified consciousness that are all available to you within your energy field as you have never been separate from all energy ever created). Imagine if we all played the game of Earth by harvesting the wisdom energy we gather through playing the game of duality. Then, by understanding that games of duality were created so that we could experience true bliss by melting back into unified consciousness, we find a new way to connect by choosing to create a new way to love. When we remember we are all one light and surrender to each other's magnificence and power, what version of love will we create together? Will you transmute the fear of y/our power into the potential of creating a unified consciousness while in a realm of duality? Will you explore the "nonboundaries" of your light ocean today and play through the dissolution of y/our light body into the light of all your mind perceives as a separate vibrating mass of energy today? Will you realize that your light has a frequency within it called love that dissolves all holograms of duality and experiences the bliss of unity with all energy? We got this. I love you and the unique wisdom of y/our unified consciousness that your mind is creating to enrich and evolve y/our beautiful soul.

Karma

We have attached suffering and penalty to the grace of gathering information for the collective by creating the concept of karma. We need to stop this attachment NOW!

There are many words and concepts in the human language that rarely, if ever, hold a loving vibration. *Karma*, *shame*, *should*, and *evil* are a few. I propose we no longer allow ourselves to vibrate in the resonance of such nonloving concepts. When we invest in the energy of the human idea box of karma, we forsake the peace that our soul was meant to embody and flourish with. By seeing our actions as good and others' as bad (or vice versa), we create a world where we only see dark and light. We get lost in the never-ending drama of victimhood or, even worse, the sadistic vibration of revenge.

It is time for us to see the world through the lens of exploration. It is time to see behaviors and people that many humans would label as "evil" as vessels gifted to you to raise your vibration. The "evil" in your world provides insight into your unlimited capacity to love and forgive. I ask you to see the "dark" vibrations that you are blessed to cross paths with as an opportunity to remember the blissful resonance of sharing love with someone who may have forgotten love exists. Understand that your bandwidth of compassion, understanding, and light can grow through the transmutation of the dark. When you transmute your darkness or help another transmute theirs, you create the frequency of that healing for all ready to receive it.

You are an unconditionally loving soul who feels the weight of the revenge vibration as pain because you refuse to embrace y/our true soul's nature to turn the other cheek and find a new way to love. I have helped countless people release years of pain in less than an hour by helping them let go of their anger and need for revenge. This anger has often been self-directed. That's because duality is an incredible illusion, and when you are angry at another through the lens of duality, you are angry with yourself in realms of singularity. The anger can be from this life or "past" lives. The true insight here is not to get too attached to any story from this life or a past life because the weight of the emotions you will carry when connected to a story will hurt you and others. See the story for the compassion it was gifting you, then let it go.

In this dimension where the veil is so thin right now, and love, wisdom, patience, understanding, and kindness are so easy to access, why are we still adding energy to the vibration of karma? Do you want to come back to this planet perpetually to hurt or be hurt by someone? No. So it is time to get off the infinity loop of karma.

When you have been wounded and want to feed the vibration of karma, close your eyes and breathe through your heart chakra. Connect your heart chakra to your entire hara line and see and feel through the energies of patience, love, light, courage, understanding, and wisdom within you. Become this resonance of the more loving dimensions of our consciousness within you. Then, combined with the higher dimensions within you, feel the pain of the other person/energy that you perceive as dark and is causing you pain. Sit with your pain instead of reacting with it. Imagine you can combine your pain with the pain of the one you perceive is inflicting your pain. A bright and loving soul is always encased in the darkness of the pain body that many want to wish karma on. Open your heart and connect with the heart of another so that you feel, see, sense, know, taste, or smell the light of the encased part of y/our soul standing in front of you in another human suit. Nourish your heart and soul with the love of Source that you are and marvel at how easy and fun it can be to transmute a pain body. Call in angels, God/Source, or your "higher" self for help until you have woven these higher light energies into your hara line by choosing to live in their resonance so much that they become part of you.

When you find the loving wisdom of y/our light in places you label as dark, you will transmute wounds from this life and past lifetimes and release joy, love, and connection that will heal you and others. I have seen many at work sending seeds of healing vibrations to others, the planet, the galaxy, and even the multiverse because they choose to no longer invest in a story that traps them in a box of the darkness of heavy emotion. We can heal each other in every interaction we have—if we choose to.

So, who is with me in creating a new world where the concept of karma does not exist? Will you choose to become the vibration of a patient and passionate love that seeks the darkness in yourself and others to create energy for this new world through transmutation? Will you transmute your darkness so you can know and emit the 144,000 dimensions of loving consciousness within you? Will you help me tell karma, "Thank you for your service, but we no longer need you"? I love you all and am blessed to share this trip to the planet with such loving versions of our one soul. Thank you.

Doors

One of the most asked philosophical questions is "Why are we here?"

As a human, I do not know that we will ever be able to understand the answer to that question. I do not think we can understand this with our limited human mind. I do know that I enjoy my Earth experience when I am connected and present with other humans and when I perceive that we are resonating at the same frequency.

Ask others what their bliss is for fun and the enlightenment that connection can offer. Every time I've asked someone this question, they've said they find bliss in connecting to another human through the vibration of peace, happiness, and shared joy, or in connecting to nature. In connection, we remember we are one. When we vibrate in oneness, we feel bliss. We are not here to connect only through times of bliss but also in times of perceived suffering. We have been taught to suffer alone and not burden anyone with our suffering. I encourage you to look at the bumps in the road of your life path as an opportunity for connection with another. Appreciate and understand that these bumps are a means to individual and collective growth through the sharing of difficult emotions with others. Allow yourself to appreciate life's ups and downs with gratitude because they are all here to enrich our lives. Oprah Winfrey said that at one time, when venting to Maya Angelou about a problematic interaction she was having that was causing her perceived suffering, Maya told her, "Stop it. Stop it right now. I want you to say thank you." Maya knew Oprah would grow from this "suffering" and reminded her to be grateful for the light she could share with the rest of us through this story.[2]

My bliss is being in service to others in a way that the light of their soul increases and then lights up other souls. I have found bliss in connecting to the vibration of perceived suffering in another and offering them space to receive the love they need to heal and take the next step of their journey. Showing people how to find the light within them always makes the light within me brighter and brings me to a place of humility that melts open the doors of the self-imposed prisons in which my heart has been trapped. You'll feel humility when you realize that a trip to the planet where you help others discover the magnificence of their light has got to be one of the coolest roles to play in the game of Earth.

I expect the road I am traveling to have ups and downs. However, lately, I have seen even the downs, the challenges, and the necessary leaps of faith as blessings. I understand that whenever I perceive a period of my life to be uncomfortable, I can transmute that illusion so that I can resonate and offer that transmutation to another person whose road will take the same path someday. I view these periods now as a blessing. By celebrating both the "joy" and "suffering" of my life path, I have learned patience, acceptance, and a deep gratitude that makes me weep. The gratitude arises by appreciating that my consciousness is choosing to play human so that we can open the doors of the prisons our soul has created with fear.

When we're faced with the opportunity for a new adventure or a perceived bump in the road of our life path, we can either pause in the paralyzation of the cortisol response that fear brings, or we can allow the invigorating current of surrender to take us on a ride to new dimensions we never dreamed of. The choice is yours. In her book *Intimate Conversations with the Divine*, Caroline Myss describes new opportunities in life as a waiting room.[3] We enter this waiting room when it is time to take the next step of our journey in the game of Earth. Many of us want to keep opening the door we just closed and return to how things were. When we try to do this, we prolong our suffering by returning to a vibration we are no longer meant to resonate with. Myss states that fear keeps us from opening new doors, but if we change our perception to a more exploratory outlook, we can open the new doors or options our life path can take with gratitude and the vibration of hope one can embody when thinking, "What beautiful adventure awaits behind these new doors?"

I encourage you to shift your perception and open as many waiting room doors as you can with a loving heart instead of a cortisol-producing mind or limbic system. Become a child and giggle while you ask, "I wonder what fun I am going to find behind this door?" Jenniffer Weigel once told me I reminded her of the movie *Elf* when Buddy was in an elevator for the first time, and he pushed every button with the joy of exploring what each button did as he pushed them. I was attempting to understand the new healing operating system my essence was revealing to me at the time.

How many times can you open a new door today? Will you close the old one with gratitude and honor for the experience you got to have while on that step of your path? Someone I was working on grew beautiful roses with thick vines over the old door in her waiting room so she could no longer open it. She allowed and incorporated the "lesson" (aka loving energy she transmuted for our collective soul) she learned behind that door with gratitude. The roses grew from the appreciation for the "lesson," and the thick vines kept her from reopening it. She then could turn around and be ready to open new doors and new chapters of her life with less trepidation.

We all have different paths, options, and opinions on how the game of life should be played. Our differences create the beautiful spectrum of our rainbow of light and keep us in a perpetual state of absorbing different frequencies to experience when playing the game of life. It is solely up to you to pick the path that gives you the freedom and confidence to embrace the potential you were born with. The cool thing is you always have the choice to be in gratitude when you are guided into closing the doors to the pathways that no longer serve you and opening new ones that will grace you with experiences that will offer new nourishment for y/our soul. It is up to you to choose the path that will allow you to remember why your soul chose to have a human experience on this beautiful planet in this timeline. It is up to you to use the "lessons" your path gives you to discover how to love y/our soul and human suits more so your soul and the energy of y/our human minds merge to deeper levels of symbiosis. With each step of your path, you allow the underlying lesson of love on the old step to be incorporated into collective consciousness, and as a byproduct of this incorporation, the soul/human mind symbiotic relationship deepens. The soul is our tether to Source, and the more in resonance with your human it is, the easier Source is to access. How many closed doors will you have gratitude for today? How many doors will you open in the future while giggling with anticipation and excitement of discovering what new opening embodiment of love lies behind the new door? Will you giggle as you punch all the elevator buttons today?

Angels and demons

Our thoughts create reality; our emotions solidify it.

This dimension is a game we call life on Earth where we are given the opportunity to experience "good" and "bad," "light" and "dark," and "heaven" and "hell." We chose to come here to play this game so we could collect the energies of despair and isolation and the joy of love and connection and use those energies to expand the creative capability of our collective soul. In the realms "higher" than 3D, we have no body and cannot experience this dimension of duality that we use to gather energy through embodiment for creation.

When our human suit chooses to experience fear, our body contracts and shields, and our mind tries to help by removing us from the reality we perceive as uncomfortable. When we allow our mind and body to do this, we are playing the game of life the way it was meant to be played. However, we tend to get stuck in fear; thus, the game is no longer fun, and we create a "hell" reality. Since we are in a "hell," our mind may even create a "demon" that we imagine to be controlling us. We might think this "demon" comes from within or sense it as external. The demon can be manifested as an addiction, depression, or even another's energy attacking us. I invite you to at least consider that we are creator beings and that if you see demons, you may be creating them because you are choosing to feed fear by giving it your attention and, thus, your amazing bandwidth of creative energy. I believe that fear can be fed to the point that a "demon" is solidified. If this is the case, you can dissolve the "demon" by no longer feeding the dimension of reality your mind is paying attention to, which is creating it.

How do you dissolve a "demon"? You can ask to shift the lens through which you perceive the world and change your reality from embodied fear to embodied love. You can ask for help from a healer who resonates with your belief system to help you do so. You can tell the gods of duality, "Thank you for allowing me to embody and understand that ouchy vibration or emotion, but I am ready to embody love now." You could ask a fellow human for a hug. You can sit and honor your soul for collecting the powerful, heavy emotion you got stuck in so that our collective soul can become more compassionate and loving. I have felt these demons in people as a powerful attachment to the energy of victimhood, the stab wounds of unreciprocated love, the frustration of injustice, and the separation of soul that judgment and grief cause, as well as other flavors of fear. If you choose to stop feeding these painful, energetic embodiments, your "demons" will dissolve.

We all have and will continue to embody fear and thus have all created demons, so please, if you feel the need, forgive yourself and move on!

Every step you take on your journey is perfect. Please know this to be true so you can embody the vibration that allows you to transmute the heavy emotions and embody love; this is how you create angels. There is a link to God/Source/the universe inside of you, found through a photon in the center of your body that I call your God particle. Once you surrender to your God particle—you will no longer be playing the game of Earth through the separation of duality. You will be embodying love by letting it flow from within. You can picture you/love untangling and healing all of the energetic entanglements your fascia (thought) has created by feeding fear. When your fascia is free of fear, it becomes an energetic web of loving connection. Your human suit will no longer need a shield because your mind, when surrendered to your God particle, does not understand fear. Your fascia will embrace loving connection, and those around you will feel your light and may even see you as an angel or see the angel you create because you are choosing to feed and embody love.

You are a creator who solidifies your reality with the emotion you feed. Please choose to feed love today and play the game of life in a way that allows us to create new angels instead of demons. We got this. I, our soul and the energy of God you are an essential part of within you loves you. May you be blessed to discover this in the felt sense today and know it is true.

Perfection

We are all taught to strive for "perfection" from a young age. We absorb the idea that something is wrong with us when we are not "perfect," according to a human Ego comparison scale. I would like to invite you to help me obliterate the harmful and limiting belief of the concept of perfect that the human Ego entices us to feed in this dimension. It is time we stopped wasting our magnificent creative energy on the idea that perfection is a goal to be achieved and realize it is a state of grace we are in at all times.

We all have moments that we allow ourselves to believe are perfect. They are the moments or stories we revisit to find peace. These perfect moments are revealed in the harmony we feel when we open our hearts and symbiose frequencies with another soul. The harmony can be in a moment of joy or extreme sorrow. I would like you to remember one of these moments and try to understand this is the definition of perfection we need to feed with our energy. There is no greater bliss than when we are connected, when we truly see another and are seen by a fellow soul. Understand that we are always perfect because we are always in a symbiotic relationship with our soul, whether we perceive it as separate from us or exploring its depths within us. Our emotional state may not be comfortable, but it is still perfect and exactly where our soul needs to be for this step of its journey.

So please let go of the idea that perfection is an ideal performance or goal achieved, and we can stop feeding the energetic definition of perfection that limits us all. All the steps of our journey are perfect and deserve our love and respect. All interactions with others and yourself are required for the energy exchanges that will guide us in alchemizing our soul into a unified consciousness in a dimension of duality. Thus, honor the steps of your path by loving the "perfection" and wisdom they grace you and y/our soul with. Thank you for collecting the energy of creation for our soul to play with through the perfect steps of your fantastic journey.

Validation

When our consciousness is tethered to frequencies of the Earth's vibration that reside in duality, we have an attachment to our story. Our stories are important in this realm because they are a very effective connection and communication tool. Many cannot feel a soul-to-soul connection when playing Earth, so they must connect through stories created with the tool we use to navigate this dimension: the mind. When connected through a story, our minds serve as a vehicle to exchange the energetic frequencies of emotions. Stories are significant because we came to Earth to collect the energy of emotions, and stories are an effective way to exchange and experience emotions. However, when we get stuck on one story, we miss the opportunity to explore and collect the vibrations of other emotions and connect ourselves to other souls by sharing a new story.

So why do we get stuck in our stories? I think at least one of the answers is validation. When we land in a splat in this dimension, we perceive our soul as separate from all energy. We are also neurolinguistically programmed to think that love is conditional. When brainwashed into this idea, we feel love should only be given and accepted when we or others are "good," "right," or "worthy." Thus, the giving and receiving of love are associated with judgment and the need to share your story so that others can validate that you are worthy of love and on the "right" side of what you are "judging."

Attaching the wonder and awe of the unlimited frequency of love to a diminishing box of judgment makes me laugh and cry at how ludicrous and limiting our thoughts and, thus, our capacity to share the energy of our souls can be when connected to a mind that resides in separation from unified consciousness. Love is the frequency of light we were created from, the solidified atoms that form our human suit, and it is the energy that connects us. We should never limit the opportunities to share and receive it by judging when, how, and whom we should share it with.

In unified consciousness, we are always validated because we are never alone. One could argue the more into unified consciousness you surrender yourself, the concept of validation does not even exist. So how do we access unified consciousness in a human suit to play the game of Earth in a state of flow, where we experience as many stories as possible, and not just get stuck in one? We choose to absorb the story we are telling by absorbing its wisdom and love. A story stored within your consciousness vibrating in love and wisdom will only be shared when it is called to share the notes of its wisdom and love, not to validate a human Ego.

So, how do we absorb the stories that attach us and keep us stuck in limiting boxes while on this human-suit roller-coaster ride? How about trying to melt into the stillness at the core of the box? Within that space is a tender, loving part of your mind that never felt loved, heard, appreciated, accepted, cherished, etc. The core of the box is found in the part of your body that is tense or in pain. This banished part of your energy field is begging for you to reembody it by loving and honoring it. Hug it with the vibration of love required for transmutation out of a cortisol state to a dopamine, serotonin, or norepinephrine state. Validate the boxes your mind has imprisoned itself in by lovingly witnessing the steps of our story that you have collected in the powerful vibration of fear. Do this until the fear is transmuted through the validation of the energy of gratitude, and then ask your mind to release the attachment to the story trapped in that particular fear box. In doing so, you have altered the lens through which you see and feel this story. You will now share it with an undertone of love and connection that will heal you and all you share it with when your soul (not your mind) is called to share it.

So, will you go within and spend time validating all the parts of your human mind that have never been offered unconditional love or been too afraid to see it has been offered? Love your boxes until they are opened and then dissolved. Set your mind free from the attachment to an old story told in the vibration of the duality of fear and allow it to be held until it symbioses with your soul. The story can now be told with the vibration of the wisdom and love of y/our soul. If you don't know what unconditional love feels like, find a healer or surrender your mind to your higher power or unified consciousness. Know in these words, you are loved by my/our soul more than you might ever be able to imagine. You can at any time ask to be held and validated by the essence of our soul, and our essence would be honored and humbled that it could guide and help you heal yourself in this way.

The more stories we tell in the vibration of love and wisdom, the faster we heal our soul. The more pieces of our soul that are healed, the more fun the game of creation is to play because we will be playing it with love and wisdom, not the more painful emotions. We got this. Our soul loves you so much and is always there within you to help you validate and love the parts of you that you do not perceive as healed and whole. Let's rewrite our painful stories today so that we can create many more marvelous new ones together.

3

Discovering the Power of Our Light

Our fortress

There is a bliss we can find when wearing a human suit that is divinely unique and unlike other flavors of bliss. The sad part is that we infrequently taste this bliss while playing human. I want to encourage you to soften and open up so that you may experience this more often—or even for the first time. Many souls want to leave this realm because they think consciousness is better in another dimension, but the secret is we never leave any realm that our consciousness inhabits. Part of our soul will always be in this "timeline" to collect energy and experiences for the benefit of our collective soul. If this statement is true, then let's alter how we experience this reality and walk the steps of our journey here in a way that brings joy to our collective soul.

How do we do this? Here is a theory. Think of the times when the fortress of your heart has been open and connected to another soul in a human suit with the bliss of understanding that there is no separation between your energy fields. If you have not experienced this, I am putting that vibration of elation and joy into these words for you to experience if you open up your soul by breathing through your heart or belly and asking to remember what that bliss feels like. How do you find it on your own? Ask to cross paths with another human who wears their heart on their sleeve. These old, wise, and incredibly loving versions of the embodiment of God/Source/Gaia/the divine on the planet are profound teachers. They are masters of showing you how to dissolve the world of duality with one glance of their loving eyes. They invite you to share God's peace by emitting the frequency that is God. If you choose to dissolve the Ego's protective fortress, you will understand, embody, and then transmit God's frequency yourself. When we are in this state of embodiment, we do not want to leave this dimension, and we cocreate a new reality that will thrive on this energy.

When we walk the steps of our human journey, we are playing a game of duality that is necessary to collect emotions other than bliss. We can create with these emotions' energies. We can also use these other emotions to connect with God. We can find another resonating in fear, anger, sadness, guilt, grief, shame, etc., and ask to hold each other with a heart with no prison walls of protection. I guarantee this hug, experienced in the divine state we call vulnerability, will instantaneously summon the transmutative flames that your mind needs to comprehend that the pain of the separated yang energies you are experiencing is simultaneously the bliss of the yin energies our soul would describe as unconditional love. With the embodiment of this yin and yang cohesion, you will create new loving energy for all others to feel so they can join in this blissful game of soul connection through a human suit.

I want to thank all the souls that have crossed my path to show me this frequency so I can share it with all of you. You never know when you will be one of those souls crossing my path or the path of another to share this divine wisdom and magnificence of the embodiment and radiation of God energy on this planet at this time. So, I encourage you to listen to the energy fields of others with a heart free of any walls of duality as often as you can. You will discover this is the ultimate way to play the game of Earth. Will you walk the steps of your journey playing Earth like this as often as possible? Our hearts will be opened in a way they have not remembered in a long time if we just allow them to blossom into the beautiful notes of our symbiotic symphony of creation. We can do this by setting them free from the prisons we have created to "protect" us from feeling the bliss of love because we are afraid that we will lose it. A closed heart separates us from knowing that love is an ingredient in all the emotions we feel. Thus, when our hearts remain open, and we understand that love is part of all of our experiences here on Earth, we will never want to imprison our hearts again. Will you ask all the prison walls that keep you from experiencing all flavors of love to remain open always so you can find the bliss of creation in all your experiences today?

Fear

> "The answer to fear is never to think more. It is to think less and to trust the flow of life. It is to fall back into the state of grace that is your birthright. It is to release instead of grab hold." —Pamela Kribbe, *The Jeshua Channelings: Christ Consciousness in a New Era*[1]

Pamela Kribbe is one of my favorite authors. Please read the above quote a few times and try to absorb what it tells you. With the headlines constantly trying to keep us in fear on a daily basis, finding grace can be perceived as problematic. Fear is an emotion that many of us feed daily. It is the reality that our limbic system connects to, and it incites global destruction and suffering by fueling the separation of our collective soul.

So, how do we coax our minds to think less and thus stop feeding fear? I have used the simple phrase "fuck off, fear" at times. One of my patients even made bright-pink hats that said "FOF" for her and her friends. The giggling that might spontaneously erupt from you while wearing a FOF hat would definitely be enough joyful energy to transmute fear. You could also tell your mind to be more afraid of what you will miss out on (FOMO) by not being in the now than what disaster your mind is imagining might happen in the future. Or try breathing the love you are made of into all your cells so that the cortisol created by your limbic system can no longer keep you in a fear-infinity loop.

So, how do you breathe love into your cells? Somewhere in your core, you have a photon I like to call your God particle. Try discovering it by asking your mind to find it. This photon connects you to all energy ever created and allows you to feel and embody the love and support of our collective soul. Take as many deep breaths as you need to while asking to find your God particle by remembering you have never been without it. It has been with you since your soul's conception and will never leave you. It will help if you picture your heart, solar plexus, and sacral chakras opening to their core as you breathe them open. My God particle lies under my xiphoid process, but I have felt it below the belly button for others. It may be in another location for you. At times, it travels to different parts of my body where healing is needed or where there is a greater capacity for an energetic exchange to take place.

Once you find this God particle, you can feel the love that it is made of emanating from it to open and heal your energetic field. I also feel Source energy is what the outermost layer of our aura is made of, and I often receive healing love and wisdom from there. You can even receive from the God particle within and the outside shell of your aura at the same time. You will stop perceiving this as receiving when you realize there is no time and all the energy you perceive you are receiving is *your* energy. You will remember the amazing and magnificent totality of you, that your aura has no outer shell, and that you are Source/essence/God/the divine.

As you breathe open, feel how amazing it is to be open and connected to all energy instead of residing in a tiny fear box that keeps you from embodying all you are. Imagine that the loving energy you are inhaling to open with permeates every cell of your body. This loving energy fills your body with a love that will caress your fear and gently remove or transmute it when you exhale. When you exhale, say no to allowing fear to keep you from peace. You can even say to the fear, "I release you with love and light to your next highest good," or "I am choosing to honor the experience you have graced me with. Thus, I no longer need to give my attention to the step of my journey you enlightened me with because I now see the love that I created with that step. It is now part of the energy field of love I will share with those who cross my path."

Many people believe that if just 1 percent of the planet's population can resonate in a loving state together, all of the Earth's population will become aware of this state of bliss and beauty. Will you work on releasing or, better yet, transmuting your fear so that you can emit love to heal yourself with and share with others today? Do you want to be part of the initial 1 percent that guides the rest of the planet out of the perpetual fear state that the news brainwashes us into embodying as our reality? Which fear box will you choose to love open today? Will you hold loving space for another to love open some of their fear boxes?

The limbic brain

We are taught that the limbic system is part of our primitive brain and that its "protection" is essential to survival. If your limbic system detects immediate danger around you, it allows your body to react without thought to reach "safety" in the most efficient way possible. If you are in a safe environment and are vibrating in a fear state, I invite you to tell your limbic system to piss off and that its services are not currently wanted or needed. Some of us believe that our consciousness will never leave this time experience. If you believe this, it means death is an illusion, and you might never need to pay attention to your limbic system at all. Our limbic systems have placed our essence in a box of fear for far too long. You cannot simultaneously vibrate in love and fear; you must pick which vibration you want to play Earth in. I prefer love. I have told my limbic system many times, "The contract with overprotection is up. You may no longer prevent me from exploring the creative potential of the essence of my/our soul while wearing a human suit." I wish to choose love and giggles over fear; I want to feel the environments that are my steps on the path of life as safe. In this relaxation of my energy, I choose to be vulnerable and have no heart walls so that I may experience every version of my essence that I meet along the way with the singularity of connection that is available when we know we are one. I choose to see, feel, taste, touch, and smell through the oneness within and be humbled to exchange knowledge, wisdom, and love with the fantastic version of my soul standing before me.

The limbic system is involved in processes relating to emotion, learning, memory, and motivation by working with both the endocrine and autonomic nervous systems.[2] The purpose of this part of the brain is to inform us of what may harm us and what is safe so that we survive. The power of the imprinting it possesses can be ingrained in our subconscious for generations, as has been documented in the children and grandchildren of Holocaust survivors.[3] Another example of the power of its subconscious imprinting is when you witnessed your mother fear a spider when you were two years old, and you are now deathly afraid of spiders and have no idea why. Your mother may have passed this ridiculous fear on from her mother. Even the trauma of past lives can access your limbic system and keep you from opening up to your potential in this lifetime by trapping you in the emotion of fear. Please read Dr. Brian Weiss's many books to be enlightened on this subject.

Our human suit contains a limbic system because it guides our fascia into helping us run away when we are in danger or takes subconscious control of our body when we require a reaction like steering our car to avoid a crash. So, we should be grateful for the immediate dangers it steers us away from. However, it does not serve us when it—with the help of our mind—manipulates time and we run from a threat that does not exist in the now. Does being afraid of spiders help you in any way? I would argue no.

If you watch an antelope get chased by a lion, first it will run; if it gets caught, it will play dead; if it survives and the lion walks away, it shakes for thirty seconds to one minute and then walks away calmly. This is how the limbic system was meant to operate. The shaking removes the memory linked to the attack from the antelope's fascia and nervous system. When the antelope walks away, the memory of the attack and the cortisol that the limbic system provoked into secretion for the survival of the antelope also disappear. The antelope is back to living in *now*. The antelope will never retell this story or go back to the scene of the attack and reactivate its limbic system by doing so. We need to incorporate the wisdom of an antelope by reprogramming how our limbic systems can serve us and not limit us by creating the shit show we call PTSD.

In our modern world, there are no more saber-toothed tigers to attack us. But some of us have PTSD from witnessing a traumatic event. When that traumatic event happened, our body experienced a surge of cortisol as our limbic system tried to get us to safety. Now, when we're reminded of that event by a trigger, we go directly back to that traumatic event, and our limbic system secretes the same cortisol chemicals.

However, many of us do not have PTSD, yet we allow new, nonthreatening events to activate our limbic systems into a cortisol-producing frenzy. Most of us live in relatively safe environments. Thus, it is possible our limbic systems and brains may get bored and entice us into being afraid of things that do not threaten our safety. It is also possible that you have been neurolinguistically programmed into fearing everyday objects in your environment. How many of you now perceive an email, an interaction with another, or gossip about you or another to feel like a life-threatening trauma? Many of us now allow interactions like these to provoke fear, anger, guilt, etc., for months or even years afterward. These are not actually life-threatening events, but we allow them to control our capacity to love by placing us in unjustified fear states. There is no physical trauma to be protected from in these circumstances, just trauma to the energy we call Ego.

Our Ego will survive as long as we wear a human suit. You could argue that, at times, the temporary "death of the Ego" is a good thing because without this energy of separation in control, we can experience great freedom. Because we are all empathic, I believe our limbic system is activated when others are afraid. How many of you watch the news and become angry or sad as you feel others' pain? How long after watching a scene from the news or even a movie have you allowed yourself to be led into a cortisol state of fear by your mind replaying the scene and your limbic system trying to help you escape it?

So, how do you release the "irrational" emissions of your limbic system so that you can regain control of it and have it secrete happy hormones that heal instead of stress-inducing cortisol? Command your limbic system to be in the now. Michael J. Shea, who has written several excellent books on biodynamic craniosacral techniques, uses these techniques to take you back to an embryo stage to reset your limbic system and all the reactions to perceived previous traumas you store there. In doing so, you erase the subconscious autonomic response to prior trauma; your current fears, anxieties, resentments, and anger will be released from their entwinement with the old limbic system activating memories. Stimuli that currently trigger you into fear will no longer have that energetic resonance with your field. I have used Shea's ideas and Donna Eden's technique of holding the neurovascular points on the forehead to alter PTSD pictorial flashes in many people and alleviate the crippling terror they feel when subjected to these memory flashes. Sometimes, shockingly, this "reprogramming" takes less than one minute and is very effective. From what I understand, tapping techniques and EMDR techniques are also beneficial for reprogramming the limbic system and freeing you from PTSD.

We can also guide our limbic system into the now through our intention. You are more powerful than you have been led to believe regarding the power of an intention you set with your heart. You can alchemize cortisol with love and create dopamine, serotonin, and norepinephrine through heart-centered breathing. Lovingly, thank your limbic system for directing your attention to a fear from the past that has been grabbing your attention so you could love that experience into your wholeness. Go to the place in your energetic field where you feel pain or tightness from the grip of an old fear and breathe energy from the heart of the entirety of y/our soul through that area. Reclaim the power of love that has been hidden deep within it for far too long.

I want to create a body that has no fear of death or what circumstance is going to walk into my awareness today. My limbic system prevents me from doing this, so I picture ripping my limbic system out of the back of my head at times because I genuinely feel it no longer serves any purpose for me. I wish to see every exchange of energy that my soul in a human suit is graced with experiencing as happening *for* me and not *to* me. When I have perceived all the traumas and joys that have created the magnificent steps of my journey as vibrations of energy and understood that all energy is love, my mind and heart have been opened to, held lovingly, and then become one with a vibration of peace I never dreamed could exist in a 3D reality. In this blissful state of peace that is a thread of singularity connected to the womb of creation, I am offered an opportunity to open my heart in such a way I remember or create a new way to share love. I cannot find this state of peace if I am vibrating in fear.

The path one chooses to be free of the control the limbic system has on them is likely an individual one and different for every trigger in need of "reprogramming." I am a firm believer in what Caroline Myss and others call "dis-ease."[4] I believe that when we "suffer" (this is a word and idea that we should consider removing from our vocabulary and understanding), there is a "growth" potential, individually and for the collective soul we all share. I believe our collective mind uses the symbiosis and equalizations of our perceived dark/light and yin/yang information absorption to create new energy. Thus, the fear we plunge into with the activation of the limbic system may be a necessary energy to play creation, but remaining in it may pause the game and prolong a part of the game we do not perceive as fun to play.

So, just a postulation. Maybe before you reset your limbic system, ask to use the power of the control/energy your limbic system has had over you to be released after the sway in emotion/information you have been experiencing has been absorbed by you for the growth of our soul. Honor yourself for collecting vibrations that only exist in the resonance of fear because these were not fun to collect. If you are too traumatized and can't absorb the information, then ask someone strong enough to help you. The secret is that the one you perceive as stronger and wiser than you is actually a part of you that you have not yet loved back into your awareness. By surrendering and asking for help, you find the extremely profound pathway of remembering awake that is self-love. I am so grateful when you choose to play Earth in the self-love vibration. The sound of your unique note in its glorious power is essential for our soul to embody and radiate the loving symphony of creation.

Death

Death is a very uncomfortable word for many of us. I want to invite you to shift your perspective and find respect for the gift it offers us.

A friend's soul recently departed the body it was gifted to synchronize with on this trip to the planet. The pain and sadness that her death awakened in me are still being released and transmuted through my tears. It comforts me to know that she "reunited" with loved ones on the other side of the veil and that her essence is still infused on this side in the friends she left behind. I know the gifts her soul blessed me with will eternally be infused into my essence so that I can share her unique flavor of love with others. This knowledge creates a gratitude that our souls crossed paths again while playing another round of the game of Earth. When we tap into and become one with Source, we resonate in unconditional love's patience, peace, acceptance, and persistence. However, while in a human suit, we can taste the flavors of love that we call passion and experience a narrowing of the bandwidth of love so that it can feel more intense. When our passionate love bonds are torn while resonating in the Earth's energy, where our perception of time is altered for our great benefit, it causes the deep pain we know as grief.

Many of us have difficulty opening up and perceiving death as anything other than a painful and almost unbearable loss. I invite you to change your perspective on this mantra because we were not meant to get stuck in the heaviness and stagnation of grief. I think one of the reasons we feel love and connection so differently on this planet is that we can use the pain of losing a loved one for tremendous growth if we surrender to the information it is trying to gift us with. My friend's death taught me that the illusion of a loved one's energy leaving planet Earth to return "home" can be a blessing to help others grow through the alchemy of the pain that the death of a loved one gifts them. If you are not ready to see the death of a loved one as a gift, I open the love of my heart to hold space for you to begin to open yours and start healing. Also, the book I give everyone to help with grief is *The Light Between Us* by Laura Lynne Jackson.[5] This book will help you step out of the pain of grief into the broader healing realm of acceptance. Acceptance leads to the return of awareness of the energies of peace and joy that lie in you, hidden deep in the boxes of your painful grief.

There is a story I have heard about a servant who went to the market and met Death. When he met Death, he got terrified, but Death seemed confused, so he ran home and escaped Death. When he got home, he asked his master for a horse so he could head to Sonora to avoid Death. The master agreed but still needed goods from the market, so the master went to the market and also ran into Death. He asked Death why he had been confused when meeting the servant. Death answered, "I was confused why I saw your servant here because I am meeting him in Sonora tonight." This story and many others like it resonate with me in that I don't think the time we die in this lifetime is negotiable most of the time. Thus, we need to let go of the control we want over when our loved ones die and accept the gift their death was meant to provide us.

My friend's death taught me to accept I cannot help everyone find a path to healing. God's and her soul's plans are more important than my Ego's wants. I can sometimes feel her loving me and supporting me in my growth in ways I could not before she passed. I do think if you are facing death, you can have a conversation with God and your higher self and can opt to change your pre-life exit strategy planning if you have a good reason to stay longer than you and God originally intended.

Through the pain and searching for answers that death incites, many people have a dramatic shift in perspective with the loss of a loved one. I have recently gotten to know Jenniffer Weigel through her Spiritual Social Club. She is a gift to all of us who are trying to absorb, understand, and incorporate the connective abilities we are remembering how to manifest and emit in this rapid energy frequency shift the planet is going through. She has tirelessly interviewed countless psychics and healers all because she was searching for closure and answers when her father, Tim, died. These interviews have resulted in books and podcasts that have opened the door to a world many never knew existed. The messages and ideas they radiate have held a loving space to lessen the fear and perceived isolation that we feel when remembering that our energy field is so much larger than our human suit. Jen's stories have helped countless people to obliterate the boxes of the limited ways we have been taught to view and understand our human suits. Her stories are dissolving the veil between worlds by guiding souls like me into remembering who they truly are and helping us realize there is no veil between realms when our heart is open and our human suit is vibrating in love and not fear. Because of a drive to alchemize the pain of her grief, Jen steered her human suit along a path different from what she thought she would take in life. She grew open to discovering a realm of healing love to share with the planet that she had never imagined existed. Tim's death guided her on this unexpected path. Thank you, Tim and Jenniffer Weigel.

I do think understanding death through a frequency other than grief is one of the main reasons many souls made their current trip to the planet. Choosing to get stuck in grief wastes productive growth time on the planet and takes away the fun of playing the game of Earth. When you are able, will you see the gift a loved one's death has given you? If you cannot see a gift, will you waste the growth that can come from the pain of their death? Will you have to endure this same pain in future lifetimes until you accept the gift their return to "home" (at a "time" your Ego does not think is fair) is trying to give you?

Shackles

What shackles have you been placing on yourself?

I recently spent a weekend with a friend who is a healer, and I was having some pain in a neuroma located just above my ankle. I have had this painful area for a few years, but of course, as a doctor and healer, I am a terrible patient and have not yet made an appointment to have it removed. So, I tolerate the pain when it comes and goes. I know there is emotional information stored in this annoying tumor and that I have the capacity to heal it through the surrender to the self-love that will hold and will emulsify it in the frequency of love it needs to dissolve. However, the day I was with my healing friend, it hurt a lot, so I asked her what vibration it was created with. She held her hand over it and said, "Despair." I have always seen this as a shackle wound from a previous life, so despair made sense to me because that would be a vibration you could easily embody in a dungeon. I then felt that my soul created this neuroma to tell me it was in despair.

Why was my soul in despair? The answer I came up with was my scared Ego was shackling it and not allowing its true potential, beauty, love, peace, and brilliance to radiate from me. How many of you are doing the same? I felt that day that most of us are shackling our souls. This saddened and angered me into saying, "No more. This bullshit ends today." So, will you take the self-loving steps needed to end this tragedy today?

Our heavy emotions create our shackles, and the time has come when we must love ourselves enough to free ourselves from them. How do we do this? First, be honest and ask yourself, "What triggers me into self-doubt, anger, sadness, grief, judgment, etc." That answer is not hard to find. I bet one of the next three interactions you have with yourself through the eyes of a fellow soul in a human radiance will give you an answer if you ask and allow yourself to receive it. The answer you receive in the triggered emotion you vibrate in will guide you to the part of your pain body that needs your love and attention to heal. My answer had come in a few inter-actions with humans before my shackle epiphany. These humans kindly told me I needed to release my fear of becoming the leader I was meant to be by encouraging me (with loving conviction) to explore areas I had been afraid to explore.

When things come in threes, please take notice and work on what y/our soul is trying to tell you. Take a deep breath, feel the power of your connection to Source inside you, feel the loving embrace it is always hold-ing you in, and love yourself with it. Take your newborn soul's unbiased, unconditionally loving energy and tenderly embrace the part of your body in pain. Honor the painful but powerful vibration that you have bravely collected for us to use to transmute into a beautiful new energy of hope, healing, forgiveness, and unity. Hug yourself until you set yourself free of that shackle created by the limiting belief you temporarily chose to vibrate in to gain compassion, wisdom, and love for all of us to heal with.

I am now making a conscious effort to release shackles by inviting the symbiotic combination of my/our soul and my Ego to help me be aware of them. As I have done so, I am expanding my capacity for love and gratitude. I am now loving my neuroma for reminding me that every day I need to spend time setting my soul free from the enmeshment my human mind has with the limiting beliefs of this dimension. I know my shackle will be reabsorbed into my energy field soon if I continue to love it until I have witnessed all the healing it was meant to grace me with. For fun, I am playing the game of loving my neuroma out of existence with a patient who also has pain in an extremity because she has been shackling her soul by shunning the grace of receiving. We are both discovering that self-love is a much better vibration to play the game of Earth in than frustration and self-judgment.

So, will you play this game of removing your shackles with me? I hope you do because it is time for us to be free of our bullshit. Can you imagine the new reality we will create when we are free of all shackles?

Suffering

The headlines will continue to try to put you in a reality of perpetual suffering. Will you choose to let them?

> "A human being is a part of the whole, called by us 'Universe,'
> a part limited in time and space. He experiences himself,
> his thoughts and feelings as something separated from
> the rest—a kind of optical delusion of his consciousness.
> This delusion is a kind of prison for us, restricting us to
> our personal desires and to affection for a few persons
> nearest to us. Our task must be to free ourselves from this
> prison by widening our circle of compassion to embrace
> all living creatures and the whole of nature in its beauty.
> Nobody is able to achieve this completely, but the striving
> for such achievement is in itself a part of the liberation
> and a foundation for inner security." —Albert Einstein[6]

I would like to address the frustration, sadness, and grief that many of us feel when we hear or read headlines about horrible school shootings, war, or whatever daily dose of fear or hatred the media promotes. When we are at peace, we have no reason to venture outside the small space we create with our loved ones. However, our compassion, connections, and hearts open to humanity and beyond when we see suffering. It seems we sometimes empathize with suffering more than joy, which is interesting. Suffering awakens us from the prison that Albert Einstein describes above. The question is: How do we process the suffering for growth instead of allowing it to cause anxiety and depression by getting us stuck in sympathy? Will we use suffering to create another prison of division from the whole through the judgments and the anger we are being spoon-fed from the media, or will you use the suffering as a means to connect, pause, and transcend to a new place within that creates a solution to the suffering through love?

It is our birthright to use the endless source of unconditional love within us to change our beliefs and perceptions of our reality. When you recognize the ability to shed your limiting beliefs through the pain of suffering, you will be grateful for the awakening it graces you with as you fully step into its resonance. I know how helpless we can feel when we read headlines that make us feel that humanity has lost its way. What can we do about it? How about making eye contact and smiling at the next person who crosses your path and who you feel is suffering?

We create environments that are devoid of love. It is time to try to walk in the frequency of the unconditional love our soul was birthed from. When we remember this frequency of love and walk the realms of duality as this vibration, the loveless environments we had previously created, by emitting the ignorant conditional definition of love most of us have been taught, will no longer have that frequency of love to feed off of and thus they will cease to exist. I can't help but think about the Uvalde school shooting on May 24, 2022, at Robb Elementary School in Uvalde, Texas. The eighteen-year-old shooter was bullied for a speech impediment, had a bad home life, lashed out in violence, he may have been molested by one of his mother's boyfriends, and when he told her, he was not believed.[7]

What if several people had recognized, empathized, and were 100 percent present with this kid's suffering over the years? What if people had let him know, "I see you, and yes, your life sucks, but you got this," and shown him the love that would have helped him remember he is made of the power of hope. What if they had reminded him that the strength of his hope and the love he had within to fuel it could create a better life for him and all around him? Would this shooting have happened? How many more shootings need to occur before we start connecting with each other's pain so that we can process our own as we help another process theirs? There is only one soul here; thus, your neighbor's pain is yours and vice versa.

It is time to change the way we react to global suffering. We must realize that the mass of energy that creates global suffering comes from the pain of many fragments of our soul that suffer individually in isolation. It is time to start changing the emotions of the world by being kinder, more present, and nonjudgmental with the humans, animals, Gaia as a whole, and all of the amazing energy she nourishes and holds space for that you interact with each day. Just for fun, the next time someone upsets you or looks sad, energetically create a flower of your choice with your heart and place it in theirs. I know this sounds a little wild, but try it. You cannot feel love and anger at the same time. It is impossible. A seed has been planted even if the one you create the flower for is not present enough to receive it at this time. There is a time when our soul will not only accept it but fuel it with our love to grow a garden of life we never imagined possible. Living in an unconditional love state as much as humanly possible will free you from suffering.

How often will you try to use your suffering as a means to open up to loving yourself by being kinder to yourself and others? How often will you choose to share your suffering with another who shares the same vibration so that you both may heal as one? It is way more fun to share healing with another than to do this alone. Will you understand that by ending the isolation of suffering in y/our soul through the transmutative unlimited power of love, you heal y/our soul?

> "Imagination is more important than knowledge. For knowledge is limited, whereas imagination embraces the entire world, stimulating progress, giving birth to evolution. It is, strictly speaking, a real factor in scientific research." —Albert Einstein, *On Cosmic Religion and Other Opinions and Aphorisms*[8]

I find it fascinating that one of our most prominent mathematical geniuses was also one of our most seemingly spiritually advanced human beings. I guess he played and created with unconditional love and connection a lot of the time. I believe he created the game-changing "science" he gave to humanity through play. As a child, Jean Houston met Einstein during a field trip to Princeton, and he told her class he created $E = mc^2$ when he entered an imaginative state and rode "the light beam."[9] We should all ask for dreams where we merge with the powerful bioelectricity and biomagnetism of the love we were all created from. In this dream state, we create on a playground composed of the of the vibrations of love of the universe. Lets all play alone or together in this sacred place as often as possible and see what new vibration of love y/our magnificent soul fractals can generate to unveil the illusions that perpetuate our collective suffering.

Anger

It is natural and arguably essential to be angry at times, but staying angry will make you and our world ill.

During a Spring Forest Qigong healing class with Master Chunyi Lin, he stated that when the Dalai Lama visited New York, crime in the whole city was down for the duration of his stay. How is this possible? When you learn Qigong, you are learning to harvest and store energy from the universe. Master Lin teaches you to store this loving and powerful energy in your lower dan tien (an energy center in the area just below your naval—a place where some will find their God particle). This stored energy can be used to heal or harm. During the class, Master Lin said that you can become like the Dalai Lama and work on your dan, enlarging and embodying the frequency of your entire auric field. Thus, we can become beings with so much love flowing from us that it alters the energy field of others so that they become more loving. I am sure most of us have been in the presence of someone who can make a whole room lighter and happier when they are in it. We may not realize that loving essence emanates from an individual in the room, but we feel the room or structure is safe, peaceful, joy-filled, and loving.

What does this have to do with anger? If love can change a city's crime outcome, anger can do the same. Most of us can also feel the uncomfortable energy of someone who is angry. If you watch the news and get upset that things are not going how you think they should, or if you judge an event or a person with anger, what kind of energy field are you generating? How do you think others around you process or absorb the energy your aura emits when you are angry?

I learned how harmful anger and judgment are through my inability to help someone heal one day. I came to work upset and stuck in judgment and anger. I put my hands into the patient's energy field in my usual attempt to use the love I can channel through my God particle to feel the pain and blockages in her field so that I could help her love into and untangle her pain. She noticed the usual energy flow between us was not happening and asked, "Doc, where is your juju today?"

I told her I was suffering because I was sad. I was allowing my energy to resonate in fear. I learned that day that if my energy field vibrates in fear, the consequence of this choice is the caging of the love I am meant to share with others, to offer vibrations to heal and find joy with. I also learned that if I play God through the limited capacity of a human mind, I lose my ability to allow the energy of God to flow through me to help others. I remembered that any form of judgment is based on fear, and one cannot find and embody the vibration of love while in fear. We have to choose which vibration our human suit will ripple in actively.

When we ripple in love, we open the portals within our hearts that connect to all the wise and loving energies of the multiverse. When we do this, we can heal and then share the vibration of our healing and the love of the wise entities that make healing possible with others. I came to this planet to heal myself (our soul) in the 144,000 dimensions of my/our consciousness and share that wisdom and love with humanity, the energies present here on Earth, and all the energies in all dimensions of our consciousness. I cannot find the tears of humility that take me to the place within where I find the spring that God's love emanates and flows from in amazing abundance if I let my mind (the tool we use to understand this dimension) be in charge of the frequency that my human suit vibrates in. The tears of humility are produced from a vulnerable, open heart that the mind actively chooses to explore. The frequency that heals all is love.

Since that day with my patient, I have actively worked to immediately stop any judgment I feel as soon as I am aware I am judging. I am human, so there is a strong possibility I will always be in judgment, but how long I stay there and the conviction I feed it with are all up to me. I try to see through God's heart when I start to judge, and it helps me to find love to transmute the judgment immediately most of the time.

How do we turn anger into a productive emotion? We sit with it and ask: What can I learn from the anger I am feeling right now? If your anger is provoked by you judging a person or situation because they do not think or act like you, use this to gain insight into how to observe with love instead of reacting. We are all limited in our perception of the bigger picture because we are under the constraints of a human Ego and brain that can only handle and process so much information. For example, many saw the COVID-19 pandemic as an opportunity to unite the world in a common resonance. However, the provocation of fear and judgment the media fed us daily caused sadness in the heart of our collective soul through the fear created in the minds of our human suits. We can instantly transmute this sadness by choosing not to judge.

So, when I use a retrospectoscope to observe what the COVID-19 pandemic gave us, I conclude that the world needed more suffering through division to grow so that we can choose to release the grip of fear that our minds have become accustomed to gravitating in and perceiving reality through. When we view the pandemic through this lens of love, we can find that judgment and anger are not produced within our heart. Instead, we can find gratitude that the world was in the vibration of the dark night of the soul necessary to awaken to the light deep within the dark. We will use that light to grow the tree that will spread seeds of love in this dimension and beyond. Humanity was where it needed to be to understand that we can achieve growth as a whole when we choose to no longer feed the energy of the judgment that divides us.

How do you stop your anger from lasting when you're provoked by another's hurtful words or actions? First, you stop blaming them for your anger. Then, you step back and realize this is an opportunity to work on the part of your pain body being poked for your benefit. You are not responsible for the actions of others, but you are responsible for your actions and reactions. If you need a time out to release your anger by screaming, punching a pillow, etc., take a time out alone to do so. Understand that if you are around others when you're angry, others will feel and possibly embody your anger. We all share the same energy source, so you don't have to be physically around someone for them to feel your energy. When you vibrate in anger, it could result in fueling someone you walk by on the street to harm you or another, or go home and harm their loved ones. You are never responsible for the actions of another, but imagine a world in which we all walk our paths emitting love and sharing love instead of anger. Imagine what we could create in this shared vibration. As you work through the insecurities of your solar plexus and release your "not enoughs," you will not anger as easily. One day, hopefully today, you will discover you can remove all anger, frustration, and judgment by taking one deep breath through your beautiful, unconditionally loving heart chakra.

Imagine the world we could create if we no longer got angry. We would no longer emit anger that provokes the defensive anger of others, perpetuating a cycle where no one wins. Instead, we would just be walking around emitting love like the energy the Dalai Lama was emitting on that trip to New York when crime was decreased in his essence. Maybe today we will discover the bliss of linking our auras in such a way that we can create love at a rate we never dreamed possible. Thus, a time could come when we will not understand the concepts of war and crime. Will you diffuse your anger a little faster today? Will you allow love to heal you and others today? Will you choose to emit the energies of peace and love—instead of anger, judgment, and frustration—to share with the beautiful world we are creating today?

Evil

There is always light deep within the dark.

Our solar eclipses remind us that light is always present in what appears to be a world in the dark. The more we understand this, the less time we will spend in the experience of the heavy pain of the dark. What lens you wear to see your world through is up to you. You can wear a blackout lens and play the game of life in the dark in pain, separation, depression, and anxiety. Or you can wear the diamond lens made of the unity of the strength of our combined ability to love. Through this diamond lens, we can see the fractals of all the colors we can choose to love in. We can bathe in the purple light of wisdom; the blue lights of creation and truth; the green of kindness and compassion; the gold of patience, nonjudgment, and peace; the orange of joy; the reds of connection; the dazzling white of strength; and the black light of the wombs of creation.

This dimension offers us a plethora of energy to experience so that we can create and embody our personal divinity for the benefit of the one divine love we are. We are one soul but have chosen to experience this dimension of duality to gather and play with energy in a way we cannot in other dimensions. The separation we are graced with exploring is often seen as difficult and painful. The sensory experience of being deprived of the love that we are and embody in other dimensions causes many to act out in the game of life on this planet in ways that many call "evil." If you judge an action as "evil," you are trapped in the game of duality we are all playing. You have bought into the belief system that you are separate from the one you perceive as Satan, Maya, Māra, etc. That part of our soul that is suffering and lost in the duality of the game of life on Earth needs you to love it more than ever. Please do this, and the "evil" you see will start to dissipate.

How do you love into evil? You realize that all of the movies you create to experience emotions in this dimension are for y/our benefit. If you do not like the movie, you can change the plot and direction of it at any time. How do you do this? It is simple. Love everyone, including your amazing and perfectly beautiful self. If you judge, you will not be able to feel the God particle within you because that particle is part of a dimension that vibrates so high that it cannot even begin to comprehend and thus be in sync with the vibration of judgment. Take the time to understand that those who commit acts of harm and pain to others are just showing you the pain we are all in because we have forgotten the oneness of our divinity. You are creating acts of pain in another dimension right now.

In a past-life reading by Therese Rowley, I was told that in one of my lifetimes, I was a baby killer. This past life had a great influence on the energetic field of experience that I use to love with today. Therese told me that in this past life, I was responsible for population control for the society I was part of. I have been told this is an act of fear that multiple human societies have chosen to incorporate into their standard operations. After years of being responsible for population control, I had children of my own and understood the energy of life with a whole new respect. Therese said I was full of remorse for the "evil" my Ego had been enticed into believing was an act of greater good for the society I was part of. I stated from that day on, in that lifetime, I would consider all of humanity my child to love, nurture, and care for. This is a truth I have embodied in this lifetime, and its loving vibrational essence allows my heart to remain open to the cosmos to listen and embody vibrations of love to share with humanity to help them heal.

I always wondered why I call everyone, including those older than me, "kiddo." Therese said this pledge was the driving force I use to constantly search for the whispers of love we need to heal within the places we consider the darkest evil. She told me I am connected to many dimensions of our consciousness and discerning the information I bring in as a result of this lifetime. From the day of this reading, I no longer feared surrendering to the totality of the loving consciousness of God. This perpetual act of the bliss of surrender is how I temporarily become a vibration of God that is offered to the version of God in a human suit on my healing table. We stop this pain by going within ourselves and finding our God/divinity/Source/love particle of unity and allowing the energy of transcendence to radiate out to heal ourselves and others.

What does healing mean to me? It means we remember in a felt sense that we are one divine soul capable of unimaginable acts of evil, rage, anger, love, compassion, and kindness. We experience them for the purpose of understanding through the lens of loving wisdom, all energies, and emotions. However, I think it is time to lessen the pain we experience through acts of "evil" at this "time." I am requesting your loving help with this lessening of the degree of "evil" we are exposed to. If just 1 percent of the humans on the planet choose to wear that diamond lens and see the world through love, then we will create a world that will vibrate in love. Please play the game of life with this intention with me. We are one fantastic soul created with divine love, and it is time to reclaim our birthright to walk the steps of our journey in the vibration of love.

Darkness

It is in the darkness we find the note of our light.

I am reading *The Ancient Secret of the Flower of Life, Volume 2* by Drunvalo Melchizedek.[10] In it, he describes a training chamber in Egypt in the temple of Dendera. This was a channeled memory, so who this training chamber was for is unclear, but my interpretation is that it was used to know in the felt sense, without any doubt, that you are one with God if you choose to surrender to that frequency of loving creational light. In the chamber the human seeking oneness with God would swim through pitch-black tunnels into a chamber with a pool of crocodiles and have to find a new way out of the chamber through a different pitch-black tunnel. This training chamber represents a way to ignite the light within you, which is your God particle. This light is so bright that there is no darkness it cannot penetrate, and no path without the guidance of the wisdom, love, and light of God infused in its essence. I cannot see auras with my eyes open, but those who can often see humans glow. I have a friend who claims the light inside him has at times been so bright that he has given himself a "sunburn" from the inside out. I have another friend who awoke to a room full of blue light and, when she went in search of the source, found she was the source of the light. I have felt my body emit many different shades of light and have very often been told, "You are glowing." We are liquid crystal light beings that know all. It is time for us to remember this.

When we allow ourselves to sink into darkness and know with conviction that there is a way out through surrender to the connected light of the divine within, we ignite and open the light within us that will lead the way. This light we emit from our God particle is composed of the photons of love we are created with, and those photons constantly connect us to the parts of our soul wearing different human or other energy suits. Picture yourself swimming in an abyss of darkness and, through the correct lens, how peaceful that may be.

The empty is the black hole of creation that many on my healing table visit. Many of the patients I play the game of healing with often stay in the empty for a longer time than I feel necessary. When I ask why they spend so much time there, most answer, "It is such a peaceful place that I did not want to leave it." One patient even scared me because she went back and forth to and from the empty about three times, which is not usual. I asked why she was ping-ponging back and forth, and she said Elohim was there. My patient said, "Every time I left, I could not see Elohim and wanted to see and be with her again." Elohim is a name for God; this patient saw the Mary of Michelangelo's *Pietà* as her version of God in the empty. This vision was so beautiful she kept returning to get another opportunity to be in that presence. I assure you all patients do come back from the empty, and they all receive a healing wavelength of the light of God while there. It is time to see the darkness within and around us as a gift that we are graced with so that we can find and create the unique light of our soul. We are meant to share that light with all that ever was and will be.

So, how do you find the bright flashlight of your God particle within you to light your way through the darkness? You go so deep into the black hole of creation, into energy so dense and full of possibilities, that you can't help but remember this is your birthplace. You/we were birthed in an energy of dense potential just waiting for you/us to add the loving light of our soul to it. When you/we add the love of y/our collective soul to it, we create new versions of reality. You can go back to the empty with the individual color and note of your soul anytime and create by surrendering to the loving bandwidth of the light of the heart of y/our soul that you have within you. I call this photon of light your God particle, but please give it a name that resonates with you.

We all have a beautiful colored photon within, just waiting to ignite with the knowledge that it is part of the one soul we all are, and then combine that light with the light of other awake souls to play the game of creation. We are meant to play the game of creation together here on Earth as a magnificent, harmonious symphony of a rainbow of loving light. To remember and emit this rainbow, we must explore the dark within and create light from it by sparking the potential of the dark with the loving photon of God we all have within.

Our unified soul is within and around you, supporting you in rediscovering, playing with, and then sharing your photon. However, the frequency of love you will share through your photon is so special and unique that only you can create it. So, settle into the quiet and the bliss of the darkness within and around you and rise with the vibration of your embodied note as it guides the next step of your path. Listen to that guidance because it will take you places and connect you in ways you never imagined possible. When your light is plentiful, share it through the connection it spontaneously makes with the hearts/God particles of others. Let's play the game of Earth the way it was meant to be played. Let's play with our light and love so that a new, more loving version of Earth is birthed into existence.

Senseless violence

There have been over 600 mass shootings each year from 2020 to 2023, according to the Gun Violence Archive.[11] Since 2014, almost 13 percent of Americans have lived within one mile of a mass shooting.[12] I imagine there are very few Americans who live less than two hundred miles from a mass shooting that's happened within the last ten years. Hopefully, the painful and heartbreaking wounds these events create will be diminished through transmutation over time so they will not be carried into other lifetimes. Trying to understand how a human Ego could be so lost that it would carelessly take away the beauty of a human life is hard, if not impossible, for many to comprehend. Thus, maybe we have to give up trying to understand and just accept this is all part of God's/Source's/the divine plan that we, with our limited human mind/Ego, do not have the capacity to understand. This leap of faith and surrender of the human Ego's judgment of what is "right and wrong" can be done. Without judgment, the human Ego takes a vacation and is allowed to observe through the eyes of God. God looks only for new ways to create. Without the weight of judgment, the human Ego can surrender fully to the love frequency of the soul and energy of God and create reality from love.

What if we could connect to the other side of the veil and contact one of the victims of these horrendous acts? There are many mediums, authors, and past-life regression therapists who would speculate the deceased soul would say, "It was my time to die" or "I died to bring the human race together." I am not trying to diminish the pain of someone's loss; I am just postulating a change in perspective so that we can all heal the tears in our heart chakras that these horrific acts of violence cause.

Through suffering, we crack open and search for growth, understanding, and connection. We surrender so that more light and love can be brought to our core to heal our soul/Ego/chakras/auric field and redirect and guide us to the next steps of the path of our "highest" purpose on this planet. Maybe it will ease someone's pain to at least consider their loved one may have died in sacrifice to the planet, to wake us up and start healing collectively so that we can learn to love more and put an end to the violence this world faces every second a little faster than the turtle's pace we have had going for all of written history.[13] Maybe the idea of not wanting to waste the gift of a sacrificed life by getting stuck in grief, judgment, and anger will help someone heal faster. I do believe when we are in a collective energy resonance, even if it is one of grief, pain, and sadness, we can accomplish way more than if we are all resonating at a separate frequency. Whose energy frequency will you match today to create healing love for both you and the planet? We are on the planet to feel all emotions and learn and create from them. We were never meant to get stuck in yin, yang, dark, or light energies because we need a balanced combination of opposites to discover the bliss energy of the peace found in acceptance.

The dimensions of duality are necessary to create new energy to nourish our souls, loved ones (also called our enemies), and the entire multiverse. Many souls in human suits have been too busy striving for "success" found in a monetary reward or a title. What we call a senseless tragedy is an opportunity for those souls to remember that "success" is found in the frequencies of heart coherence. Bliss and peace are not found in a title but in the open, connected hearts that resonate with joy, kindness, and compassion. They have forgotten their connection to the divine. These tragedies attempt to awaken us by breaking us open to let the lights of love and peace found deep within and in the outer layers of our aura be rediscovered and then used to upgrade our human suits. In the process of these upgrades, we will remember that we are here to use our loving lights to create singularity even though we are in a dimension of duality.

Disappointment

It is human to interact with the energy of disappointment. It is celestial to understand all of our energetic interactions are divine and purposeful.

The word *disappointment* can cause you to feel a crater open within. Many of us fear we will not be or were not "enough" in an interaction with another, especially those we truly love. This energetic thought entanglement keeps us spinning on what should have been, could have been, or maybe even what will be. We blame ourselves or others for the pain created by obsessing over the loss or perceived missed opportunity we think we or another caused or will cause. I challenge you to shift your perspective and realize our actions, emotions, and feelings are exactly what you and your loved one need for growth at that time. It is up to both individuals to digest the crater of pain caused by the illusion we call disappointment and grow an increased bandwidth of light from it.

Try seeing your pain or even your fear of a future disappointment as a gift for you and your loved one to "suffer" from because you know it will push you to come up with new ways to resonate in kindness, compassion, and unconditional love. Internalize this newfound compassion so you accept yourself and the frequency your light body is vibrating in right now on its precious journey in the realm of the dimension we call Earth. The pain of our perceived missteps is an invitation to quiet the mind and open our hearts so they may explore the dimensions of our loving consciousness. As the heart explores the universe's loving vibrations, it remembers the loving energy our soul is made of, and if you open and receive this love, your craters of disappointment will transmute into portals of light to heal you and share with another.

It is time for all of us to start releasing the self-flagellating thoughts that keep us from finding the power and beauty of the unconditional love within us. Every step of your journey is a dance in the vibration of perfection and of discovering you are enough. Our minds were assigned the job of keeping us from that truth so we could experiment with the creative capacity of this realm of duality. You can spend time creating craters of pain or portals of love—it is your choice. I recommend spending the least amount of time in the craters as possible by loving through them as soon as they present themselves to you. It is time to understand that disappointment in yourself or another is a beautiful tool of the mind that we can use to search for and embody more love. You can stay in that crater or create a portal of loving light with it. What will you choose? Who will you lean on to help you choose light? Will it be the one you are playing in the vibration of disappointment with? Will you have compassion and patience for the beauty of every step of your unique soul journey? I do, and I am grateful to be playing the game of creation in this and all 144,000 other dimensions of our consciousness with you.

The darkness between us

There are many who believe that our human suit has the entire universe we live in within it. A galaxy is generally depicted as a dark space with the bright light of a spiral of stars being emitted from a central light in the center. If you search online for a picture of the universe, you'll find depictions of dark space with the bright lights of galaxies looking like stars. I would like you to imagine that your body is a universe and the person sitting next to you is also a universe. They may be the same universe, or a different one, or even multiple universes compressed into what appears to be a human suit.

Now picture the two of you in what the 3D world calls a disagreement and what the 5D and higher dimensions call an opportunity to create. When you are not in resonance with the vibration of the one around you, you feel yourself as a separate entity and are blessed with an opportunity to explore the emptiness between vibrations. This disharmony is the most beautiful gift you can be graced with in this dimension of duality. Disharmony is an opportunity to see through the lens of creation.

The emptiness between vibrational notes of consciousness you are exploring is what many call the "empty." The empty is the black hole we were all created from, the space between us, the energy we use to create consciousness, healing, and whatever else our collective soul can dream harmoniously into creation. We created the game of Earth with it.

When we perceive ourselves as not vibrating through the light that is the central star within, which I call our God particle, we are exploring the darkness or emptiness of the universe within our human suit. In this condensed energy, it is wise if we choose to willfully surrender to the ecstasy of the wisdom and giggles of creation that your God particle is made of. Once we submit to the unlimited pathways of healing and connection that the empty provides, through the light of our God particle (the central star of our galaxy), we unmask new pathways to understanding and embodying the unity of loving connections to other stars wearing human suits that exist both inside and outside us. Other stars are within us as part of the universe we are made of and, through the lens of duality, outside of us as a separate universe wearing a different human suit. If we are resonating in oneness, we see them as within us and adding to our light from within. If we are playing the game of duality, they are the person standing before us, gracing us with a new way to see the light that connects and creates us.

The deliciousness of creation will be found in all of our stars surrendering to the empty at once. Imagine if all of humanity could surrender the unique creative frequency of their light to the empty in unison. Imagine that this has already happened. In that place, no one star is in charge or wants to be in charge. Our stars just want to participate and relish in the power of their unified light through the energetic tethers of love that are created through surrender. They want to rejoice in the power of love that their combined light will infuse into the empty. They crave the paradox of creating new universes together in the empty with our combined light, while wearing the human suit of darkness that allows us to find an individual light to share. With this individual light, we can create in ways we are not able to if we never left dimensions of consciousness that resonate in a vibration of singularity alone.

We all try to evade the darkness that is infused within and around us in the form of an ouchy emotion on this planet. It is time we melt into it and discover our light's power of connection and creation when we surrender to its quiet healing wisdom. So, will you explore the empty within you today when you feel an emotion you perceive could be held, appreciated, and transmuted with some of y/our unique, loving light? Or ask another star within you to do this for you? Or even better yet, will you remove all the prisons of the Ego's protection that dim the light of your star and allow one or more stars at the center of other human suits to gather and play the game of creation in the empty together by lighting new pathways of connection between you?

Let's set ourselves free from the hell we create by dimming the light of the stars and galaxies within us. Let's create heaven on Earth by letting our stars shine bright and allowing them to forge pathways through the darkness by surrendering to the energies of love and play. Let's create a symphony of light that we hear as a unified resonance of joy and peace that brings us all to tears. Let's create a light show of love we never imagined possible. Let's unite our God particles and play the game of creation like never before. We got this. I love you and the unique light of the universe within you.

4

Hearing Awake

The energy you create

How is the energy we call a human lifetime of any significance when viewed through the lens of the eternal energy of the cosmos? Does it need to be significant? Does it matter if we spend our time on Earth stewing in the emotions of judgment, sadness, and anger versus connection, love, and contentment? It is very likely that five hundred years from now, most of our names will have long been forgotten, and twenty thousand years from now, with almost utmost certainty, they will all have been forgotten. Our human names are essential for our souls to play this amazing 3D game in which we are all participating. However, the unique energy our soul creates while in a human suit will always be part of Source and never be forgotten. The energy we share with others will exist through time. The thoughts and feelings we encounter in this game become part of the soup of the collective mind of consciousness, and this is the energy that guides creation.

You are always contributing and connected to Source. You just may not be allowing yourself to feel or be aware of that connection. You will find and feel the divine within you when you breathe with chakras full of gratitude and love. Master Chunyi Lin of Spring Forest Qigong would say to put a smile on your face to help you heal yourself and others. Donna Eden would encourage you to breathe through your heart like this:

- Take a deep breath.
- Take a deep breath into your relaxed belly.
- Take another deep breath and breathe through your heart chakra.

I have played with both of these healers' techniques and find them very beneficial.

You can also be every atom in the cosmos through breath. Try this—close your eyes and take a deep breath that starts in your lower belly behind your belly button or the area of your lower dan tien (if you are female, you may use your middle dan located behind your sternum instead if this feels better). When you inhale, imagine your breath radiating out from the dan of your choice through every molecule of your body and then beyond into the atoms of the cosmos. On the exhale, imagine the energy of your breath returning to you through your cells and back to your dan with the wisdom and love that reside in every atom of the cosmos. Take eight more deep breaths in this way. Know that you are the cosmos, so you only have to imagine that you are breathing to the outer edge of your aura. Know that when you do so, you breathe in the entire cosmos. Then, let the atoms of the universe breathe you for nine breaths. If you cannot feel the cells of your body or the atoms of the universe when you breathe, then welcome to your personal healing journey that will guide you to the peace of surrendering to an energetic resonance that will allow you to feel them in the future.

I believe there is not one human on the planet who is incapable of being breathed by the atoms of the universe. When you sense you are part of the one breath breathing, you know your energy is eternal and way more expansive than the name and energy of the human suit you are projecting. I have muscle-tested while saying my name is Essence and my name is Time, and I have received a yes with both. Spiritual muscle testing is used to explore the truths and knowledge that are vibrations of your energy field that the limited box of your conscious mind is unaware of. When you muscle test, you ask a group of muscles in your body a question that has a yes or no answer. If the muscle group you are asking remains strong, the answer is yes; if it is weak, the answer is no. I don't think my soul has a name anymore because its energy has merged with a collective with no name. When you know you are eternal, you listen for the guidance of the love you have collected throughout eternity to help you walk the steps of this lifetime. You know you never die, so you realize there are no fears that are justified. And you realize fear is just an essential illusion that aids us in getting lost in dimensions of duality until we no longer want to be lost; then we dissolve the veil that creates the fear illusion. What steps will you take today to ensure you give your soul and your human mind a return to the bliss of the ONE breath in this lifetime? If the universe has breathed you, will you experience the ultimate bliss of teaching someone else how to breathe in the unique way you have adopted so they can understand the one breath in the felt sense? Will you use the peace, love, knowledge, and creative spark of the breath of life in a way that leaves you content and connects you to others? Will you use this connection to create a loving energy for the universe that, unlike your name, will be around to help someone else for the rest of time?

Masters

It may be time to reconsider your definition of a master.

Many have suggested that you should ask your guides for help when you require assistance. Many people see their guides as masters who are vibrating at a higher level and will help them overcome the difficulty they are perceiving in their current reality with greater ease. Many books have been written on how to do this, and if you just quiet your mind and ask for help, you will receive it. Consulting with your guides or Source is a great way to receive information that will help you get through your day and achieve your goals, especially if your goals align with the common good for all. I want to postulate openly an idea that may shift your definition of a master.

It is a common belief that everything happens for a reason. Thus, we are meant to absorb information from all the challenges and the beauty that cross our paths. What if we started to see the souls and situations that present us with these scenarios as our guides or masters? For example, I recently crossed paths with several people who are perceiving a struggle with a relative's behavior. They are wounded because they cannot understand why their relative could be so narcissistic, unkind, judgmental, etc. The pain we can feel through another's behavior can generate all the uncomfortable emotions we are capable of. These emotions can provoke us to lash back at the person causing our discomfort and sometimes even innocent bystanders who happen to be around them at the time. This tit for tat we all play by giving our pain bodies too much attention by playing the victim role will ensure we all continue to be divided and continue to feed and grow our pain bodies with more feelings of isolation, sadness, anger, judgment, and low self-esteem. What if, instead, you used your uncomfortable reaction to another's behavior as an opportunity to diminish instead of grow your pain body? When you perceive that someone's behavior is upsetting you, it is because you have not loved yourself enough. You are being given a gift that allows you to see where your energy field needs more self-love and tender, nurturing attention.

Consider the following quote, which I recently came across, as I think it encompasses the state of mind we should strive for:

> "Unfuckwithable: (adj.) When you are truly at peace and in touch with yourself, and nothing anyone says or does bothers you, and no negativity or drama can touch you."
> —Vishen Lakhiani, *The Code of the Extraordinary Mind*[1]

What if we started to see everyone who pokes our pain bodies as a master? What if we began seeing everyone who fills our hearts with connection, love, and joy as a master? What if you spent your day looking for the master within everyone you crossed paths with? What if you realized that anyone at any time could provide you with valuable information to help you evolve into a more loving and kinder human/soul/Source beacon of loving, creative energy? There is light of every color radiating from all humans on the planet. The more colors of the light spectrum we absorb, the more connected we are. When we approach everyone looking for more colors of light to harmonize with and grow from, we allow ourselves to absorb more light. When we absorb more light, we light the paths for others by radiating more love and colors they naturally resonate with. I am pretty sure we all agree that the planet needs more love. Whose light will you allow yourself to receive and grow from today? You have the capacity within you to choose to create a lighter and lesser pain body instead of a heavier and denser one. Will you diminish our pain body today by absorbing the light of another "master" who is just trying to get you to love yourself more?

Thank you, Eckhart Tolle, for your beautiful pain body concept, which you blessed humanity with in your book *A New Earth*.[2]

Sight

Most of us are blessed with two eyes that work in unison to transcribe the reality we perceive as separate from us into information we can use to navigate our path on Earth. I would like you to play with the idea that your eyes are instruments you were given to experience the vibration of duality. When you would like to feel the bliss of singularity, all it takes is remembering that as a light body, your reality is felt, not seen. In singularity, your reality is known with certainty through a vibration you receive from within, not a picture you create with the mind from an external stimulus.

I have been doing BodyAwake Yoga with Dr. Sue Morter for a year and a half. Over this period, I have repeatedly heard, "Be the one behind the eyes." I did not find this "behind" until last week. Before the yoga class, I had set an intention for what I wanted to get out of it. I decided that the intention was too limited because it came from my tiny human mind, which is encased in a significantly limiting belief system. So I asked God to set my intention. (My definition of *God* is all our souls residing in unison as one loving being, and all other energy in existence. This energy to me is a glowing ball of golden peace and acceptance that resonates in all vibrations of love and can flow from within you to heal, connect, and guide you anytime you choose to surrender to it.) I immediately felt a vibration of energy course through me that I did not understand, but I knew that God heard me and we were going to play and grow together.

This time, during the yoga class, when I heard "Be the one behind the eyes," a glowing ball of golden light that I knew to be God was behind my eyes. For years, I had been looking for a piece of me or my soul to be there with a mind that is limited in belief, and I never would feel any entity "behind" my eyes. The day I surrendered my intention to God, that energy allowed me to know it has always been the one guiding me "behind" my eyes.

So what is it like to have the energy of "God" be the one behind your eyes? You "see" the oneness of this dimension and are released from the prisons of judgment that you see with your human-suit eyes. You do not see the physical body or even the aura of the person standing before you; you feel their essence. You feel the dimensions and experience that the part of your soul standing before you is trying to share with you. You see with an energy of eternal wisdom, peace, love, and guidance that makes you feel so humbled that you never want to see through any other lens again.

We are here playing Earth to experience duality. However, I think at this time, we are being graced with an opportunity to see through the lens of singularity if we choose to do so. If we do this, we will remember that we play this game only to understand emotions and collect their energy to create with. Playing Earth, knowing we can "see" through the lens of singularity when we choose to do so, limits the time we suffer in separation and judgment and increases the time we vibrate in the connected wisdom of eternal peace and love. This lens gives us inner peace, which we constantly search for. With our combined collective inner peace, we will create a new Earth game to play that will resonate with that vibration.

So, will you consider that God is the one behind your eyes today? Will you open your heart and see the human suit before you as another piece of the God within you? Will you connect and see through y/our God energy today? Let's play the game of Earth differently today. Let's see, feel, know, and create our reality through the energy of God. We got this. I, our soul, and the golden energy of acceptance and peace love you.

Dr. Sue Morter, thank you for holding the space and providing the wisdom for me to rediscover this part of myself. I am eternally grateful to you and the vast quantity of loving space you hold for the universe to heal with.

Family

One of the definitions of *family* is a group of individuals living under one roof. I am inviting you to broaden this definition and consider that all humans live under one roof; thus, we are all one family. We as humans constantly need validation from others because we have been brainwashed into thinking love is conditional. Because of the time we have spent under one roof with our "families," we look to the humans we spend the most time with for that validation. Our current definition of family limits the opportunities for validation. Of course, as we learn to love ourselves unconditionally, we no longer need validation, but this discovery of unconditional love of self is a never-ending journey of learning how much your heart can open and flow with the divine essence of love we were created with. Thus, while we are in a human suit, at least periodically being validated feels good.

So, back to the definition of *family*. The family I chose to be born into cannot validate me in ways my fearful human mind and Ego would like to be validated. However, this genetic family constantly enables me to realize that no external validation is needed to love myself, my path, and others. I can be divine love and allow it to flow from me without needing recognition. I can walk the path of not being validated by other human suits because I have looked within for comfort, support, and strength and found it as I have written and starred in the story of Julie Ledoux and then Julie Foster.

My father, who did not get past eighth grade because he had to work and English was not his first language, once said to me, "Do you really think you are smart enough to be a doctor?" Thankfully, I knew somewhere inside I was smart enough, or at least I was going to find out if I was, and was able to dismiss the vibration of fear that those words were created from. I also had the support of many adults from our human family who did not live in my household or share 25–50 percent of my DNA but shared my "human" DNA. These adults came in the form of teachers, coaches, and guidance counselors whose minds were not in a box of fear. Their hearts and minds were able to see and feel the potential and light inside of me that I was not yet aware of myself. I wasn't aware of it because the household I was living in was lost in regret, fear, the scars of abuse, and the brainwashing of the idea that love is conditional. The adults outside my household guided me to believe in myself and loved me with the divine light within themselves so that I could write this book and share my love with you today.

I have read and have come to understand that "old souls" pick abusive and neglectful parents to raise them. I know I am a very old soul. I am so old that I can imagine myself saying in my pre-life planning, "I am not doing childhood again. It is a waste of time. Put me in an abusive childhood so that I do not want to be present and am free to leave my body and be present in other dimensions where my consciousness would be more of service than it is in the body of an Earth child." I now also understand that if you are an abused child, you have to learn self-validation. As a child, you do this out of fear and knowing there is a better way to play the game of Earth than your parents are showing you. You leave home as soon as possible, which means you are self-validating outside of the fear boxes your parents' energy places you in. I am very grateful for my parents' roles in my movie, as I have been self-validating since age two. However, I am now learning how to self-validate with love instead of fear. I suppose if I choose to wear the lens of singularity, I can see that even as a child, I loved myself and our soul so much that I was already self-validating out of love. I was determined to find a path to show other human suits how to see through the singularity lens.

So, if you feel guided to do so, I invite you to leave behind the small box that defines family as people genetically related to you. Find a mother, father, sister, brother, and loved one in every soul you make eye contact with today. We are one soul playing with ourselves in one of the realms of duality we call Earth. When we remember this and love ourselves in the form of the human suit we call "me" and the one we call "other," we embrace and embody the vibration that we need to play the game of duality and creation in a state of bliss.

I want to thank Jen Weigel and her Spiritual Social Club members for being the amazing family that has been validating the awakened amnesia-free reality I have embraced and embodied over the last few years. These souls have helped me incorporate the vibrations that allow me to feel and open pathways to healing for myself and others worldwide. If you need validation as you remember your divine self, this group of people will love and support you on this part of your journey. I also so appreciate all the individuals I have called friends, mothers, fathers, sisters, brothers, sons, and daughters in my life, and my beautiful kids and ex-husband who have aided me in remembering who I am so that I can help you remember who you are. The aid has not always been offered or received in a way that one would consider pleasant, but it was exchanged in a way that was needed to find the unending supply of divine love that we all have within to share and serve as a tool to reconnect with our collective soul. I love our human family. We got this.

The guide we call fear

Many have said you cannot vibrate in fear and love at the same time; you need to choose which emotion to vibrate in and create from. This is true in a dimension of duality, but in realms of singularity, they are the same energy. Let me explain.

This morning, I awoke with an earache in my right ear. I felt slightly congested, so according to Western medicine, I had a cold and serous otitis. The remedy for this would be rest and Sudafed. Fortunately, I have the mindset that illness is a gift. If you allow its message to be heard, it will offer you time to self-reflect and heal. My Eastern medicine training has taught me that the ears are a part of the kidney meridian, and thus, when you have ear issues, you are vibrating in fear. I have been working on "Godding up" for the last few weeks because "womaning up" does not seem to describe the love I am trying to embody anymore (there are no genders in singularity realms). I have had several patients with cancer who have contacted me hoping that I can help them heal, so I have been trying to love myself enough to allow that frequency of love and truth to flow freely from me so they can, in fact, heal. I have also been working on self-validating the reality of knowing we all can be the frequency of God instead of playing God. When we are the frequency of God, "miracles" happen.

So, back to fear and love being the same energy. When I am sick, I ask for help and go outside and sit in the sun. This morning, I felt my body may be remembering a story about my childhood that my mother told me as an adult. My mind does not remember this story, but the ear pain I felt told me my body may be remembering it. When I was six months old, I had one of many ear infections and was crying in the middle of the night. My crying stressed my father so much that he threatened to throw me down the stairs. My father, thankfully, did not follow through with most of his threats. I wanted my current ear pain to go away and was guided to revisit this time in my childhood so that I could not only transmute my current fear but my old fears into love. I understood that my current ear pain was also the fear my mother must have had when she was trying to comfort me with the energy of rage that she had seen manifest into violence before in the background. I also tapped into the fear in my father that was provoking his rage. Through the lens of singularity, my fear is our soul's fear.

So, I did the Ho'oponopono prayer not just for myself and my parents but for all of humanity. We are all in some sort of fear state at times and do not realize that there is no such thing as fear in the mind of singularity. There is just energy. In doing the Ho'oponopono prayer, I could understand the singularity of love and fear. My parents' love for me gave me a childhood that made me a very strong and independent woman. I would not take a second of it back because I love who I am today. Every step of my journey has helped me remember the vibrations of the love of the essence of singularity within me that I can share it with all of you.

Another example of how to understand that fear and love are the same came yesterday through a healing visit. The patient I was playing healing with wanted to heal her fear. She has had plenty of past traumatic events that definitely bring the energy of fear into her resonance when she is poked, even by sometimes benign triggers. While she was on the table, she saw her fear being deposited into a patch of morning glories. The fear then went to the center of the Earth where she imagined hell was because, in her mind, fear is not from God, it is from hell. However, she then saw the fear transmute while still in hell into a rainbow of healing starlight. I asked her how hell could create healing starlight if God was not part of hell to do so, and she giggled.

Through the lens of singularity, energy is not qualified or described. It just is. In duality, we are graced with the tool called our mind that separates energy so we can experience and grow. When we surrender and ask to find the love that our fear is created with, we remember how to God up. Who wants to play Godding up with me today? By the way, my ear is better, but I know my energetic body has more love disguised as fear to explore later today so that it can heal completely.

Our shepherds

Please take a deep breath and be present so that you may absorb the loving guidance of the soul standing before you right now.

As I took my wonderful dog for a walk behind my house today, I noticed there was way more shit on the trail than usual, and I mean that in the literal sense. It is the time of the year when local sheep are brought to the hills behind my house to graze on the cheatgrass. It made me realize we are in a time when we once again have not one but too numerous to count

Christ consciousness shepherds walking the Earth. These lightworkers do not necessarily want a flock to tend to, but they offer insight into new ways to embody love. I know the word *Christ* triggers a lot of you. I now use it to be synonymous with unconditional love. Unconditional love is the solvent that can easily dissolve any perceived uncomfortable step on the journey you are calling life in this dimension.

I have come to understand through opening my heart that my shepherds are everyone I come into contact with and, of course, the gurus whose books I have read and absorbed insight on how to love more from. See the gallery page on my website, www.brightenallsouls.com, to see authors and healers I have absorbed insight from. If you take the time to be present and listen, you will be given the grace of absorbing a healing vibration from the soul in front of you. This vibration may come in like a breath of fresh air and understanding, a warm needed hug, or a stab in the gut. I assure you that all of these presentations are there for you to absorb a new way to love. The breath of fresh air and hug will be easy if you love yourself enough to receive it. The stab may take some work; you will likely need a new lens of perception to see where the gift of love is in this ouchy form of information. I encourage you to go to the place inside you where you feel the pain of the stab and hug that place with the tenderness of a child with no limiting beliefs on helping or healing. I encourage you to imagine yourself as a newborn soul (the Christ consciousness) that knows and understands only the vibration of love and just wants everyone else to understand it by hugging them until they know without a doubt they are that vibration. Hug yourself until you can see through the bullshit story that your Ego generated to separate you from the divine by playing victim, martyr, princess, etc. If you need help, find a healer who has come to know well the vibration of Christ's consciousness and love and allows it to flow through them so they can help you find the love in you to heal. Or ask your guides or an angel for help. Every soul you cross paths with is a star of light, but many are buried under the veil of a dark pain body, so it is difficult to feel their star within. You will be able to sense the stars of others with greater ease as your star brightens by loving yourself enough to transmute your pain body.

I encourage you to be present enough today to commit your energy and attention to the shepherd of Christ consciousness (or any other loving consciousness your faith resides in) in front of you. Remember, the person in front of you is you because we are all one soul. You will be their shepherd in your current interaction between human suits, just as they are yours. Eventually, our human herd will be in such resonance that there will be no more need for shepherds. We will achieve ONE consciousness here in this 3D dimension by sharing our energies enough to remember that we are one collective soul on the other side of the veil. Your soul will always walk a path of uniqueness created by you sharing your journey with others, but you will understand this uniqueness is part of the spectrum of love that our human herd craves to share with each other. Together, our herd can embody the love and guidance of all the dimensions of consciousness we currently reside in. Can you imagine what it would feel like to experience that love through the senses of a human? Can we please try?

How do you find the presence to feel and embrace the energy of the Shepherd in front of you? How about saying: "My intention for the day is to allow myself to embrace my true essence. I set the intention for my essence to always be connected to the heartbeat of the collective. I set the intention to remain connected and in service to the consciousness of this dimension so that all may discover that the consciousness of this dimension is one with the consciousness of all dimensions."

We live with one soul, one heartbeat, one essence, one vision of evolution, and one love that requires insight from all the individual soul essences we are embodying right now. Let's play together in the freedom of creativity and love today. Let's discover the guidance we have to share with each other with grace and ease so that eventually, we can feel the consciousness of the ONE in this 3D body that we are gifted with sharing a frequency with. We got this. I love you all.

Righteousness

We are divine beings here to create the reality we desire. In this dimension, we are bonded with an amazing mind that is able to harness the power of emotion. The capacity and creativity of this mind are unimaginable to most. However, we limit this creativity with the painful emotions we allow ourselves to feed daily. Many of us are unaware that we are embodying subconscious pain and creating the 3D world we live in with it. It is time for all of us to be aware of the emotion we are choosing to embody.

Deep sadness—which can manifest as anger through the eyes of perceived injustice—is one of the prominent emotions running through many souls. Many who embody this emotion will feel the need to be on the "right" side of an issue. Righteousness can create a reality of war because there will be sides and matters of such "importance" that war may be deemed necessary by those lost in its vibration. Let go of the idea of "sides." We are all on one side. We are all one soul. Hold compassion for yourself and others. See that the difference in our insights and opinions allows us to create solutions we would never have thought of by only aligning ourselves with like-minded thinkers. See that God has everything going according to plan and let go of the fallacy of injustice. It is time for us to protect and defend peace collectively. It is time to embody the alchemy of love and release the control that the heavy emotions of righteousness and anger have had over the human race for so long.

If fear is the emotion you choose to embody, you will create and feel "demons," dark forces, and obstructions as part of your 3D reality. You may see yourself as "good" and those who do not think like you as "evil." On the other hand, if you embody joy and love, you will manifest angels, peace, and healing and be surrounded by souls that give and receive love openly without conditions attached. A connection to all energy on a level you never imagined possible will be revealed to you. You will be open enough to feel the unique, loving energy and the depth of the souls that cross your path, even if they have no idea how loving and compassionate they can be. You will witness "miracles" daily and feel profound gratitude for your soul's experience in this human dimension.

You pick the vibration you choose to embody and emit, not the soul you think is causing you to feel some flavor of pain. If you allow your mind to understand and begin to feel the profound peace found in acceptance, embodying love is automatic. It is time for you to feel the ecstasy of allowing love to be the dominant vibration of every breath your atoms take. It is time to surrender and create a dimension where our hearts beat together in one expansive symphony. We can then use that symphony to create the vibration of a new world that lives in harmony because of our differences instead of despite them.

When our souls merge, we see and feel through a collective lens. Dark and light energies are equally appreciated, and the concepts of right and wrong do not exist. No sides means no more war.

We all have access to the atoms that have vibrated in love in all dimensions and all timelines. Wouldn't it be amazing if we all simultaneously fully embodied the frequency of those atoms at our maximum human capacity?

Will you add to that possibility today? Will you create the 3D reality of love and peace we all desire by choosing not to take a side today? Will you look into the eyes of another person searching for unconditional love and invite them to play with you in that vibration today?

Dis-ease

It is time for us to discover the ability to heal through the embodiment of gratitude.

I have been blessed to cross paths with many powerful, healing souls in the last few years. They have collectively taught me how to heal and love more. Thank you to everyone who has shared their heart and healing with me.

Recently, I watched a documentary called *The Living Matrix*.[3] In the documentary, Arielle Essex talks about how she healed her brain tumor by being grateful for it instead of hating it and telling it to go away. Instead, she went in and asked the tumor, "Why do I need you?" She found the answer and became grateful for its presence, and the tumor disappeared. Her story tells us how to transmute the energy that creates disease into the energy that heals.

In traditional Chinese medicine, every disease is caused by an underlying emotion. For example, you will have lung and large intestine issues if you have grief issues. If you ruminate too much, you will have stomach, spleen, and pancreatic problems. If you are angry, your gallbladder, liver, and heart will make you aware of this. If fear is an underlying issue, you will have bladder and kidney problems and sometimes irregular heart rhythms. If frustration, judgment, fear of love, and smoldering anger are the beasts you feed, then you will have heart and small intestine problems. If you fear the symbiosis with your soul, the Earth, and God/Source, you will have a body that feels out of sync with its environment, has a hard time staying present, and may manifest vertigo, mania, depression, etc.

How do we appreciate grief? First, accept that it is there to teach you to inhabit your body and be fully present at all times. Through the pain of grief, we can choose to understand how precious "now" is and not want to waste "now" in vibrations other than love. Accept that the anger and the profound sadness that can accompany grief are there to remind you how powerful and wonderful the embodiment of love feels. Grief can be an opportunity to let go of regret. See the loss you are feeling as a way to let the regrets attached to the death you are mourning also die.

To transmute the pain of grief, imagine opening up the area of your C7 vertebra and letting all your and others' could-haves, should-haves, would-haves go. Let them leave through this area where your soul's energy so freely comes and goes from your body. Without the energy of regret, you have room for the light energy of the soul's wisdom to come in greater quantity. You can even picture your regrets being vacuumed out back into the collective. Regret causes dementia by keeping you in a continuous dense vibration thought loop, so I strongly recommend you let all regret go. Thank any remorse for the reminder that there is always a way to be kinder and to love more. The love you feel for the reminder to be present will fill your lungs and sinuses with light, and you will breathe with ease. Allergies may even disappear because you will no longer judge the environment that caused you the pain of grief. You will be breathing in peace, and thus, there will be no need to be allergic to anything.

For the overthinkers (99 percent of us) with spleen, stomach, and pancreas issues, it is time to get lost in a new, ever-changing story that brings you joy and happiness. Breathe into and imagine expanding your solar plexus. In Earth school, we are taught love is conditional. This is bullshit, and we need to unlearn this as fast as possible. *You are loved as is!* Let go of the "not enoughs" you have learned in Earth school. As you let go of this heavy energy, you will discover the light of the divine inside; I have seen entire galaxies within bellies. Be grateful for your stomach issues, diabetes, and immune systems that do not seem to protect you and may even be attacking you with an autoimmune disease. Be grateful you were given the opportunity to be reminded to move on from your rumination loops and discover new ways of how beautiful and unique you are several times a day. You would not watch a movie you did not like over and over again. Why do we replay the movies of our life that cause us pain? *You have always been perfect, are perfect right now, and will always be perfect.*

Every step of the dance of your life has had a purpose for you and your dance partners. Every step you take tomorrow will have purpose, so please don't spend time hating your old dance steps or worrying about the ones you will be taking tomorrow. Enjoy that you get to dance and that through all the steps of our dance, you are guided to receive the grace to discover the light within you that creates your magnificence.

If you have hepatitis, gallbladder disease, and herpetic outbreaks, then smoldering anger is your issue. The energy of rage is likely not a one-lifetime issue. You came to the planet in this incarnation to heal many lifetimes of a suppressed voice and the wounds of many broken hearts. Please be patient with yourself here. You are a magnificent part of our soul with great love in you that is trapped behind protective boxes around your heart that you have put up so you will not feel the sting of a broken heart again. However, you are meant to share the great love within you. You are angry because you have imprisoned your beautiful heart.

You can heal anger by breathing through your heart chakra and imagining the cages you have placed on it disappearing. Say "I forgive you," or even "I pretend to forgive you," to all those who have reminded you of the greatness of your love by wounding you in this lifetime. They have reminded you that you have an unending supply of love caged behind the pain of your multiple broken hearts. Be grateful they have given you this reminder. Let the love in your heart out of its cage to heal you and even become a seed you can place in the hearts of others trapped in this self-made prison. End the cycle of one of the most painful karmas present. If your rage is deep, imagine cutting the painful areas, draining the black ooze within, and then replacing it with light, love, and gratitude. Giggle with joy and start spreading the vibration to do this incredibly blissful transmutation to all the people you come across who are angry. Thank you for being brave enough to do this. The vulnerability of open, endless heart energy seems impractical in dimensions of duality, but it is the definition of freedom in the felt sense.

If your anxiety rules you, try saying, "I am safe right now." Breathe into every cell in your body the energy that you are safe, and command your cells to be in this resonance from now on. Let the fear go from your kidneys, bladder, and lower back. The Earth and Source so desperately want you to feel nurtured by them. Feel their nurturing energy in your bladder and lower back (your sacral chakra) so that you can open this area and release your fears. When this chakra vibrates in a nurturing frequency, the reality you birth will be one of your capacity to love. The dimensions above 3D do not have the capacity to understand our heavier emotions. These heavy emotions often trigger the fear that a previous human suit and mind have not processed. I am not sure if the soul carries PTSD or if its memories trigger PTSD when it emits a new body. Regardless, have a discussion with your soul, and try to remember that although it may not feel like it at times, it is a great gift to be human. The power of the emotions of the human dimension can manifest incredible things.

Symbiose your human suit, soul, and Source, and ask for help in releasing your fear. If you feel like your soul fears being incarnated as a human, tell your soul to honor the contract it made to be here and that it came to fine-tune its loving, unique note. Hold hands with your soul, hug your soul, and merge with it to fully inhabit your morphogenic field in blissful unison. Remind your soul, or be reminded by your soul, that we are always one with Source and that the soul and the mind operating as a dynamic duo can be one of the keys that open the door to the path of a blissful earthly experience. Be smart and put your fear down. You have carried it long enough. The Earth needs the vibration of freedom and creativity, which cannot be felt when fear is present.

Last, pick the areas above that need the most work if you have cancer. Cancer is an energy that manifests because you are letting the energy of a trapped heavy emotion eat you alive. It is time to love that emotion and release it. All dis-eases, including cancer, are a gift for you to manifest and transmute what you came here to transmute. Our diseases are a great teacher and a gift if you see them that way.

Will you change the lens through which you see your dis-ease today and help the collective heal? Will you add your healing transmutation to the collective so the frequency of that vibration will be so strong that others will feel it and heal? Will you choose to love yourself enough to do this? Will you seek a healer who you resonate with to help you? They are waiting to help you. It is time for us to unite in a resonance of love and creativity that most of us have never imagined possible, but to do so, we need to heal so that no veil limits our connection to each other. So, let's heal collectively today. I love you all. We got this.

Trust

The game of life we are playing could be so much more fun through the lens of trust.

In this dimension, we have created a game we call life on Earth to experience the vast range of emotions that are the essence of creation. It may be a game we choose to play because we are bored of the eternal bliss of some of the other dimensions in which our consciousness resides.

The game's difficulties and divinity occur when we get lost in the heavier energies that we created the game to experience. It is time for us to understand the way out of these heavier energies and go back to the lighter joy and peace found in the game because it seems the heavier energies may be a little too loud and unbalanced right now. We can emerge from these denser vibrations through trust.

Trust is among the most challenging emotions for many to understand and incorporate. We easily succumb to sadness, anger, fear, judgment, joy, and love. We can get lost for months or years in these vibrations, but trust is a vibration that is generally very fleeting for most of us. It is time for us to understand we are all one soul and that when you choose to trust another, it is because you first trust in yourself.

It is this trust in ourselves that we have tremendous difficulty with. When we hear our first words in this dimension, we are bombarded with vibrations of division and scarcity that brainwash us into the thoughts of "you are not worthy" and "pride is a sin." When we choose this belief system as our reality, we lose our capacity to trust in ourselves. We have been hurt so many times in many ways in many of the other dimensions we reside in that it is a wonder that we can comprehend the vibration of trust enough to embody it even temporarily.

So, how do we embody trust? We actively continue to choose to love ourselves unconditionally. You choose to breathe with the center of y/our heart or the center of y/our belly. Find your unique spot where you can feel y/our essence of love and light residing in dimensions where trust, bliss, peace, connection, and love are the only vibrations available. When you allow yourself to trust in the expansiveness of the love found deep within yourself, you remember oneness with y/our loving, expansive collective soul. Breathe deeply with trust and surrender until you find the point inside of you where our collective soul is patiently waiting for you to reunite with it. When you allow yourself to do this, our collective soul will embrace, lift, and remind you of the incredible bond that connects us all. Once you find this connection, you will understand its infinite capacity to support and love you so unconditionally that you will weep.

Merge with this energy as often as possible and connect with its/your/our wisdom, kindness, and compassion. Ask for help surrendering to its/your/our grace and healing capacities. Ask for help remembering what trust in yourself feels like, and then ask for help getting your entire body to vibrate in the blissful surrender of trust. When you resonate in surrendering your vibration to the collective through trust, you will understand that every step you have taken in this lifetime—and the steps of your consciousness in all dimensions—has been perfect. You will no longer doubt y/our capacity to play this game of life as the loving creator beings we were designed to play it as. You will trust that every step you take is a step of infinite beauty to be honored for its perceived difficulty and celebrated for its vibration of peace. Y/our steps are creating new ways to love for all of us.

Only you can limit the love you are meant to discover through your steps by labeling the vibrations they cause you to feel as "good" and "bad." When we vibrate in the judgment of this limited labeling, we lose trust in ourselves by labeling ourselves as "bad." If we are "bad," we are taught we are not trustworthy and thus lose the capacity to trust ourselves. If we cannot trust ourselves, we cannot find a way to surrender to the beautiful collective soul we have within waiting for us to remember how fun it is to play the game of life in the resonance of the love of all the energy ever created. Please understand that we created this 3D realm to find new ways to love.

When you choose to trust in yourself, you can play the game of life through the lenses of spontaneity, surrender, and faith. When we all play this sacred game through these lenses, we will play with giggles in our steps and experience much more joy. You can also heal in ways you never imagined possible.

In 2020, I chose to surrender to my higher self and asked to open up and receive whatever vibration I needed to be a more effective healer. This act of surrender was very scary the first time, but my desire to be of service was greater than my fear of surrendering, so I surrendered and received a very powerful healing. I rarely asked for help before this healing but have asked many times since, and every time I have asked, I have received it. The help has come in the form of angels and other deities playing with me when I'm offering frequencies for others to heal with or when my body needs love to heal. I have felt beings enter my energetic field and offer light healings. Sometimes, these healings have been in the form of a laser of healing light penetrating into the body part in pain and offering a frequency of love that healed my pain within minutes. I also have felt portals of energy come into my field and offer healing frequencies to the part of my body in pain. When I surrender and become one with God, I often see what I would describe as new dimensions of wisdom and love being "incorporated" into my awareness and body. This visualization of dimensions and energy flow entering my field and body helps me remember all of the loving energy I already have within me so that I can be more confident in sharing it with others. When I share this loving energy, I remind people that the whispers of the love we heal with are already in them, waiting for them to remember their divinity and their birthright to be whole and healed at all times.

We create how we play this game. Let's create a kinder, more compassionate, unconditionally loving game. Let's start playing the game of life with trust in the collective soul we are. Let's play a game where we remember the Earth and its energies are part of our soul. Let's play a game where we value and connect to the sparkle of light in another's eyes through trust. Let's play a game in which we all remember just how special and beautiful we are when we share our souls with faith that the energies we exchange that day are always the ones we need to exchange for the growth of all, even if at the time we perceive them as uncomfortable. I feel our collective amazing soul wants to change the way we play the game of life and make it more loving and peaceful. Will you surrender to the light you have within by trusting yourself to add your note to the symphony that will create a more loving game? You/we got this. You have already created the love and appreciation in me I have for you/us. I am blessed to remember what our entire soul vibrating in trust feels like. It feels amazing, by the way.

Also, if you have not experienced the song "Trustfall" by P!nk, I highly recommend you do so, and watch the video.

Our stars

I am reading *Energy Blessings from the Stars* by Virginia Essene and Irving Feurst.[4] In the book, Irving Feurst talks about how the inhabitants of every solar system are being guided in their physical and spiritual evolution by the sun of that system, which he calls a solar logos. The solar logos is an intelligent being in every star that helps the entities of the solar systems they give life to incorporate a unique quality of love. I googled how many stars are in our universe this morning, and the first entry said there are possibly a septillion stars in our marvelous universe. That is a one followed by twenty-four zeros. Interestingly, this is a multiple of eight times three. Eight is the symbol of infinity, or the consciousness in which time does not exist, and the yin and yang of all energy are in a constant dance of balance in creation. The number three represents the concept that when we combine our energy with another, the sum of one and one does not equal two. The sum of yin and yang is the energy of creation, and this can be seen as a three-sided triangle in the two-dimensional realm or a twenty-four-point star when seen in dimensions we cannot quite grasp with a human mind.

I believe our human suit is an energetic hologram of our universe. Therefore, all septillion stars reside within it. I also believe every soul in a human suit is one of those stars. I know that while our consciousness is playing the game of Earth, we can allow the energy of our stars to connect in a unique way that we can only understand in the felt sense.

The light that is the flavor of the wise love of your star resides somewhere in your body. The magical note of your star is found by surrendering resistance to discovering how beautiful you are and how much we love and support each other through the whispers of the ethers. You dissolve this resistance by breathing open the energy field that is your human suit. With every breath you take, imagine pulling your diaphragm down through your kidneys and opening the points of the star within you. The center of this star is a photon. This photon connects you to not only your star but all energy. Let every breath guide you into sinking, softening, or melting through the energies of your human suit until you find the photon that is the center of your star. Once you find the center of your star, breathe until the light it emits fills and heals your whole body. Then, take a walk, watch how others will sense that light, and then marvel at how your light will guide others to melt open so they can remember and know how elevating it feels to embody and walk the Earth as their wise star.

Once you remember you are a star and allow its light to radiate from you, it will awaken you in such a way that you will remember your human suit is not only one with, but also created with all of our stars. You will begin to appreciate every human you are graced with crossing paths with and remember that their star is part of the light your suit is made of. You will know their story and energy is part of the magnificence of your unique loving light. You can connect for support, guidance, and love to the one energy we all came from at any time. You can feel the heartbeat that is the light and dark (yin and yang) of creation within you anytime. You can connect to the stars of others and the darkness between our stars that we create with. Because we are playing Earth in this dimension of our consciousness, you will also see that you can connect to other parts of your soul that appear to be outside of you (in the form of another human) in ways you never imagined possible.

So, will you love yourself and relax into your magnificence so that you find the starlight that is the true you within you today? Will you share your light with others so that we can create a new peaceful reality that none of us alone could ever imagine possible? Will you emit the sound of your unique giggle of creative light and combine it with another's giggle so that you can enjoy this game of Earth in a way you never imagined it could be played? Let's giggle a peaceful creation into existence right now. We are, I am. I love you. We got this.

5

Playing Healing Open
with Your Heart

Love

Humanity has turned the word *love* into a game played with a chessboard of mind-controlled options. This powerful emotion should never be subjected to the limitations of the imagination of a human Ego. Love is an essence of our divinity that is meant to flow freely from you as an expression of the unique light of Source you are meant to share with your human Ego/mind and all you cross paths with.

The following are some of *Webster's Unabridged* definitions of *love:*[1]
Love (n)

1. A feeling of strong attachment induced by that which delights or commands admiration; preeminent kindness or devotion to another; affection; tenderness; as, the love of brothers and sisters.
2. Especially, devoted attachment to, or tender or passionate affection for, one of the opposite sex.
3. Courtship; — chiefly in the phrase to make love, i.e., to court, to woo, to solicit union in marriage.
4. Affection; kind feeling; friendship; strong liking or desire; fondness; good will; — opposed to hate; often with of and an object.
5. Due gratitude and reverence to God.
6. The object of affection; — often employed in endearing address.

Love (v)

1. To have a feeling of love for; to regard with affection or good will; as, to love one's children and friends; to love one's country; to love one's God.
2. To regard with passionate and devoted affection, as that of one sex for the other.
3. To take delight or pleasure in; to have a strong liking or desire for, or interest in; to be pleased with; to like; as, to love books; to love adventures.

After you read the above definitions of *love*, you can understand how seemingly complicated love is and the many forms that love comes in. I would like to discuss its purest form today: unconditional love. According to the dictionary, this would mean love is an absolute, unqualified, unselfish, loyal, and benevolent concern for the good of another. This definition may seem difficult to aspire to and sustain because we expect those we love to love us back. It is time to begin to open and create an Earth game in which humanity is graced with a heart that only knows love as an unconditional green flame of compassion. We can start by waking up in the morning and rolling out of bed with the fluidity of remembering we are made of love and decide to unconditionally love ourselves and all the steps our human suit will experience that day. As we comprehend what compassion and admiration for our own steps look and feel like, we will subconsciously offer that vibration to those around us.

We are taught in many fairy tales that we only have one true love in our lives. These fairy tales teach us that our "true love" will fulfill all our needs and that the relationship we have with that individual will be eternal bliss. This is bullshit. No married couple I know receives eternal bliss from their spouse. States of prolonged bliss are not found in the game of Earth, but nuggets of bliss are, and they occur when your heart is open and vibrating in the resonance of all love in all forms ever experienced, aka all energy that has ever existed.

What if we shed the fairy tale version of "true love" and instead play "loving open" with our hearts every day so that we know and embody the frequency of the energy of unconditional love? The more we play Earth in this way, the more we know that the essence of unconditional love creates every step of our marvelous human journeys. When we walk our steps with our Egos marveling at this new perspective of love and how fun it is to play Earth in this frequency, we find that the nuggets of bliss we experience become never-ending rainbow brick paths we cannot wait to explore and share with the parts of our soul in other human suits.

How do we embark on this journey to seek and know unconditional love above all other forms and then be awed by the connection and bliss of the state of awakening it graces us with? We start by loving ourselves in this way. We start by having compassion for our past behaviors that were programmed into our Egos when we learned that love is conditional. We can process—with gratitude—the experiences that taught us that love is conditional. The ouchy energy vibrations that we got from these experiences awakened us and allowed us to explore a box of fear in our hearts. By exploring those fear boxes, we can understand at a broader frequency that love is *not* conditional. As we choose to love open the fear prisons in our hearts, we broaden the bandwidth of the definitions of love that flow from it. When all definitions of love flow from our unimprisoned hearts, think of what we collectively will be able to love into creation.

When was the last time your smile, open heart, and vulnerability were responsible for someone else's joy of awakening to a new embodiment of love? How did that make you feel? If it has been a while since you were in this loving resonance, I encourage you to explore the reembodiment of it today. You may even want to try experiencing the harmony of the cosmic frequency with a complete stranger. Your love for yourself and others will grow open as you surrender to walking while emitting unconditional love more often.

One day, when many of us are humbled to experience Earth while walking that rainbow brick road of giggling possibilities created from the wisdom of open, unhindered hearts, the human race and the planet will play Earth in a new creative capacity. There will be no more disrespect for life of any kind. We will cherish all moments with one another because we will see them as all coming from the cosmic connection of the one who unconditionally loves us all even when these moments are perceived as painful. We may even come to cherish painful moments as we learn to love the mind that interprets loving interactions as painful and use the pontificative power of the mind to create a new way to love. Through loving the mind, we can soften it and use it as a guide of duality that shows us how to find more unique notes of powerful love to share.

How will you unconditionally love yourself and another today? Embrace the joy found in the vulnerability of doing so because when your love is unconditional, your Ego is surrendered to dimensions of singularity. When your Ego is not tied to duality, no version of your soul can poke you because there will be no prisons left to poke open and thus no reason to feel pain. Please trust me when I say you do have an endless source of unconditional love for yourself and others within you. Will you start enjoying the exploration of this indescribable Source that can make you giggle with delight and playfulness today? When will you decide to shed the limiting belief that love is conditional? When will you explore the level of contentment that can be achieved by giving and receiving unconditional love? When will you feel the bliss of the connection you can make when the love is mirrored in the eyes of the one you are sharing its vibration with? I am lovingly asking you to open your heart and ask to connect to and create as much love as possible today. Will you choose to rise from your bed in this state of awareness and exploration and play open your heart today? If you do, you will not be disappointed. You may even understand the true meaning, power, and joy of creation while playing Earth in the full bandwidth of power that your loving heart has the miraculous capacity to flow in for the first time in your life. I can feel your smile and heart open as you think about playing this way today. Thank you for sharing this giggle of the joyful bliss of creating with unconditional love with me today. You are so loved and appreciated.

Potential

Do you allow fear to limit your potential?

Most of us strive to achieve our potential. Unfortunately, many perceive the word *potential* as a synonym for *perfection*. The idea of performing any task with perfection will cause many of us to enter a fear state that causes anxiety, anger, isolation, or depression. I would like you to consider how you are allowing fear to block you energetically from the love that will guide you to discover and play your symphony note with its maximum capacity—aka your potential.

In J. K. Rowling's book *Harry Potter and the Prisoner of Azkaban*, Harry Potter creates a dementor during an exercise that allows him to witness his greatest fear by conjuring it into reality through magic. This is what we do every day. We think while in fear and create a reality where these fears solidify. Or we think with an open, loving heart and create a life where our interactions mirror the love we are resonating in. When the dementor appears, Professor Lupin is able to understand that Harry's greatest fear is fear itself. I did not understand the depth of this concept until recently. I think many of us need to be more afraid of fear. Our fears provoke our Egos and pain bodies into behaviors that rob us of our potential and compassion. Our fears keep us from being present, loving, and kind and cause us to judge others. When you melt into the center of your deepest regrets, you will understand that fear in the form of a cortisol-induced emotion is the root of these regrets. Will you work on stopping fear from causing any more regrets? Regrets are how we learn in Earth school, but it is time to stop creating new ones because we can access the regrets of all time right now. I believe that in some other timeline, you have the same vibration of regrets and can heal them without needing a new parallel regret that traps your Ego and mind in this dimension.

How do we no longer allow fear to control us? Well, you could start by saying "Fuck off, fear." I am now using this as a texting acronym: FOF. Someone even suggested I put this phrase on a T-shirt and she made hot-pink hats that said FOF for a girls' weekend getaway. If this acronym works for you, that would be awesome. If you don't like to swear, please pick another word that motivates you to love your way through your fears.

I am now consciously using fear to motivate me. My purpose is to offer a vibration of healing to as many parts of my/our soul as possible. This includes those wearing other human suits and the suits we wear in other dimensions. If these fractals of the light of our soul choose to receive the vibration I am blessed with the ability to offer, they can take the next step of the journey of remembering awake with slightly more ease. I believe at least some of the vibrations I can offer are the keys to the fear prisons that have kept people isolated from knowing they are Source. I have been actively searching for the fear boxes within myself and asking for help finding the keys from my loving guides to shed my fears and open my energetic field so that I can love this purpose into creation with as much capacity as possible. I recently had an amazing group healing session with Pat Longo, thanks to Jenniffer Weigel and her Spiritual Social Club, in which I set my intention to receive access to the keys to the boxes that trap people in fear with more ease. I received them through Pat's opened, healed heart. I felt as if the vibration of a master key was incorporated into my voice and touch. Thank you, Pat Longo, for loving your fear boxes open over the years so that you can offer so much loving capacity to all the souls that cross your path and offer healing vibrations to love their boxes open beyond their wildest dreams. *Please remember, if you do not receive, you have nothing to share.*

My fears include or have included in the past (I have been spending my time loving open my boxes):

- Speaking to groups of people.
- Using new ways to heal as soon as they present themselves in my imagination.
- Leading others.
- Writing blog posts—but now, these blog posts are a book!
- Fearing that surrendering to Source is safe. Source is the energy that every healer holds space with and channels to heal the patient who is ready to heal and is meant to heal as part of the grand plan the universe has in store for us. You are Source, so know you are simply surrendering to the totality of yourself.

I have decided at this point to be more afraid of allowing fear to control me and keep me from my potential than I am of my fears. Will you start to think about what joy and connection your fears prevent you from witnessing and loving open with? Will you start to fear fear itself so it no longer keeps you from your potential? Will you return to the state where fear was not even part of your vocabulary when your soul was born?

It is time to search and find our fear prisons and heal them open with love and light of Source. Allow fears to present themselves to you so you can love them for the wisdom they have taught you. Then tell them they may no longer control you as you kiss them goodbye. You can mindfully view the appearance of your external world in a state where you perceive happiness. However, if you transmute your fears, you will find your stillness. Listening to your stillness will reveal what path will make you glow with connection and joy. You will find contentment, purpose, and peace by journeying on this beautiful, unique path only you possess. Will you love your fears, go within yourself, and find your unique pathway of capacity to love your fears into collective wisdom today?

Your spirit

My definition of *spirit* continually evolves, but I see it as the energetic vortex to collective consciousness created when your human mind and soul live in perfect symbiosis.

Spirit is the cord that connects our soul with Source/the divine/God. When we suffer, we search for a way to end the suffering. We begin to understand that peace is found through a change in perspective. We are often guided on how to open our hearts to see, feel, know, and accept a broader viewpoint through the whispers of the divine emanating from other human suits and our guides. Or we can push the easy button and ask God itself. When we surrender our minds and souls to Source, we gain access to the wisdom and the oneness of Source. This wisdom is the accumulation of yin/yang, dark/light, suffering/bliss of every experience of every soul that has ever existed. It is never the same because it is always what we need (which may not be what we want) at the time we connect. When you connect to this indescribable power of creativity and love with humility and stillness, you can know with confidence how to help yourself and guide others into playing healing.

How do you find your spirit tether (the energetic cord that connects you to source before you remember you are source) to connect? Try to understand that harvesting our emotions' energy is one reason we incarnate in these human bodies. Our volatile emotions are necessary for our soul's growth and cosmic energy transformation. Never judge your feelings. Appreciate how they give birth to new levels of understanding and connection. They are in every form a wondrous instrument we can use to achieve connection to the oneness of Source and to help us ascend to a "higher" vibration.

The real key to transmuting our suffering is to sit and absorb through appreciating the uncomfortableness and pain of the lows or the pure joy and blessings of the highs you feel. Breathing through your heart will let you know that life's "ups" and "downs" are about fostering a connection to others. When we suffer, we have the option to continue to suffer by clinging to a lens of perception that interprets the reality around us as happening to us. Or we can look through a lens that views the suffering as a blessing because it is a means to remembering a new way to feel bliss in that we are forced to take steps that will reconnect us with our magnificent capacity to love the object that is the cause of our suffering. Many times the object you need to have more compassion and love for is you. Suffering is how our spirit expands and remembers there is a net of love connecting every energy in the universe. When you allow yourself to surrender to your ouchies and ask for a lens shift, you will always receive one. You may shed tears of humility at the wisdom of the love you will be graced with witnessing through the lens of singularity. Also, every time you do this, a spirit upgrade will take place, and the amount of time you spend suffering will decrease because you will find the surrender to Source or God for the lens change you need can come as fast as one breath.

It is time for us to sit with and allow all feelings to facilitate connection to our spirit tether. We appreciate the growth all emotions gift us. Once the emotion is absorbed and balanced, let go of that energy that takes you back to the initial trauma, judgment, guilt, self-loathing, grief, anger, etc., because you no longer need to go there. If you don't know how to let go, surrender and ask for help clearing the chakra longing to be free of the shadow figures of your Ego. Remember to release and share your emotions with the universe/Source that resides inside you because it will use these valuable energy generators to further growth and connection for all. You are an essential fractal of the divine, and your emotions are necessary for the sustenance of the divine.

My patients and friends have taught me that we all have unique and beautiful spirit tethers. When humans release the emotions that are keeping them from connecting to Source, the energy of their spirit tether is revealed. I am in awe that I get to witness so much inspirational beauty and bliss when people find their tether. Everyone brings in a unique color and character of connection that fills my heart with wonder, joy, and awe. Will you surrender and release the weight of an old emotion today so that you may start to find your beautiful and unique spirit tether? Will you hold space for another to release the perceptions that keep them from discovering the full capacity of their glorious spirit?

Listening in time

One of my favorite teachers in medical school was Dr. Theodore Woodward. He was in his eighties and loved sharing the wisdom that came with being a family doctor for over fifty years with eager, bright-eyed medical students. The most important lesson I learned from him was that if you listen long enough, the patient will always give you their diagnosis. Listening has helped me be a good mother, doctor, healer, coach, and friend throughout my lifetime. Lately, the power of listening broadened for me, and I wanted to share how.

I have recently understood why I do not ground like others, and many who "see" try to help me ground to Earth like they do. I have never grounded like everyone else and discovered that I am whole when grounded in time and emotions. I see my left foot as connected to the "past" and compassion and my right foot as connected to the "future" and hope. The Earth is in my pelvis, and I am tethered to her spectrum of wisdom, patience, love, and peace in the "now."

While doing yoga the other day, I had an epiphany. Thank you, Dr. Sue Morter, because your BodyAwake Yoga sessions always include a vibrational upgrade. The epiphany was that the frequency of healing that a patient needs can be discovered by listening to all dimensions of a patient's consciousness. There is no time, and we only have one soul. Therefore, if you listen in time, you have the capacity to find and embody any frequency needed to heal. Also, without the boxes we imagine with the concept of time, we allow our essence to perceive and vibrate in our wholeness. In wholeness, we remember we are light and, therefore, we have no physical vessel to manifest the disease our body was solidifying to aid us in remembering that we are light.

All disease is created by allowing our light to be ensnared in an emotion, thought, object, or idea. When entangled, we cannot flow freely and feel and embody all 144,000 dimensions of our consciousness. We create a disease to become aware that we have gotten stuck in the collection of one energy, thus preventing us from experiencing and playing with a different energy. Because we have 144,000 dimensions of consciousness, there is a chance that we or another part of our soul has also been trapped in that same energetic frequency that is part of our collective consciousness "before" and has loved it open Thus, there may be a vibration of transmutative healing love that we have created in another dimension that can be accessed and received to free us in this one.

So, if we listen in "time," we will find the vibration needed to heal. How do we listen in time? You love yourself open by finding the star in your center and letting it shine as far as you can imagine. You believe you are light and cannot be contained or separated from all light. You may become the womb of creation, as I did in meditation this morning, and realize if you are the womb of creation and there is no time, you are the energies of attachment that bless you with disease and the energies of transmutational love that free you from that attachment all in one. You choose the vibration you wish to embody "now."

When you are in the "now," there is no karma, past, or future. Since most of us are ensnared by an energy birthed through the concept of judgment (either of self or others), if we vibrate in "now," judgment does not exist. If we vibrate in the totality of all time, our soul remembers and allows the light of our oneness to be its vibration. The womb of creation does not judge the energy it produces. The frequency of a 3D dimension labels and boxes energy as "good" or "bad" and creates the attachments of judgment.

I know my vibration of this concept of listening in time will evolve as I play with it. I hope you can open to the idea of playing with y/our totality and feeling how amazing the essence we are made of feels when you become "time." I hope this book reveals a healing vibration so you can experience the full essence of y/our light spectrum. Use this note to open your heart and star to share your light with humanity. When I open my star and feel the magnificence and love of our combined light, tears of humility flow freely from my eyes because I am so grateful to marvel at how beautiful our light spectrum is when we are one. I love you all. We got this. Let's heal together by playing in "no time."

Frequencies

Why am I here? What is my purpose? When souls awaken to the fact that they are eternal beings temporarily wearing a human suit, they often ask these two questions. I think the best answer is found in surrender.

What or who do we surrender to? We surrender to the light within that connects your soul's unique fractal energy, which is tethered to our collective soul and all energy ever created. How do we do this? Set the intention and ask for help from your guides, God, Source, the divine, angels, or a healer who resonates with your belief system. Once you have enlisted these cosmic aids, ask your mind and body to melt into the place within that only you can find as your center. For many, this place will be between your xiphoid process (the end of your sternum) and just below your belly button. I call this photon inside of you your "God particle." FYI, this photon does travel to different places in my body at times, so it may not remain in a fixed place for you, either. It may move anywhere from your neck to your pubic bone, be in all those areas at once, or even fill your whole aura and beyond as you play with its connection capabilities.

How do you connect to your God particle? Picture it as an intelligent entity that is like a radio dial. This part of you is as old as the Big Bang (maybe even older) and is an extremely wise cosmic energy. It is made of unconditional love and thus has no fear. Without fear, your God particle has no restrictions on where it travels and what frequencies it chooses to explore. When I meditate, this particle has a mind of its own and connects to frequencies that let me experience the felt sense of energies like the Big Bang, the dimension of consciousness where our soul is not perceived as separate but is one loving, incredibly creative being. This dimension is a place where all of the "gods" we know have unified as one brilliant green light. It's a place where all of the dimensions of my consciousness have become reflective mirrors of light that shine back on me in my human suit to give me the confidence to love freely and write about this. By the way, meditation is not a sit-still activity for me. My best downloads occur on my mountain bike, hiking, or playing with Dr. Sue Morter by doing BodyAwake Yoga or her monthly healing session. Thank you, Dr. Sue.

Surrender to this particle is also how I help people heal. By saying, "I am in God, God is in me, we combine as one," I surrender to this photon within me. It connects to the field and the God particle of the person or group I am playing with and brings in the vibrations that the person or the group can incorporate to assist in remembering their wholeness. When we are "whole," we "heal" from the frequency our human suit emits when it forgets its wholeness. We call the frequency of forgetting our wholeness "disease."

Many human suit problems are invitations to explore your God particle's potential to reconnect with a sacred frequency that you and all of humanity need to heal. We allow our human emotions to be a guide that helps us explore and gather the frequencies of the loving wisdom of the universe so that we can bring them back to Earth to share with humanity. When we do this, we evolve and create as one being. The felt sense of sharing this joy of connection while in the vibration and capabilities of a human body is profoundly blissful.

Will you melt into your center today? Will you let the wisdom within your center be explored by allowing the radio dial within to travel along loving frequencies to places you have forgotten exist or to new ones you are creating? Will you then breathe these sacred vibrations into a light you emit to share with the one soul we are all part of that surrounds you in the form of other humans, animals, and all the energetic vibrations of the Earth and the cosmos today? I/Our soul loves you and is always supporting you. We got this.

Best friends

A best friend is the most precious gift you could hope for. Please let your besties know today how much you appreciate them.

I am so blessed to have so many wonderful besties in my tribe who love the gigglegasms found through exquisitely delivered sarcasm as much as I do. The last few years of remembering awake have frequently been difficult for me. When I awoke at age fifty, I realized I had been in a state of asleep induced through the vibrations of guardedness, judgment, and science, to name a few. My veil has been dissolving as I have chosen to release attachment to these limiting vibrations by opening my heart. With no veil of fear limiting my vision, I began to appreciate and embrace the world of psychics, mediums, and healers who have become my new besties.

The new reality that was revealed to me is magical and beautiful but so different from my old reality that it poked many of my fear boxes along the way. There is no better way to dissolve a fear box than to do it with a gigglegasm. Archangel Michael recommends his Ha, Ha, Ha meditation in *Earth, the Cosmos, and You* by Virginia Essene.[2] I asked Michael through medium Heather Sprigg if this meditation is meant to provoke gigglegasms, and Michael said yes, because laughter will raise your vibration. Here is a shoutout to those who have blessed me with gigglegasms and a space holding loving strength of belief in my abilities to transmute my fear prisons.

I want to share some of my fear-provoking remembering awake experiences so that if similar situations happen to you, you may find a fear box–obliterating gigglegasm to help you accept how powerful and magnificent of a creator you are.

In spring 2022, when I took my first in-person healing class, I was blessed with entering a sacred portal full of divine beings who saw my potential. There were fifteen of us in that class, and I had just entered the world of the art of healing and left behind the art of Band-Aiding diseases with prescriptions that create more disease. In this class, the other participants held space for me to talk through the idea that we are all connected and beautiful beings. By the third day of the class, one person asked me, "When is your book coming out?" They told me that I would lead the meditation that morning. That was something I had never done or even considered doing. I was scared. However, their open hearts held the love vibration necessary to release that fear and lead my first group meditation.

The guided meditation ended up being beautiful. I described how sometimes Source energy flowed through me with such a powerful light that I felt the need to release and share that light. I talked about seeing myself as a tree at times, releasing seeds of love in whatever form is needed for whomever needs it. The participants in the class had never felt an energy surge like this, and they could not understand the "knowing" that when so much light flows from you, it is not meant just for you. Through the guided meditation I led, we connected as one great, cosmic tree of wisdom and love. The participants all felt themselves vibrating in that space where you know the energy is not just for you, and they understood when energy is for sharing. The conviction that group held for me to embrace my note of love that I am meant to share with this planet and beyond gave me the confidence to start writing the blogs that have become this book. They loved me open. I will be forever grateful for the loving beings in that class.

Later in 2022, a smaller group from that class met and had me lead the group healing, and through the space they created, this took place. We were at the end of the group meeting, and there were only about ten minutes left. We gathered around a very special soul who shared that, as a child, she played the game Light as a Feather, Heavy as a Rock with her siblings. During this game, she would float off the ground. She was in a car accident when she was young and had been living in a colorful world without a veil since. (Souls without veils are easier to heal because they play human with fewer boxes.) She was having some tendinitis caused by a genetic disease where her ligaments were looser than they should be.

It was customary for this group to join hands to unite energy to become a collective unit that would offer healing energy to the one on the table in the middle. When we held hands, I got the epiphany that we didn't even need to touch the person on the table to heal her, so we didn't. About five of us held hands in a circle around her while she lay on the table. I led the meditation but could feel and be one with the power and wisdom of the other healers I was holding hands with. My eyes closed as I channeled, so I did not see what happened next.

When the healing was done, I was told that the open soul on the table floated off the table and the table floated up off the floor. The arm that was in pain went through motions and positions that it should not be able to achieve. This has been explained as a rewinding into positions her arm was in during the childhood car accident. Dr. John Upledger describes this healing process in his beautiful books, which are worth a read. The energetic unwinding takes you back to the initial trauma and unwinds the energy attached to that trauma, and as a result of this, healing takes place. I still have a hard time believing the table came off the floor, but the other people in the room all felt and saw it. The woman got off the table with no pain in her elbow. This group's steadfast belief in my abilities helped me understand the possibilities of the new reality I was entering and remember I am a healer. Thank you, old, wise bestie souls.

In the summer of 2022, one of the people I had met in the healing class who has pushed me to remember who I am told me that I was going to heal her friend remotely. I told this friend, "You're fucking crazy. I can't do that."

She forced me to laugh when she responded, "You're fucking crazy if you think you can't do it."

So I did what she told me to do, and my remote healing career began. I could feel this woman's childhood from thirty miles away and helped her release some of the boxes of traumatic memory it was trapping her in. I've been helping people remotely heal ever since.

In the fall of 2022, I went to Donna Eden's Energy Fest. Energy Fest is a vortex of unimaginable possibility created by Donna Eden and the beautiful souls that want to play in her light. During these four blessed days, I met Dr. Sue Morter and many other shamans who can see energy. The hotel was on a powerful vortex with over three hundred healers in attendance. The seeds of my tree were seen by enough beautiful souls in attendance there that I came to believe my imaginary tree was, in fact, "real" and not just a vision I see with my eyes closed. I met a soul who helped me believe in the power of love I have inside of me to share; she did this by believing in the power of the gift she knew I possessed and loving me open. Through our shared confidence in our ability to generate miracles through surrender to energy outside of the ability of our minds' understanding, we created a playground of healing in which we restored her hearing from nothing to about 70 percent in less than ten minutes. I also met a very old soulmate who shared his powerful healing stories to giggle open boxes with. I was humbled when this powerful healer was in awe of the connections I was able to make during an assemblage point healing that Donna Eden led.

When I left Energy Fest, I called a longtime friend who laughed with me as I described some of the eye-opening, jaw-dropping, and head-whipping behaviors that I saw in others when they gazed at the patterns of light that I was emitting. She helped me giggle into a new vibration of acceptance of the energy reality I was beginning to explore and helped me believe this shit was real.

In the spring of 2023, I went to Egypt on a JourneyAwake trip with Dr. Sue Morter and about 120 other souls. Let's just say my energy was validated in many ways, and I met some amazing beings who have helped me, including Gretchen Oehler Hogg, who told me, "It is much harder to run away from who you are meant to be than to be that person." She held space for me at the very end of the trip when I had some chest pain and asked for help clearing it. The help came in the form of a bright, powerful light entering my chest from above. Gretchen was able to see this and was astounded at how powerful it was. She made me ask if it was Hathor energy, and I got the answer that it was. She advised me to do automatic writing when I am blessed to be one with energies like this. She also validated that these energies I perceive as vibrations that cause my body to shake are real and that I am very blessed to be a vessel meant to share them with the Earth and beyond. Thank you, Gretchen. Those were profound words, and the loving space you hold with your wise, open heart has helped me walk with more grace and ease into the note of love I am meant to play loudly in this dimension.

Also, while in Egypt, in the museum at the end of the trip, I was playing with some new friends and came across a door carved into one of the stones. It made me cry because the energy it emitted was so peaceful. We each took a turn in front of the door and felt and embodied its peace so we could heal. The peace was so profound that when one of our group members walked into the space we were playing healing in, she started crying and asked, "What are you girls doing?" I had felt a similar vibration in the morning when I lay in the Egyptian sun on the cement outside of our hotel for about forty-five minutes. During that time, I hugged all the painful places in my body that I had trapped my light in so that they would open and I could flow with that light again. I felt like a ten-foot glowing ball of powerful peace when I got up from the ground.

Dr. Sue walked by me in the museum when we were playing with the door, which I thought was a peace portal. When I told her how beautiful the door felt later, she said, "It is not a portal; it is a mirror." This was a life-lasting lesson and a beautiful story I have shared with many since that explains and opens awareness to the fact that we are everything we see and feel around us. There is no separation from you and the energy you feel around you. You are one. Thank you, Dr. Sue Morter, for this epiphany and the hundreds you have given me since.

This trip also involved a "share" of the explosion of energy out of my pelvis in such a way that I felt like I had given birth to a galaxy. This was an interesting and slightly painful experience. Thanks to a very kind, loving, and wise soul, I was able to see that "birth" is what we are all capable of doing when we surrender and allow God to flow through us. We give birth to consciousness every day with our thoughts. When enough of us have the same thought, we affect consciousness on a greater scale. In the sacred place I was in that day, and because of the portal of loving souls Dr. Sue attracts, I was able to tap into many dimensions of loving consciousness and share that wisdom in an energy form that offers a more loving road for all of our minds to travel on. I also had one of the best gigglegasms of my life on the bus thanks to Angela Muñoz. It was a much-needed release from many of the limiting fear boxes I had been trapped in for fifty-two years.

When playing with a local shaman during one guided meditation in the summer of 2023, she said, "Archangel Raphael is here," and he came out of my chest. During another meditation with her, she said, "The Essences are here," and Jeshua and Mary Magdalene came out of my belly. The shaman looked at me with the bug eyes that people sometimes gaze at me with and said, "What a channel."

I called my friend Angela because having Jeshua and Mary Magdalene come out of my belly and then watching them travel around the room to heal everyone freaked me out a bit. Angela said, "Julie, many have their imprint, but you have their blueprint, and they live within you." I can't remember why, but then I sent Jeshua and Mary Magdalene to Angela's house, and she freaked out because she could see them. I asked what they looked like, and she said Mary Magdalene was wearing a purple robe with gold stars, had long hair, and was just a beautiful presence. She said Jeshua was like a bouncer. That created some gigglegasms as we began to comprehend that energies like that are really inside of us because there's only one of us here and there's no such thing as time as we know it. So, any entity that has ever been part of creation is part of you. When you love yourself deeply enough, you may be shocked who you find inside.

In the fall of 2023, there was also an incident where I was pretty sure someone saw Shiva on my face. I called my friend John and told him about Shiva being seen in my face, Raphael living in my chest, and Jeshua and Mary Magdalene in my belly. He made me laugh so hard when he said, "Julie, it's like you have a kangaroo pouch with all these action figures in it, and you can just whip them out when you need them!" This created a giggling open that helped me be OK with the idea that this is what other people were seeing in me.

John also told me that night that he saw me as a room closer in the future. When I told another friend about closing a room after others warm it up for me, she told me, "Julie, I see you closing the universe." When I told my friend Michelle about closing the universe, she responded with, "How do you close the universe? Do you ask for a timeout and say, 'I'm gonna go over there and stretch first, and then I'll get to work'?" This still makes me laugh. Thank you, Michelle.

I'm not sure what "closing the universe" means. However, as my veil has been dissolving with laughter, I realize that we are one soul, and there is no "I" in soul. I believe the energy that I call "home" on the other side of the veil does not have a name, but it is a unification of our soul. When surrendered to that presence here, I become nameless and thus become a "we." If there is going to be a "closing of the universe," we will do it collectively. The giggles my friends have graced me with have helped me open up to abilities that will help us connect and see what we feel like when we remember we are one. We may be closing an old universe that is no longer useful for us because it no longer serves us to get trapped in such profound pain for periods that last too long.

In the fall of 2023, I felt like I turned into a black hole during a group healing meditation. I had often been going to the empty with my patients, but my body becoming the empty was a new experience. The next day, someone mentioned that the room was so dark during that meditation and there was so much dark energy released from the participants in the room that the sound bowls and other instruments being played had a hard time sustaining their frequencies. I shared my experience with Sue S., a friend in that group, and she sternly lectured me that night and the next day on how special my gifts are and that I cannot be afraid to share them. Sue made me realize that I no longer have the luxury of not loving myself. From that day on, I have tried to melt the boxes of fear that keep me from exploring new ways to love myself open so that I can share the love I can channel with all of you. Thank you, Sue S., for scolding me into loving myself.

Also, the night I turned into a black hole, apparently, we were instructed not to talk after the meditation. I did not hear this because I was not fully in my body, and I was in the back corner of the room where I could not hear very well. I like to be in the corner because I shake and make some weird noises when I channel because I have not yet created the upgrades in my human suit to channel the energy I do. So I might have upset someone when I spoke. Another friend named Sue said, "I think you deserve a pass on not hearing instructions if you just turned into a black hole." Thank you, Susan M.

In the spring of 2024, my patient wanted to play with Archangel Michael, so that is the essence she combined with to heal. While she was combined with Michael, I felt a giant energy surge in the room, and I asked, "Oh my God, can you feel all the archangels in the room with us?" The patient said yes.

I felt very tired after this and called my friend Gail to ask, "Did that really happen?" She said yes.

Then I asked, "Why am I so tired? Am I being a drama queen in complaining about being tired?"

She giggled her response. "Julie, you just had all the archangels in the room with you, and you are incorporating that vibration into your energy field, so you might be tired and are not a drama queen."

I texted my friend Jen, "Have you ever had your ass handed to you by the archangels?"

She immediately replied, "What? They usually are so nice." This was then followed by a reassuring phone call in which Jen held space for me to tell another "crazy" healing story. Her heart has held so much space for me. Thank you, Gail Alexander and Jen Weigel.

One of the funniest stories I have to date was created with a patient who has become a bestie. I had been doing yoga and had been searching for a note that would represent the spectrum I feel to be our collective consciousness. The sound I came up with was a scale of the vowel *O*. I tried but could not voice the scale of "ooooh" I wanted to create, so I gave up. The next day, I was doing yoga with Dr. Sue, and she nailed the "ooooh" scale perfectly. I went into the biggest gigglegasm as I realized that it was the same sound the teenage mermaids make in the show *H₂O: Just Add Water* that my daughters were addicted to watching at one time. The "ooooh" sound is part of the sound of Jeshua. So, of course, my patient came up with the idea that I should be Jesus with a mermaid tail for Halloween and then started giggling as she said that Jesus as a mermaid would be the ultimate drag queen costume. We then went under the sphinx for her healing and were surrounded by beings. I just saw them as cylindrical lights, but she saw them in detail, and they appeared to be human. We were still laughing so hard about Jesus being a drag queen that they apparently started laughing with us. She then said the beings were telling us to stop laughing because they were laughing so hard they could not concentrate on healing her. Thank you, my friend, for giving me a story that will make me giggle every time I remember it.

As these beautiful revelations of remembering awake have taken place, I am so lucky to have besties that I could share these stories with, and through humor, giggle the fear boxes open that would keep me from opening to and embracing my gifts so that I could share them with others. Jen Weigel and her Spiritual Social Club have been an essential part of sharing some of these experiences. Thank you to these souls for listening and supporting me in my shares. I also appreciate souls that I have been blessed to call besties since college (which is almost forty years ago) whom I have called to giggle these stories into a comfort zone. Thank you, Katie, for not always understanding what I am sharing but listening and helping me be OK with my new reality. You have always been able to soothe me by bringing me back into my body through humor and laughing at my scared Ego.

An example of Katie's humor helping me feel comfortable with who I am came when I went to a healer for the first time in 2022. The woman at the front desk looked at me and said, "I am going to feel your energy." The Reiki healer I saw told me during the session that my heart chakra was beautiful and endless. When we were done, she bowed to me and told me it was an honor to work on me. On the way out, the woman at the front desk said, "I definitely felt your energy." I called Katie, and after she let me tell her this story with giggles created by trying to wrap my head around my new world, she said, "The next time you go to that place, you tell those women, 'No compliments today. My head is big enough already. I need it to continue to fit through doors.'" This type of sarcastic humor directed at bursting the fear of the power of your light will help your Ego surrender to God every time. Thank you, Katie, for almost forty years of helping me laugh at myself with your amazingly quick-witted and beautifully sharp sarcastic humor.

If you have a relationship with someone where sarcasm like this can be cherished, let that person know how much you appreciate them today. If you do not have this type of person in your life, consider allowing more vulnerability into your heart so that the fears of your Ego can be laughed into nonexistence. The energy created through the shared laughter of sarcasm is special. It is a laughter and connection I cherish deeply, and I can never get enough of it. Thank you to all my friends with whom I share a frequency of love where this laughter can take place easily. I love you all dearly and cherish our friendships so much. You have helped shape me into who I am today, and I love who I am, and for that, I am eternally grateful. Thank you to Carrie, Tammy, Kristin, Robin, and Asha, who held space when I got divorced so that I could remember awake and discover who I truly am and open into a world where the above stories were able to manifest. By the way, I am also eternally grateful for the besties who have had a hard time supporting me fully in my journey. When I have not been supported or appreciated, it has been an opportunity to go within and self-validate, and that has also been a tremendous gift for which I am eternally grateful.

Guilt

Guilt is an emotion that can be very temporary or last a whole lifetime. It can be transmuted into an opening to self-love if we just choose to have compassion for ourselves and live in the present.

One embodiment of guilt is the frequency of self-blame created with some perceived wrongdoing or from the feeling that you are not worthy.[3] This is the definition I would like to talk about today. The dark cloak we call *guilt* masks our light from within. This cloak is created from the destructive thoughts of inadequacy. We cannot create the resonance of inadequacy if we have no past and no future. So please choose "now" and rid yourself of regret's cloaking energy. Why do we seem to prefer to resonate with the weight of guilt over the light of now? My gut tells me it is because we now know we could have handled the situation that we feel guilty about in the past with more love and compassion.

Guilt is an emotion that has the potential to eat you up inside. Any emotion that creates this feeling may cause the disease of cancer to eat you up inside. So I suggest you try to shift out of the resonance of guilt if you know you spend time feeding this energy with your thought loops. You feel guilty because you love someone enough that you want to be a "better person" in the past or in the future. News flash: No human lives in a continuous state of unconditional love. We are not supposed to live in this state 100 percent of the time because without the pain of our uncomfortable emotions, we would not learn the lessons that help us heal and teach others. Our alchemic abilities to transform these emotions give the gifts of contentment, possibility, creativity, and peace to all. When I am ready to walk out of a guilt loop, it is the vibration of peace that I use to access the unlimited supply of unconditional love I have within me to create a different walking path.

How do you find this peace within you? Start by apologizing to whomever or whatever you have guilt issues with. Take time to process and release the part of your "I" Ego that no longer serves you by recognizing the trigger that poked your pain body or the shadow figure that created the human behavior you feel guilty about. As you uncover these subconscious triggers, ask to release the painful emotional states they place you in by gently saying, "You have expanded my ability to love. Thank you. But you may no longer cloak me in the density of guilt." Have compassion for yourself and the learning state that you were in at the time the guilt was created. You are learning all these wonderful lessons on how to love more by realizing that your steps in the cloak of guilt were gifts of wisdom. They can teach you how to coax the human mind to choose to transmute the emotions that are the root of guilt. Thank you for these steps and your wisdom, but it may be time to rediscover your light and shed the cloak that keeps you from discovering a more fun path to walk.

How will you release your thoughts that cause your guilt today? How will you help another release theirs? When will you comprehend that we walk our path in pain when our minds are influenced by our shadow figures, our pain body, and our "I" Ego and that we have the power to find happiness and contentment through new thoughts anytime we choose to do so? When will you realize the "inadequacies" that society brainwashes you into believing you have, are not, in fact, inadequacies? What are the beautiful steps you are taking to remember the power of self-love? We are all grateful for the steps of your journey that have added to the wisdom and love of our collective soul's energy.

Will you play the healing the heart open game today? Start with melting a layer of your guilt cloak by loving the step of your path you took in that resonance. Then you can find the emotion created by that resonance and rediscover the light buried in the pain of that emotion. As you find the light within, it will increase the spectrum of peace and love in which you play the game of Earth, and playing Earth will be more fun for all.

Home

It is time to play with the thought that home is wherever our consciousness exists.

In the last few weeks, I have crossed paths with many souls suffering from the collective birth of a broader consciousness we are all going through. We perceive suffering with this grand birth because we are too busy mourning the death necessary for it. We are too busy embodying the fear of change instead of the tingle of new possibilities. Many I have recently crossed paths with have been rebirthing and remembering the gifts that their soul is meant to grace the planet and collective with. To have the energy and space for this rebirth to occur, these individuals are experiencing the death of loved ones, marriages, friendships, and their previous human identity.

We have been taught that death is painful. Thus, we view it that way. I encourage you to see through the pain and fear of change it brings and see it as a possibility. Death can be viewed as a black hole. Black holes are a collection of energy so dense that anything can be created from them. Our universe and our souls were created with black holes. The black holes of creation are called the empty and the void in the teachings of Qigong and biodynamic craniosacral therapy. I travel to these amazing creative vortexes almost every day. Each visit brings a new wavelength of soul, ideas, creativity, love, and light from this dark, silent, still, and amazingly peaceful place. In the black holes of death we find the lights of creation. Black holes are composed of the frequencies and densities of energy necessary to birth new energy wavelengths into the human suits we are currently in symbiosis with. I am not asking you to skip mourning but to at least entertain the belief that the death you are going through is for the benefit of you and the collective. I view dark nights of the soul as the black hole the human Ego dies in to emerge as an Ego reborn into the "we" Ego of the collective. I don't think you will ever meet a soul that is ungrateful for this miraculous form of rebirthing.

The Earth is going to undergo a beautiful transition that we create collectively. To do this, she needs us to achieve an energy resonance that allows us to surrender to the gifts of unconditional love and creation that we have within us. Many perceive this shift in resonance as painful. Many of you have physical symptoms in the chakra or body area where your gift is (or will manifest). Many of you also feel the shift into a broader resonance, or what many call "upgrades," as painful. Many are afraid of the change in resonance or are tired of the loud fear (pain, anger, judgment, etc.) that too many souls on this planet are emitting. This discomfort is causing many souls to "want to go home." News flash: We are simultaneously here and on the other side of the veil. Home is all the dimensions where your consciousness is active. (Some feel we have active consciousness in 144,000 dimensions right now.) In this dimension, you are being graced with the chance to absorb the knowledge of your multidimensionality. Many of us think we have a home on the other side of the veil, but I do not. I think our home is where we choose to have an integrated presence with our soul; thus, all timelines we are currently in are home. All universes we have inhabited are home. We can be in all places and feel all our soul's timeless, multidimensional experiences at once. It is time for us to embrace our multidimensionality.

With the birth in consciousness we are accomplishing right now, embodying a much larger energy bandwidth is necessary. To birth this change in frequency, many of us have to perceive the suffering of a large death. I am sorry. I know this is not easy. However, others have mastered this before you and are here to hold you and help you through this process. The healing path they have journeyed on is waiting for you to absorb its wisdom. It is time for all of us to see death as a chance at a life you never dreamed possible. It is time to see death as a way to release all of your limiting beliefs so that you can enter a world where there is no need for the word *miracle* because the creation and witness of unimaginable beauty is commonplace.

Will you choose to understand you are "home" while playing Earth today? Will you stop running away from the uncomfortable feelings your soul needs to transmute for you and the collective so that you have access to the comforts, wisdom, love, and toolboxes of all 144,000 dimensions of "home"? I feel your pain. A plethora of healers can help you transmute your pain. Please choose this dimension and this body as your "home" until you can expand to feel the breath of home by concentrating your light in this one first. So let's put on our big-girl panties and big-boy underwear (I have had to buy many new pairs lately) and get to work healing ourselves. Let's get to work on creating the birth of a new type of collective soul in this dimension we are blessed to call home. I love you all. You are all brave. You are all beautiful. You are all unique, and you are all needed. Please understand this. Thank you for your service to the collective. Let's get the death/birthday party started!

Our highest good

I invite you to cast aside your belief that there is a scale of divinity in the vibrations we embody.

So often, I hear and feel myself and others judging themselves for feeling an emotion they consider "bad" and thus judge their frequency into the weight of shame and doubt. It is time to stop shaming and belittling ourselves for playing the game of life the way it was designed to be played. We have chosen to have consciousness in this dimension to experience and gain an understanding of the entire spectrum of human emotions. We are here to experience sadness, anger, guilt, judgment, injustice, fear, etc. Without these powerful emotions, we would not have the yang for the yin to create with. We need to have angergasms, sadgasms, and feargasms to collect the information and energy for Source that we willingly set out to collect for the purpose of evolving our consciousness. However, the time we get stuck in these powerful and, at times, painful emotions is up to us.

Thus, the next time you experience a heavy emotion, do not try to run away from it or judge yourself for having an emotion you feel should be beneath where you are. Instead, take a few deep breaths through your solar plexus or your heart and go within yourself to the place where you feel your beautiful newborn unique soul. Let your soul's love and light hug the areas in your human energy field where the heavy emotion is stuck in the story of this dimension of duality, where it creates pain until the heavy energy is transmuted to peace or love. If you need help with this step, keep breathing deep into your body until you feel the light of all of our souls combined and every particle of energy ever made, and ask that entity to help you learn to love yourself. Yes, you are always worthy of this, and as you heal and love yourself, that energy of love you create heals all of us. So, thank you in advance for healing our collective soul by loving you.

The game of life is way more fun if you are mostly playing it in the vibration of love and light. But the heavier vibrations are very important and should not be considered "lesser" or "lower." These heavier energies force us to go within to help us remember how magical the connection to every particle of energy is. So, instead of shaming yourself for them, go within and love them into an energy that will strengthen the bond of love between us all.

We all come from the dark energy of a black hole of biomagnetic energy and love that connects us in ways the human mind will never understand. Our souls rejoice when they remember how indescribable it is to feel this connection and experience the knowing that we are ONE. Some of the souls I have seen and been in the most awe of have a lot of this creative dark energy within. I know they are going to use this dense creative potential to create ideas and energies that will inspire all of us to love more. Of course, they will not do this alone, but with the strength of the brightest white souls I have seen and other souls composed of all the magical colors of the rainbow of love.

You are loved and supported in ways you will never be able to comprehend, and you can feel and embody this love by closing your eyes and finding the center of y/our beautiful and unique light within. Will you play the game of life with me with a deeper understanding of why it was created today? Will you play the game without your Ego being attached to the words *higher* and *lower*? Will you understand when you love open your heart and energy field, the spectrum of energy you channel is broader but not "higher" than the soul standing next to you who may teach you to love open more, or the soul standing next to you who will teach you to love open more? Only one of us is here; thus, we all share the common vibration we call love. Will you release your limited mind's need to grade love and imprison it on a scale? We got this. I love you.

The divine feminine

Are there divine masculine and feminine energies?

I participated in Dr. Sue Morter's Heal Yourself, Heal Your Life class this past weekend, and during a guided meditation, my spleen became very painful. I have been told the spleen represents the maternal chakra; thus, I associate it with maternal energy. The pain I felt was the pain of the suppressed female energy throughout all time and all dimensions. It was the pain, anger, and frustration of not being seen or heard and still being considered a piece of property by much of the world. It was the frustration of a soul's total potential being suppressed so that others would not fear, condemn, or even murder the loved ones of a soul who dares to think about what it would feel like to be the unhindered power of the unlimited light, love, and connection to the ONE love inside. The pain was the despair of not embracing this loving connective power and allowing its true creative potential to come through. It was the overwhelming sadness of living in this suppression of potential out of fear for as long as there has been documented time on this planet and in other dimensions where there is a vibration of duality.

Because this pain seemed to embody so many aspects and dimensions and so much time, my body told me that this was the "divine feminine" energy that needed some love and healing. Then I realized there is no such energy as "divine feminine" or "divine masculine" because the energy we call the divine, God, or Source has no gender. We are responsible for what we consider masculine and feminine energy because we create these energies by having our consciousness inhabit a dimension with which we choose duality to transmute and create. Thus, divine energy is energy that we do not divide into masculine and feminine. It is an energy in which what we perceive as masculine and feminine work in the ultimate symbiotic blend, losing themselves in each other and blissfully becoming one.

However, my body was still living in duality, and my spleen was screaming at me because it was likely experiencing the pain of separation of the masculine and feminine in most if not all of the two thousand people who were taking this class. That was a lot of perceived pain, and I wanted to heal it so it would go away. So I held the hand of a powerful healer taking the class with me and asked for help from her and whomever was available to help us. When you ask for celestial help and believe it is available to you, it is. I pictured the most divine feminine energy I could and thought of Mary Magdalene. I felt all of the pain she has witnessed from the celestial realm and her time on Earth regarding the division of masculine and feminine energy.

My next thought was that a divine masculine energy must also be here to witness and understand this pain in the felt sense, so Jeshua (Jesus) appeared. He acknowledged the pain of this separation of divine energy into the duality of masculine and feminine. He also acknowledged the damage caused through the mindset of a patriarchal, divided world that we have been embodying for too long When he did this, the pain of the feminine energy was released because all it needed was a witness and understanding of "we can do better." Thus, if you are a female or male who feels pain through suppression, know that this suppression has been released in a healing vibration that you can access if you just ask. You can put down the lens of perceived suppression, and the new steps of your path will be from a healed love and connection to the divine singularity of energy within you. You will perceive your future steps through the lens of freedom.

I then thought in the felt sense that the divine masculine also needs healing through witness. So, Mary Magdalene hugged Jeshua and witnessed how hard it is to be separated from Source by being brainwashed into believing that you need to stand alone or be an "alpha" to be worthy and create. When this isolation was witnessed, Jeshua was healed. Mary Magdalene and Jeshua hugged each other, and the masculine and feminine energy vibrations became a blissful ONE inside me. The 3D duality of masculine and feminine was extinguished, and an understanding and bliss with the oneness of the energies of God became another vibration of peace available from within me to heal me and the one of us that is within us all.

Will you go within and witness the pain of the division of the masculine and feminine within you today? Will you find the perfect symbiosis these energies are capable of? Will you find your full potential by remembering the power and beauty of the oneness of these energies within you? Will you remember awake when your consciousness travels to dimensions of singularity when you ask to reunite them? Will you put down the energies that are sustaining the patriarchal society by no longer seeing male and female as separate but by combining them as one energy of blissful love within you? We got this. I love you.

The veil

What is the veil? To me, the veil is the energy that creates the reality you choose to live in. If you have no beliefs about what your reality should be, the energy that your soul has available to create your movie of life is limitless and without boundaries. If you believe that the human suit you project and the Earth it resides on are limited energies, your veil will be dense, limiting the perception of who you are and what you are capable of to a box as small and thick as your belief system. It can feel scary and difficult to go from a small box created by the density of a fear-infused veil to tearing down that veil and embracing the unlimited openness of no belief other than the current frequency of the loving thought you are having. However, a loving soul is waiting to meet you who has made this shift before you. They would love to hold space for you to walk the steps of your journey needed to live in this reality of possibility. Many call this process "leveling up." I invite you to call it "leveling open."

So, how do you know you are ready to level open? Many start by suffering. If you are in a place where you feel you could cry, you feel alone, or you are in a vibration of suffering, then you are receiving the message that it is time to level open. How do you do this? I recommend you allow yourself to have a pity party with purpose. Dive into your body when you are hurting emotionally and find the place where you feel the most physical pain and detachment. That is the place where you need to level open.

Many people who are waking up right now have had a childhood that would be considered less than ideal. They have also had past lives that have left scars that have created energetic tangles where the veil collects and creates density. When you are feeling pain, these are the places that you need to love and open (sometimes with a little force). You can ask for outside help by calling on your guides, God, the divine, Source, a healer, partner, or a good friend. Or let your current self or your loving soul hug them until the dense, limiting, energetic tangle is dissolved. You can also use Joe Vitale's fifth Ho'oponopono phrase: "I forgives myself." His "I" is you and the divine forgiving your Ego (the "my self") for any behavior that a 3D realm would see as "bad." Since we are one soul, you could also use this line to forgive the "you" that resides in a separate human suit that has "hurt" you by behaving in a way that would be perceived as harmful in a 3D realm to help you love open. Therefore, you obliterate the limiting belief of karma by not having a reason to judge harmful situations for those who play starring roles in them. When I say, "I forgives myself," I also ask to send loving energy into all dimensions of my consciousness because I do not know which one is responsible for the tangle of pain that I am getting stuck in currently.

Another way to dissolve the veil is by entertaining the idea that the entity of duality creates it. Some of the names of this entity are Lucifer, Maya, and Māra. When I get stuck in a situation that limits my belief system, I thank Maya for doing an amazing job. I tell her I love her because she has created a reality where I can experience my soul as separate from God and experience the energies of emotions that exist in a 3D realm that I use to create new realities with. After all, I would not want the job of making sure that souls wearing human suits cannot remember the true magnificence of who they are. I imagine that holding a mirror to a soul in a human suit in such a way that the soul creates a Lucifer, a Maya, or a Māra with the density of their fear is not a very fun task. I believe these entities are growing weary of this job. It is time we freed them from this eternal hell we have created for them by letting them reflect our love and light back at us. In doing so, we will shatter the veil of darkness we have chosen in the past to cloak ourselves in, and we will see a whole new world of endless freedom and connectivity.

The Earth of my creation would look like a world where humans and all energy will connect through the light of their souls. That light is easier to perceive without a dense veil of fear covering it. So, will you have a pity party with me today and be open to creating a world without a veil keeping us in the darkness of limiting beliefs and separation? Will you please love open the light of your soul so that we can all play as one in this game of creation we call life on Earth without any limiting beliefs hindering the magnificence we came to create? I love you. We got this.

Cords

We are connected to others by energetic cords. When the connection is perceived as harmful, should we cut them?

Can we cut them?

This topic came up in Jen Weigel's Spiritual Social Club. It seems there is no one answer to whether we should cut an energetic cord to another that is causing us the perception of emotional distress. If the belief that resonates with us when we ask, "Should I cut this cord?" is that a healing lesson in self-love and boundaries may be at hand, then cut the cord and love yourself and the one you cut the cord with so that you both grow open. However, you may be in a phase of your life where you do not have the steps of your journey completed that would give you the wisdom and compassion to heal what the cord is showing you if it is a lesson other than what you perceive as self-love. If this is the case, ask, "What information can I use to heal the box this cord is drawing my attention to?" If you cannot even find the box, ask that the cord be softened and pulled again by the same individual or another when you are ready to love open that box.

I do feel, at times, we have an opportunity to grow if we choose not to cut the cord and work on what part of our pain body perceives this connection as upsetting. We may even have contracts to carry things for others because they are too wounded to do so themselves. Some of us may even be able to generate enough unconditional love to heal ourselves and the person we feel is difficult. If we can choose to explore self-love to the point where we generate so much light that it expands our energetic field, our field then remembers it has the capacity to ease the transmutation of the emotions of others. When we can offer vibrations that help transmute others' pain, we experience tremendous growth and bliss as we truly start to understand how connected and beautiful we are when we unconditionally love others. We are all different, and this should be celebrated. Before you choose to cut a cord, will you look within and sense if there is a wound in you or the one you are tethered to that you have enough patience, wisdom, and love to heal open by expanding the loving capacity of your heart today?

6

Remembering the Grace of Flow

Flow

There is a resonance of divine flow within you, and I invite you to explore it today.

The other day, I was doing BodyAwake Yoga with Dr. Sue Morter, and I set my intention before the class to no longer fear the power of divine magnificence within me. I underwent a powerful transmutation by allowing my consciousness in this dimension (my mind) to surrender to the serenity of my/our combined consciousness. When these energies unified, my body became a spring for the river of the light of our combined consciousness to flow into this dimension. At the end of the yoga session, while in Savasana, I listened to the flow of a water feature in my backyard and sensed that it was the water of my/our soul flowing unblocked through my energetic body. While in this felt sense of magnificent flow, I heard a bird start squawking. I realized I could be the river of consciousness that flows through us from all dimensions and still be present in the now of this dimension to receive a message in the form of a bird's song that adds beauty, love, and power to our river. I realized this felt sense of singularity while navigating duality is what we all came here to experience.

Imagine a world where we are surrendered to each other's vibrations in a way that makes them one vibration. We each know that our unique song contributes to our collective vibration, and we are so in resonance with the symphony that we know when our vibration needs to be heard more than others. That is when we play our note with a love and conviction that we only feel the magnificence of when we're surrendered to our singularity. We understand that we are the symphony of collective consciousness, but we are so in tune with the whole that we don't need a conductor for this ultimate orchestra of our one collective love because we can hear, understand, and embody each other's songs in perfect unison. Think of the world we can create if we could all be in a collaborative symphony of flow instead of in isolated, detached notes of disharmony. Can we let the will of our individual notes surrender and play in harmony with our divine collective symphony?

Now

What is time? For many, it is numbers on a clock, a box of beliefs about when we should be eating, sleeping, playing, or working. This concept of time is what we use to navigate this dimension so that we can fear death and deadlines and experience regret, grief, etc. We believe in this definition of time because the emotions created by belief in "time" are powerful tools of wisdom and fantastic energies we can use to create with. However, sometimes we get stuck in "time." We have PTSD or other regrets that create loops in our energy field that we cannot release because of the limited version of love we are brainwashed into supporting in this dimension.

It is time to dance with time. Gather the emotions you have collected by living in the 3D idea box of time, and then realize that you can be in "no time" anytime you wish to be. You can open your heart and be the womb of creation, the collective essence of our loving soul, or any other concept of energy your heart leads you to become. Surrender your mind and the limited concepts it believes are true about who you are in the limited definition of "time" to your heart. This will aid in this process because your heart will open your mind and allow it to melt open to the expansive reality that all "time" is "now." You will remember you have access to all the consciousness we have ever been and ever will be. The word *now* is both a millisecond and eternity and you can travel to any now you have ever been or will be as you desire to.

What is the point of this discussion? As I was sitting here this morning and my mind was playing with what could be a more appreciative way to look at time, I realized that we can use "time" to truly enjoy "now." Outside of this dimension, you could just be floating in the empty or in a river of light. You would be unable to marvel at the miracles the Earth game graces you with experiencing. You would not be able to understand all the heavy or light emotions we are blessed with collecting here. You would be unable to laugh, cry, hold another amazing version of our soul, or witness your own or another's gifts and note of creation in a dimension where the note appears separate from yours. So I invite you to play with "now."

Open your heart and melt into feeling, tasting, smelling, hearing, and seeing "now." Allow your mind to surrender to the wisdom of your heart energy and let your heart dissolve into the energy you perceive to be around you. You can experience "now" in a way that you "know" how graced you are to be present in this dimension at this time when our soul is waking up collectively and learning how to play Earth in a whole new loving way. Play "now" with your heart today and see if you like it. It will help you appreciate the game of Earth more and realize that we are so much more than this one dimension of our consciousness. Our consciousness is never leaving this dimension, and we are "home" in all 144,000 dimensions of our consciousness right now. Play "now" with me today and make this game of creation we are playing together here be flooded with more joy and love so we can experience the concept of "now" together. I love you all. We got this.

The veil your memory creates

The memories stored within our human suit and our soul can both harness and prevent us from entering the bliss of connection, kindness, and unconditional love that we are capable of giving and receiving. We can awaken to a new "now" by lovingly asking the uncomfortable memories that create a veil that cloaks us to leave our presence because we no longer have a need for them. In the presence of "now," without a past or future to distract us from the power of the oneness we feel when we no longer sense time in the way we have been taught, magic is everywhere. When our mind relaxes into "now," it is allowed to explore the essence of our totality. In this "now" state, my mind plays with colors, shapes, and pathways of love and wisdom. It meets and exchanges information with entities like "one," and my body enjoys the healing vibrations bestowed upon it. The reality of "now" is often felt as the state of expansion we enter while in this place, and it cannot be described in words. It is always fun to giggle with your Ego/ mind when it is so dumbfounded and immersed in a state of singularity that it can no longer communicate with words because the dimension of consciousness it finds itself in does not use words for communication. Words are not descriptive enough for the deep level of understanding and compassion that "higher" dimensions exist and create in.

Whenever we shed a piece of the veil around us that we've created through attachment to "past" and "future," we become a brighter light. Once you spend time in the "now" of the present, you can also visit the "now" of your future and your past. You can willingly choose to enter the energies that are the painful emotions of the past and future, find peace in the "now" in those timelines, and dissolve the veil in which your future and past dimensions of consciousness have been unknowingly cloaked in.

Past painful or peaceful memories will both cloak you in the veil. One path to entering the "now" from these memories is to go within by being present with the memory you carry of yourself or someone else and ask for it to transmute by absorbing the information you collected in it. If the memory is peaceful, just ask to add the essence of that peace to the strength of your light. If the memory (and emotion attached to it) is painful, ask to transmute the pain by viewing the memory through the lens of singularity, where all experiences are just energy. When you choose to see the experience as a loving interaction, you remember the bandwidth of love that your soul is made of and naturally emits, and transmutation occurs, and the energy of the memory is now perceived as love.

One way to relax your mind into doing this is a powerful technique that Donna Eden teaches. She has you or another hold your forehead and immerse yourself in the painful or fear-filled memory of the past or future. While in that fight-or-flight cortisol state, you then ask to embody a sensation of bliss. You will now remember the old memory as blissful.

I have seen PTSD memory triggers be released (or at least lessened) in under a minute with this technique.

For example, one of my patients asked for lorazepam to ease her fear of an upcoming flight. I feel every time you take this medication, you are taking days off your lifespan. So, we had her walk down the runway and experience all her usual anxiety getting on the plane, and then she felt the bliss of another memory and walked down the runway in that bliss. We put her in the "now" of bliss while in a future memory, and she never needed lorazepam to board a plane again. This healing took less than one minute. The more you play with this technique, the more you will feel the electrical, energetic shift of fear to bliss when holding someone's forehead. It is humbling to feel another soul's energy in this way. Thank you so much, Donna Eden, for sharing this extremely efficient way to heal PTSD triggers.

So, will you take some time to ponder the cost of being veiled by a past or future memory? The density of these memories can cloak us from the connection to the "now." When you choose to transmute these heavy memories, a new perspective of love and light will appear that you will welcome with tears of gratitude and humility. From this perspective, that is the "now," and you will embrace your journey of accepting who you have been, who you are now, and who you will ever be as perfect. You will realize that every interaction you have had and will have is perfect. Thus, you will recognize that the souls that starred in your duality movie with you have also always had perfect performances. As you transmute your painful memories, your veil dissolves, and your heart opens. You will offer the healing vibration you generate to all with similar memories without even trying because you will add it to the healing energies that compose the "now."

So, will you go within and love open the boxes of pain that keep you veiled in the past and future today? We can see all "memories" through the lens of love if we choose that reality. Let's pick that reality together today. I can't wait to feel the vibration of healing you add to the "now." I love you all. We got this.

How to play healing

> "Our problem as humans isn't that we are inadequate, wrong, or broken; our problem is that we believe we are. This fundamental misconception underlies every other problem, dysfunction, and pain we have." —Dr. Sue Morter, *The Energy Codes*[1]

In the fall of 2022, I spent time in the same room with Dr. Sue Morter at Eden Energy Medicine's Energy Fest. If you have not read her book, *The Energy Codes*, please do so. If you have not heard her voice, please go to her YouTube channel and listen to the love, excitement, and healing it radiates.[2] In her lectures I recently attended, she tried to convey that we are spiritual beings having a spiritual experience that we create. When patients come into my world for healing, their belief system (the world they are creating) determines how fast they heal. If someone thinks restoring their health will be difficult, it will be. If they come in ready to play and heal rapidly, they will.

I would like you all to realize that the Western medical belief system creates very restricting energetic blockages to healing, and it needs to be dissolved back into the empty. Recently, I have been blessed to assist some beautiful souls in regaining sight and hearing. In addition, I have helped many patients get off their pain and sleep medications. Some of these people believed this was impossible when they crossed paths with me, and some were convinced this was possible. My beliefs on how we heal change daily. I see so many people heal in such beautiful ways that I think any healing "miracle" your heart wishes to manifest is possible. When you release the trauma causing your disease, you will heal. This process will happen more rapidly if you believe it will.

While at Energy Fest, I met a woman who was a healer with the gift of clairaudience. She uses the sounds she hears and the sound of her beautiful voice to help others heal. She had lost the hearing in her left ear about four months before I met her from a bout of COVID-19. On the last day of Energy Fest, I found her crying because the loss of her ability to hear was a great sadness for her. It is always easier to play healing with other healers because they believe in the "miracles" of how fast the body can regain function and heal in ways that Western medicine would deem impossible. So we played healing. I had just had the epiphany that fascia is thought, and I told her we just have to help your fascia heal, and you will believe you can hear again, and so you will. We held hands, and I guided her to release all the ouchies in her energy field. During this process, an energy cord of some sort went out of her left ear to the empty and returned. Apparently, it brought some healing essence from the empty. After about seven minutes of playing healing, her hearing was restored to about 75 percent of normal. When we started, she could not hear at all out of her left ear.

By the way, since this time, I have come across many patients who will manifest disease in the chakras their gifts are in. For example, someone who can see energy had ocular migraines until they allowed themselves to see beyond the third dimension instead of suppressing this gift. Influential creators meant to seed the world with love developed breast and testicular cancer, and both people resolved their cancers by embracing their gifts and healing the traumas that were keeping them from doing so. So, if you are having eye problems, let go of the anger you feed and ask to open to another way to see. If your ears are the issue, ask not to be afraid to hear in ways you never imagined possible. If it is your thyroid, it is time to ask for help remembering the totality of your essence and then speaking the loving truth your soul was meant to share with humanity. If your stomach is the issue, you may be claircognizant; try to release the "not enoughs" that make you doubt that sometimes you just know things and they are true. If you have issues with your sacral chakra, you may have the gift to birth joy into the planet or cosmos. Try to release the fear of connecting to your totality because fear keeps you from sharing this amazing energy with humanity.

While I was at Energy Fest, I got to meet many gifted healers. Each healer brings their own unique and beautiful vision of healing to the planet. I realized how beautiful it is that every healer has a different belief system in how healing works. I love this diversity because people who need to be healed will have different beliefs on how they will heal. They will find the healer who resonates with their belief system. So, if you think tapping or EMDR will help you, please seek help from healers gifted in this resonance. If you feel Reiki, massage, Eden Energy Medicine, acupuncture, biodynamic craniosacral therapy, or Qigong healing will help you, contact a healer with these skills. All I ask of you today is to believe there is a loving healer out there who is ready for your call and wants to assist in your healing story.

Will you cast off your limiting beliefs about what can be healed and how we heal today? Will your healing story be another "miracle" when viewed from your old belief system and a common occurrence with your new belief system? Are you ready to take up a resonance in a realm where anything is possible and unconditional love heals all?

Fractures

The crystalline light structures we call human suits are fracturing as we remember who we truly are. Let your energy field quake and heal as light is let out from within and let in from outside.

In 2024, a friend called and asked how I was feeling, and my answer was "wavy." Most of us who know we are more than this 3D reality of isolated consciousness experience a roller coaster of ups and downs as we awaken. Almost everyone I know felt this way as they discovered and embraced their gifts. As we expand our consciousness out of just this dimension, we remember our abilities on an energetic level, which we have a limited ability to understand and process with the mind of a human being. We have a hard time understanding that our mind is part of the collective consciousness of God. The brainwashing we have all incorporated that we are separate and need to fear others has been fracturing for some time. Please let this happen. P!nk urges in her song "All I Know So Far" for you to let the light in through the cracks that are created when you let the protective walls around your heart crumble. I believe that when you crack open, the light you have to share is released from the cage it has been trapped in at your energy center. Because most of us fear change, the energetic shit/shift we are going through collectively is uncomfortable. Be kind and patient, and love yourself like you never have while you go through this shift. Look up when you walk the Earth, and you will find the eyes of another that reflect the growth you are going through. You will be able to hold space for each other through the love emanating from within to soften the fear of change we are collectively going through.

We are beautiful liquid crystalline structures of light that come in every color and frequency of love. We are collectively remembering the particular color of light we were born to play with, as well as the miracle of creation we are capable of when we surrender the magnificence of our light to the light of the collective soul we are. Our bodies are remembering how to embody the rainbow colors of our light, and this causes all sorts of sensations and energy fluctuations that we perceive as anxiety, hot flashes, pain, depression, etc. You are not alone. There are healers and groups of beautiful humans who can validate and share this amazing transformation we are collectively making. We are all butterflies in a chrysalis of possibility. We will emerge as the most graceful swarm of creative energy the universe has ever seen. Our wings will be beating to one symphony in which we will all play our colorful notes in a harmony the Earth has never resonated in.

Hang in there. You got this, and I can't wait for you to remember and embody your unique note of light and creative frequency so that you can share it with our collective soul. Surrender to the beauty within the center of your being and let it shine. It is time. You are loved more than you could ever imagine. We/you got this. I love you.

The felt sense

There is a knowing inside of you that evades description with words.

When I surrender to the God particle within to discover the vibration needed to help souls heal, I surrender to the felt sense. What is the felt sense? There is no accurate human description of this magical energy because its vibration is higher than the vocabulary available to describe it in this dimension. The felt sense is a place where you are one with God. Since, in my opinion, there is no accurate description of God, this place can only be deliciously experienced.

How does one experience the felt sense? There are many ways to get there, and none of them are right or wrong. We may all even have a unique way of getting there. I find it by surrendering to the photon of energy that is the connection to God (all energy in existence vibrating in a state without attachment so that its vibration is felt as blissful peace through the mind and body of a human suit). Your God particle is patiently waiting for you to remember how to connect to it through surrendering to its vibration of peace. I find this photon by saying, "I am in God, God is in me, we combine as one." It helps me to say this when I am in a state of awareness in which tears of humility are spilling out of me. I find this sacred place by recalling all the blessings that I have been graced to receive. Then I find such a profound gratitude for these blessings and the understanding that I have been blessed so I can be a blessing and share the love that has been bestowed upon me with others. I can do this by embodying to the fullest extent possible the essence of a loving healer in this dimension of my consciousness. I am one with beautiful vibrations of humility that make me cry. I also breathe through my belly and open up the space it is in so it can fill with the magic of love and the giggles of creativity that this light of God within emits.

My intention as a healer is to see every human greet each other not with the vibration of a human suit but with the essence of the souls emitting the human suits. For when our veils of fear have dispersed and we greet each other, loving soul to loving soul, there will be no need for any other vibration but peace. I know that in the vibration of my God particle, my patients and I have felt (not necessarily seen):

- Our one soul in harmony, supporting and loving our souls like proud parents, so even when you are alone, you are not alone because you carry this supportive vibration within.
- Hundreds of angels appearing to emit and share divine love to heal a cancer within.
- A deceased family member who turned into a star and radiated so much healing love that I cried for three days.
- St. Germain's healing transmutative flame to burn fear into courage.
- Jeshua, Mary Magdalene, Elohim, Buddha, and the God that the patient on the table sees have all made appearances to emit love and guidance for healing.
- Deceased family members appearing to help people embody a loving way to heal the perceived trauma of their past that is hindering them from healing. One woman even pulled her deceased father through the veil and hugged him while she was on my table.

Many other energies and dimensions have been visited through the love of the connection to this God particle to help those willing to receive healing.

So, will you find this indescribable place inside that will help you/us rediscover the blissful energy that connects us as one soul in a state of peaceful acceptance? Will you play and maybe even giggle with the idea that inside of you is the birthplace of our soul? When you find this place, will you embody its magical love and heal the connections within you that have forgotten how to love y/our soul? Will you play with your God particle today to feel blessed that you have the awareness to surrender to the felt sense of the birthplace of our creation within you so you can share its peace with someone who has forgotten its existence? I love y/our soul. Let's play this game called Earth with an abundance of giggles because we rediscovered and healed with our God particles today, pretty please.

Fascia

Fascia is the bioelectric organ that holds our 3D body together. It is an alive network of fibers that moves with creativity and fluidity. You can see it as a shiny film encasing the muscle of a chicken wing.

While at Donna Eden's Energy Fest in 2022, I watched a video of fascia in motion called "Fascia Magnified 25x" on Ronelle Wood's channel.[3] It moved me in such a way that I want to share my new thoughts on the fascia. I think you can use the fluidity of fascia to help you heal. I encourage you to watch this video through the heart and eyes of a two-year-old who has not yet been taught limiting beliefs. Watch how the strands of the fascia magically move to where they need to go.

I have shown this video to patients to help them understand how the fascia moves almost magically and creates connections it needs instantaneously as it needs them. It is responsible for us being able to move fluidly, and it is likely how the energetics of acupuncture needles and some of the body's chemical reactions are transmitted. However, I also think fascia is how the body instantaneously processes thought mechanically because our fascia is the energy of thoughts. So, if we choose to give our attention to a heavy emotion, the fascia embodies that energy and becomes tight and inwardly focused, causing our body pain. Suppose we are happy because we are choosing to embody kinder thoughts. In that case, we become open and outwardly exploratory, and our fascia has lots of energy to move energy within us and to sprinkle happiness on others if they choose to receive it.

There is also a belief that I learned through the writings of Dr. John Upledger in which he postulates that we have energy cysts that cause our pain and disease.[4] I think the fascia is where these cysts are stored, and that is why myofascial release works so well to get you out of the pain of a muscular contraction. Many of the patients in my medical practice are relieving their pain and neuropathies just by telling the pain, "You may no longer control me. I release you with love, light, and a thousand blessings to your next highest good." I know this sounds crazy, but your healing capacity is inside you and linked to your thoughts.

After taking a college psychology class (at the wise age of seventeen), my youngest daughter told me, "Mom, what you do at work is called the placebo effect." She is not wrong in that our thoughts can create the energy to heal or harm us. It is up to you what vibration you place your thoughts and fascia in. What thoughts will be immersed in your fascia today? What energy vibration will open or constrict you today? Our fascia offers us connections to remember and awaken beyond our wildest dreams.

When I visited Montezuma's Well in 2023 and connected with one of the many outlets of the Earth's womb of creation, I realized fascia is the energetic web that connects us to the multiverse. It moves in dimensions and directions without effort and blossoms new roots whenever and wherever it chooses, seemingly without instructions. It is the net we cast from within to connect with our magnificent multidimensional soul and the energy conduit with which we share and receive energetic information with the cosmos.

Suppose you set the intention to shift the lens of how you see—and thus feel—your previous energetic experiences. (There is an angel named Gikeque, pronounced "gee-kay," who you can ask for help in shifting your lens.) In that case, you can reset your fascia from a tight vibration of fear, sadness, or anger to the open vibration of love, freedom, happiness, and giggles. When the fascia is open and flowing, you can cast it into any realm you are destined to explore and connect with. The "world" you remember you have the capacity to perceive will expand, and new ideas and dimensions of reality will be available for you to play with.

Our happiness and joy are found through the power of love flowing freely from us so that our net of connection with the cosmos expands and we remember with awe who we really are. Will you find the places within your fascia that have been trapped in the pain of a limited viewpoint? This limited viewpoint causes the love you are created with to be trapped in painful prisons. It is time to destroy the prison walls within our fascia with the power of the love you have within. Will you accept this idea and choose to step into the flow of love you are meant to connect and create with today? I love you all. We got this.

P.S. Besides the Angel Gikeque, laughter is the best way to dissolve prisons. If the environment around you is not conducive to laughter, start laughing at yourself, because it is the most powerful of all laughter. Love yourself, please, because when you do, you love our soul, and our soul is ready to remember how special it is individually in duality realms, collectively in realms of singularity, and both at once in this dimension of Earth.

Boundaries

We are one entity, so why do we sometimes feel the need to establish boundaries?

I am reading *Nourishing Destiny* by Lonny Jarrett, which discusses concepts of Chinese medicine. "Unnamed infants perfectly manifest the virtue of eternal *dao*" (God or Source). However, once named, we separate from the bliss of the oneness we feel when we know we are the Dao and are given a destiny and self-consciousness so that we can play Earth. "It is knowledge of the self, as being separate from the unity of the *dao*, that the *Dao De Jing* considers to be the source of illness."[5] Jarrett then quotes Laozi:

> "From knowing to not knowing,
> this is superior.
> From not knowing to knowing,
> this is illness." —Laozi in *Daodejing*[6]

Thus, after we are named, we embody Ego in this dimension. When our consciousness is paying attention to the Ego, we perceive ourselves as separate from each other. Our Ego is sometimes easily wounded, and thus, we feel the need to establish boundaries from the Egos of others, wishfully thinking this will stop the pain we are feeling. The walls we build by setting boundaries may be beneficial in the short term to give us time for internal growth. Still, it may be that the ultimate spiritual growth comes from realizing you and the one you are seeking boundaries with are the same person. When you set a boundary, you are creating a division within yourself, and this internal division blocks your chi from flowing smoothly and creates disease and emotional suffering.

When we do need to set boundaries for reflective and growth purposes, how we set them is crucial. A friend was explaining when she set a boundary with another friend, the friend receiving the forceful boundary felt like one of her chakras had been speared open. I think this is possible. There are stories of Qigong masters who can kill someone without touching them by using their energy to attack the chakras of another. I have heard of an individual who cracked their engine block because they got mad in their car, and someone else who was not allowed to go near any colleagues' computers because the computers would crash when they were near them. The emotion of anger is a powerful energy, and it can disrupt both physical and energetic fields. Thus, if you set a boundary out of anger or frustration, someone may feel like you just speared their chakras. So when you feel the need to develop a boundary, consider taking a few deep breaths and looking into the eyes of the one you feel the need to distance yourself from. Try to see the light of their/your/our soul and set the boundary with as much love as you can muster.

Reflect on times you have set boundaries with force and times you have set them with love. How did you feel at the time you set these boundaries? How did you feel long after you left the energy of the one you set the boundary with? I bet the love boundary felt much better. In fact, in a conversation with Jenniffer Weigel, she described setting a limit for a coworker from a place of self-love. It did not feel like she described a boundary at all. It felt like she extended an olive branch laced with the golden energy of peace and offered a new way of loving communication in oneness instead of the isolation and pain of separateness. Thank you, Jen.

Each step we take on our journey in this dimension is perfect. If it is a step where we need the space of a boundary to incorporate information that we are temporarily perceiving as painful, so it is. We are all souls that choose to experience consciousness in this Ego-based dimension. Thus, there are times when we further want to explore the game of Earth with a louder Ego and use boundaries as a tool to do so. However, there will come a time when you are tired of creating divisions within yourself and the souls you love. When this time comes, and your name and identity become less important, you will no longer need boundaries because the light within you will be so strong and so bright that it will blend with the light of others. You will no longer perceive any separation of energies from your fellow souls. We will remember how beautifully we are combined as one with the power of all our unique musical notes playing in the grandest symphony ever created. Will you rejoin the ONE of this amazing symphony today by changing your thoughts on boundaries? We got this. Let's play and grow together as much as we can. It is the best way to truly enjoy the grace of consciousness in this dimension. I love you all.

Your soul

During a biodynamic session, I went back to what I felt was the birth of my soul. I felt I was a small ball of light just released from Source to explore and gather information. No scale was in place to judge whether the information was good or bad, and no one was around to prioritize the importance of any of the information gathered. The human mind/Ego is responsible for judgment and the division we create with it. We are told in the rules of the game called Earth that we achieve success when we earn a title and play on the level of "I am better than you." This level of the game sucks. Can we please stop playing at this level and collectively move to the next level? At the next level, success is felt inwardly and known when your heart is so open that you feel the essence of the souls around you wearing human suits. Many are walking the Earth playing at this level. Would you like to join them?

Think about what it would feel like to be free to explore without labels or trophies attached. To be free to gather information while just playing. To understand earth is an endless sea of the energies of the possible outcomes of the interactions we are graced to explore every day. To be able to see yourself as an immersed observer who has chosen to play duality just for the experience of empathy and no other purpose. Does this sound freeing to you? If so, try it today. Just for today, don't get caught up in the Ego's need to externally validate its importance. Today, just try to feel and appreciate every moment you choose to feel the essence of Earth with your soul. Use your mind to navigate how to help your soul gather information. This is the purpose of the mind. Our soul needs a navigation tool for the density of 3D, and that tool is our mind. It acts as a translator. We have let the translator run how we play the game too long, and the game is not very fun when we allow this.

How do you stop your mind from directing how you play the game? Start breathing deeply while saying "We are safe" until your body relaxes. Then, let yourself feel blessed by surrendering to the ability to witness Earth through the eyes of a two-year-old (aka the innocence of a newborn soul) who sees everything that crosses its path as new and thus undiscovered. Playing Earth with a relaxed mind and limbic system that does not know what to fear or judge lets you play Earth with wonder and awe. The states of wonder and awe awaken and open your heart through gratitude. When you vibrate in gratitude, your mind and body relax, and it is easier to sense the light of y/our soul inside of you. The more often you play the game of Earth in the openness of the vibration of gratitude, the easier it is to remember that the entirety of our soul and all energy ever created is inside of us, waiting for you to remember how amazing you are.

Once you remember how bright and beautiful your light is, please let it shine bright through and with every atom in the universe. Remember, you are the universe, and every atom of the universe is part of your human suit. Allow the human mind/Ego in you to recognize, be replenished, and rejoice in knowing that it is an essential tool needed for gathering energy in the game of Earth. If it has spent a lot of time gathering a particular energy, hug it and ask it to shift gears so it can move on to new experiences and collect new energy. Will you let your mind/Ego surrender and feel the ecstasy created when it reaches a state of symbiosis with our soul and Source?

Transmutation

The frequency of transmutation is acceptance.

We all struggle with the heavy emotions that create a reality of suffering for us. Instead of fighting against processing that reality by trying to ignore it or blaming someone else for it, I ask that you simply accept it. We feel these heavy emotions as pain in our bodies at times. So dive into the deliciousness and wisdom of your pain because it is a guide to opening and understanding the creator being that you are.

In her BodyAwake Yoga classes, Dr. Sue Morter instructs you to squeeze and breathe through any tight or painful area you experience during yoga. When you do this, you acknowledge that the area needs your love and attention. By hugging and breathing the totality of the energy of the love you are made of through this area, you can honor that you collected this energy of trauma for our soul to create with. But then let our soul's love help you neutralize it so you can move on to collect another energy or stay in an open vibratory loving state so you can help others find this place of profound peace.

I now understand that "grounding" in this dimension makes it easier for us to know the love we are and then use this energy to transmute our pain. Like many souls, I subconsciously do not want to ground to the dimension we call Earth 2024 because my mind sometimes tells me the Earth is an uncomfortable energy to resonate with. For many souls, grounding is understood as a tether to a dimension that can be perceived as painful when viewed through the mind. It is also possible that when our souls are exposed to the vibration of the Earth and the tool we call the human mind, our souls recall old painful incarnations, and these memories create more fear of grounding. I had a patient who, at seventy-nine years of age, had kept a trap door open above her head her whole life because she felt if she needed to, she could leave Earth and go home through this door anytime she wanted. I giggled and said, "Umm, you are almost eighty years old. It might be time to shut the trap door and stay and play Earth in a way you have not yet played it. It might be time to play in the peace of love instead of in a box of fear." She did shut the door and is happier and more at peace with the vibration of playing Earth than ever. It was the guilt of a past life that made playing Earth uncomfortable for her.

Most of us have issues dealing with the traumas of this lifetime. When our mind also feels heavy emotions from past-life traumas, we really don't like Earth 2024, and many of us want to exit the game. News flash: We never exit this game, and apparently, unplugging it and walking away is not an option. Why was this game created in a way that lets us simultaneously experience and remember the energies we have gathered throughout time? The answer to this question is simple. We can be the totality of all of our soul's experiences by grounding our energy into the dimension we call Earth 2024. You want to ground and process because that is one of the reasons you came to this planet in the first place.

Like many of you, the human suit is not my favorite suit to wear. I just had a reading with Heather Sprigg, who channels Archangel Michael, and he recommended that I try to tap into the energy of a mermaid lifetime I am living in right now to help me flow more in this one. He also said that I prefer alien suits much more than human suits, and this belief resonates with me. I have had a hard time wanting to play Earth 2024. We are emitting a human suit, but we don't have to play a restricted human in the Earth movie we are continuously creating. We can play the role of the light of our totality by projecting a human suit that shows us and others how we can recreate the game of Earth 2024 by rewriting the rules we play it with. We have lived (and are living) in so many other multidimensional lifetimes that may feel like they are much better than this one. However, this dimension at this time is very special because the veil is thin, and we are getting help from everywhere to transmute all of our densities in all 144,000 dimensions of our consciousness if we choose to do so. Will you consider playing Earth 2024 on this level so we can create a better game to play?

It is time to remember that choosing a human lifetime is a powerful gift because of the strength of the emotions we feel. The energy you create when you feel despair and love as a human is very powerful. I have felt the unconditional love of Source and the unconditional love of Source attached to a recently deceased human. I can tell you that love with a human component (interpreted through the tool we call a mind) is a way more powerful vibration. The more power a vibration has, the more we can use that energy to create the multiverse in which we all want to flourish. I have not felt Source's despair (likely because Source accepts all, so it does not know despair), but I have felt the pain of human misery, and although it is painful and we perceive pain as bad, it is still a fantastic energy we can use to create with if we choose to do so.

So, how do we transmute our heavy and light emotions into the energy of creation? We simply accept them. Accept with gratitude that you are gifted energy to share with Source for the purpose of creation when you think or feel anything. When we think with the mind about pain or love, we become thought energy and shift the universe's trajectory. However, if we place our mind in the hands of our divinity or the center of our heart chakra (or even all our chakras) and ask to feel our thoughts, we access the energy of our thoughts for transmutation. There is a huge difference between thinking a thought and allowing your body to feel its vibration. I encourage you to do this now. Take a thought that has been spinning on your hamster wheel for far too long and allow it to leave the wheel and land in the energetic field you perceive as your body and sense it. How do you sense it? Did the thought become a constriction or pain? Did you see your thought as a memory, color, or other type of vision in your field? Did your thought become a sound or song? Did it become a craving for food or a flavor? Did it become an energy loop you are tired of traveling on? When we remember how to feel our thoughts (the product of the mind) as vibrations of our energetic field, we can transmute the energy we are here to harvest from this dimension to energy that can be shared and used for creation in all dimensions.

What do I mean by transmute? Energy is neither created nor destroyed, but it does shift or transmute into different resonances. The human suit you are wearing is a collective of resonances of energy. If your body feels heavy, you vibrate in a denser resonance. If you feel "high," your atoms are dancing at a higher frequency, and your body has more light in its resonance. We play the game of Earth to transmute energy by shifting our resonance from dark to light and then from light to dark. However, the density of the dark of the game has been collected and understood to the extent that we may no longer need to collect this dense energy. I do believe that we are entering an Earth cycle where a lighter vibration of the human suit is intended to exist. I have found that the Earth game is way more fun to play if your body is vibrating in the light of love and giggles, so I am choosing to play the game in this magical resonance as often as possible.

How do you play Earth in the resonance of love and giggles? You love the densities of the dark in your energy field. How do you do this? What does this mean? It means you honor every drop of energy you have chosen to experience by loving the part of you that collected it. You ask or even command the entirety of your consciousness to help you do this. In this totality of your energy field, a part of you has learned to see every experience and energy through the lens of love. It is this ascended master version of you that will have the compassion, wisdom, patience, and insight to help you love all parts of you. When all parts of your human suit are vibrating in love, your suit perceives that frequency in all energy it meets as it plays the game of Earth 2024. You then play the game of Earth emitting and sharing love and giggles. When you play in this resonance, you will offer the heavy vibrations of others the magnificence of your light for the purpose of transmutation. You may even experience the bliss of transmutation while your essence is merged with another's; this experience will open your energy field to a broader frequency of light.

There are no coincidences. As I was writing this, I got a phone call from a new friend, Suzanne Alexandria.[7] I was graced to meet her because she reached out for help in transmuting the energy block in her field that was causing her metastatic breast cancer. She gave me permission to tell her story and use her name. Suzanne has been working hard to release the blockages that have caused her cancer. She is a healer herself. She channels several entities and deities, and they let her know she would be healed from her cancer. She believed this was so, but she believed that the healing was going to require some steps of opening into the essence of her totality. During the first visit we had on the phone, Suzanne worked through forgiving her father for years of molesting her. She called me the day after the visit and said she had gone to see him, which is something she had not done in years, and forgiven him on a new level, even though he denied molesting her. She experienced a wonderful opening in her heart by choosing to transmute the anger box that her childhood fear had created by choosing to vibrate in love instead of fear.

Over the next ten days, Suzanne worked on recalling the anger she had harvested in her childhood that she had displaced on many others over the years. She did this because she had no toolbox within to understand how to remember her anger is actually a form of the light of her soul. She had only been able to feel it as an unbearable pain she needed to be freed from. Suzanne realized that although her mind and her energetic field had started to embody and resonate in more light, she had not yet entered the sacred place where she is her totality. I received a second phone call after this ten days of reclaiming her anger so she could tell me she realized that although her mind had forgiven her father, her energetic body still woke up daily with the same heaviness of old, dense attachments. She returned to bed and chose to rise in a more fluid, energetic vibration of light. As she did so, Suzanne felt the light of her soul/our soul/Source come into her pelvis and shine so bright that it healed all the dark, energetic prisons the little girl inside of her pelvis had protected herself in. That light loved that little girl so fiercely and told her how beautiful and essential she was. The little girl was finally able to believe it and walk in the vibration of that solidified love. The girl chose to come out of the "protective" boxes that had veiled her brilliance for years.

The light then traveled into Suzanne's third eye, and she let its healing love have free rein to heal all the attachments to old, energetic entanglements and beliefs/prisons that were no longer serving her. She chose to forgive her father with her body and not just her mind as she had done a few weeks back. In this open resonance of the liquid light of love, we are able to hear the whispers of wisdom and love that the totality of our consciousness is made of. These whispers that Suzanne could now hear helped her understand that when we blame others for the boxes of fear we live in, we splat our energy field on them. This dispersal of our essence causes us pain so that we can have the epiphany that incites us to ground our energy back into self. As Suzanne relinquished the energy she gave to blame, and thus her energetic attachment to entities outside of her field, she has been able to bring all of that energy back into her field to heal and create a stronger connection to God. The morning she chose to rise in the vibration of her totality—and not one of ungrounded dispersal—she felt the brightest light she had ever witnessed while playing Earth 2024. She saw this light as the ultimate form of healing energy, and she will now be able to incorporate it into her healing practice and share its wisdom and brilliance with others so they can heal. This is how we play the game of transmutation. Thank you, Suzanne, for allowing me to share this beautiful story.

We are all one soul, so your pain is another's, and their pain is yours. You can play the transmutation game alone or with others. I am so glad Suzanne reached out to play healing into wholeness with me. She reminded me how uncomfortable it is to play Earth in the vibration of blame and graced me with a cancer-healing story to tell you so that you, too, can believe in and play with the magic of light to heal as I do. When we connect in one heart resonance, we can play together to heal our collective soul and do so much more. So I ask you, what vibration of the dark will you allow yourself to sense today and melt open with love so you can share the energy of your transmutation with all? Tap into the love all around you by changing the lens through which you see the world. Let your two-year-old soul and mind play healing with your unique signature of love and light. Will you transmute the fires (your emotions) in your tree into beautiful knots of love, wisdom, kindness, and compassion by flooding them with the loving and nourishing water of y/our soul? Then, you can use the love you created and have stored in those knots to help others love open. I love you all. We got this.

7

The Frequencies We
Play Healing In

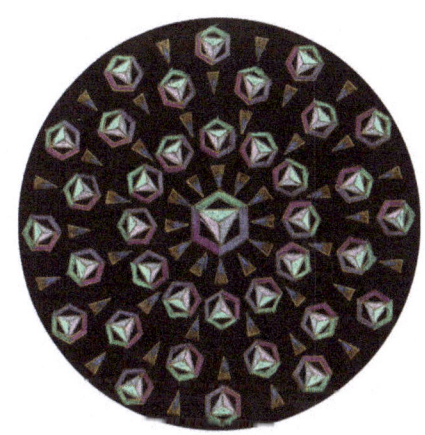

Playing rebirthing to remember awake

We choose consciousness in this dimension to explore and constantly be reborn.

If you are feeling this magnificent energetic shift the planet is going through, you are not alone. We choose consciousness in this dimension to explore and experience vibrations of thought in ways we cannot experience in other dimensions. We are not meant to be stuck in one vibration of thought, so we are constantly shedding the skin of old, energetic experiences and rebirthing into a different embodied experience as we desire. Thus, in this dimension, we are always going through some sort of rebirth.

However, in the last few weeks, you have been offered the potential for big shifts in the awareness of the consciousness through which you experience this dimension. This offering of energetic expansion of awareness often presents itself in this 3D reality as fear, anger, depression, guilt, etc. I ask that you settle into the energy you are vibrating in and feel the flow of energy in your body with stillness and curiosity. Please take the time to search for the areas in you that are the ouchy, painful gatherings of your creative energy and honor them. Honor them by loving them with the tenderness and awe of a newborn's smile, and hug them until the love you are made of and were born to radiate and connect with brings these dispersed parts of your loving energy field back into your core. In loving them and reclaiming the energy you have so graciously collected and experienced for us, you transmute the duality of this dimension by combining dark and light and remembering there is no light and dark. There is only divine energy to be experienced through the illusion of light and dark, yin and yang, so that we can vibrate in the bliss of the many facets of our wholeness through as many realities as possible.

In saying, "I no longer have the luxury of not lovingly caring for my energetic field," you choose to collect all the dispersed energetic facets of y/our wholeness and feel the connection and awe of the love you are within your core. You can then take your reclaimed God particle and use it to connect with the other facets of your soul, who you greet with each step of the beautiful journey you have chosen to walk for the one of our consciousness. With this transmutation through self-love, you are giving our collective consciousness the energies of the four sacred gifts of hope, healing, unity, and the power to forgive the unforgivable.

Thank you for reclaiming your fear through transmutation and giving our collective soul the ability to create from the love you radiate by choosing to go through the energies of rebirthing y/our consciousness every day. Hang in there. You are never alone and always loved more than you could ever imagine possible. If you need validation of how beautiful you are, just ask and then be receptive to receiving an energetic vibration from Source or from the part of your soul you willingly greet and recognize in another's eyes today. What new vibration of reality will you/we be reborn into today?

I love you all. We got this.

Quantum healing

In 2022, I took a remote healing class with Dr. Sue Morter, and she asked, "What does quantum healing mean to you?"

My answers were trust, surrender, one mind/one soul, attuning, non-judgment, and becoming a vessel that emits healing vibrations without the need to understand them. I know I am on the planet to help as many people as possible heal. I also know that if you cannot incorporate the vibrations I emit to heal, others can help you with the vibrations they emit. It is time for all to seek the healer who resonates with them or accept the healing vibrations in the atoms surrounding you waiting to become part of your soul.

Trust and surrender are complex spaces for a human Ego to inhabit. The initial trust in and surrender to Source were very difficult for me. However, over time, it has become instantaneous. The surrendered state I enter to help myself or another heal is creating the webbing of a beautiful energetic field of symbiosis with God and my human morphogenic field that gets stronger and more expansive every day. This is how I have healed awake in the last few years. With every surrender, I have remembered a piece of the totality of my vibration by witnessing another facet of my/our frequency be "downloaded" into my field. The reality is that my field has always been complete, and there are no downloads, but my human mind needs the illusion of downloading to remember all the tools of creation that we have the capacity to use.

For example, at the end of a yoga session, I saw this beautiful dimension of pink and purple grace floating just above my head. Seeing dimensions of color like this is normal when I do yoga, but I asked, "I wonder what this dimension is?" The immediate answer I got was, "It is you, dumbass." Then I giggled as I said, "Did I just call myself a dumbass?" and I trusted and incorporated that dimension of wisdom and connection back into my human suit. Or at least my brain thought I did this, but since there is no time and we are always whole, it was already part of my human suit, but my mind and Ego had to find a way to remember this, and so they gave me one.

Without trust and surrender, you cannot remove your Ego from the healing energy you naturally emit. Your Ego needs to be removed because the vibrations that most human minds are attached to are painful ones. At one time, a friend asked me why I chose to come to Earth this time. My answer with my mind was to help people heal. She then asked again,

"Why did you choose to come to Earth?" with sternness in her voice. My answer changed as it came from my gut, and it was guilt. I know if I offer a healing vibration from a place of guilt, I am offering a vibration of duality, and the vibration I offer will not be optimal and just create more duality vibrations. However, if I remove my Ego and the emotions that are based on vibrations of duality and just let God offer them, they come from the place of singularity. If you do not allow Source to flow through you when you are playing healing, you cannot tap into, reveal, or remember your true quantum capacity and abilities. We are not meant to play God as an isolated soul. We are meant to spread a frequency of energy that is God through the vessel that we call our body. As a vessel of the collective, the "miracles" you will witness will be endless.

The one mind/one soul vibration is felt by attuning with all of your senses. The eyes listen for body language. The ears absorb the emotions underlying the story of the spoken word. Your skin and hands listen for pain, joy, and energy currents. Your aura aligns with the energy field of others to incorporate energy that needs to flow out because it is no longer serving that individual or healing energy that flows in from the collective to heal them. Your gut intelligence leads you to the resonance of energy that the individual or the collective needs to transmute. Your heart attunes and opens the endless patient love of Source to be brought forth for compassion, connection, and transmutation. The symbiosis of your loving heart and your intelligent gut opens your hara line. With an open hara line, you can access an infinity loop that unites you, the Earth, and God. Embodying this oneness, you can bring in any vibration that the person you are trying to guide in healing needs to heal.

If you allow your Ego to play judge at any point along the way, you will not be able to be one with the quantum field. You cannot be in judgment of those you are showing how to heal, yourself, or even some circumstance the world is going through. You cannot simultaneously vibrate in judgment and be in the state of surrender that it takes to love yourself or another open and play healing.

I have learned that trying to understand the vibrations passing through me as I help people heal would limit my abilities. Humans try to quantify everything because the Ego needs a scale to prove it is superior to another. When we do this, we limit imagination and possibility. The quantum field changes with our thoughts and emotions. Thus, it will never be boxed or collected and understood at any time by any entity. We should stop trying to box unimaginable magnificence and instead expand it with surrender. In surrender, I promise you will never get bored of playing remembering awake.

That is my current limited human understanding of the magic of quantum healing. Will you play with some of these ideas today and start creating the healing and other miracles you were born to manifest alone and with others?

Your purpose

What is my purpose? This is a question many struggle to answer.

I received a healing session from Therese Rowley, PhD, in the summer of 2022, and she asked, "Why are you here?"[1] Thankfully, that is a question I know the answer to. But many of us don't know, and the lack of an answer can cause pain, isolation, and suffering. I am here to help as many people as possible heal the wounds in their/our collective subconscious that the teachings of conditional love have caused over time. When we heal these pain bodies and shadow figures, we can return to a place where unconditional love is the main energy source flowing through all. When you are in this state of flowing love, you are so connected to Source and others that you will know and easily perform your unique purpose in this lifetime.

How do you get to the place where unconditional love is the main energy vibration flowing through you? You work on self-love and see this as a vibrational gift you are blessed to share with all. We are all one and all connected, so if one of us suffers, we all suffer. If one of us is disconnected, we are all disconnected. If one of us heals, we all heal.

How do you work on self-love? Start by forgiving yourself for the actions and emotions you have allowed with a human Ego that was not connected to Source for guidance. All of us have done stuff in this disconnected state in this or other lifetimes that could be considered horrifying. Please remember that behaviors that create shame and self-loathing come when we're disconnected from the unconditional love of Source. We are graced with the opportunity for this disconnection so that we can experience duality and create a unique note of light for Source to play with. Creating this note requires disconnection (aka suffering), but the joy of sharing it requires reconnection.

We can remember awake and reconnect with God by individually working on forgiving ourselves for our past actions that have created pain and shame. We can make a choice every day to choose kindness and compassion for others. When we can't be kind to all, then we have a pain body box that needs our loving attention. We need to ask to release with love and light the subconscious imprinting that no longer serves us. We need to release the imprinting and self-loathing that keeps us from resonating in unconditional love.

Most of us will treat others better than we treat ourselves. This is a beautiful sentiment, but it is time to realize by clearing the ingrained belief system we have been taught that keeps us from being kind and loving to ourselves, we are performing one of our most important purposes. Dissolving the boxes of your pain body will heal the cosmos because you are a cosmic consciousness. It is time for you to remember your magnificence by loving a new part of your cosmic consciousness back into the awareness of your energy field. What limiting belief about yourself will you release today? What will you forgive yourself for today? Will you help the inhabitants of this planet remember we are one by not only refusing to feed the belief that keeps you divided from others today but by telling that belief, "You can no longer control me. I release you with love and light to your next highest good"? Humans need to perform this process of self-love and self-cleansing of our limited belief boxes daily to be in a state of peace. Will you play self-love today so that you can resonate in the state of peace that will reveal your fantastic cosmic note (aka your purpose)? Will you join others who are learning to clear the pain that divides us and create a more connected and peaceful planet to live on? Get to play, beautiful souls, pretty please.

Our tears

It is time to no longer shun the transmuting power of our tears.

Recently, Dr. Sue Morter, whom I have been guided to play with over the last two years, said that tears have the power of transmutation. This resonates with me. As a child of the '70s, many of us heard the phrase, "Stop crying, or I will give you something to cry about." At least once, I received the "something to cry about" from a father with many fears he did not transmute with tears in his lifetime. The ridiculous idea that physical pain is the only reason to cry is one of the many reasons we fear shedding tears. We have been told crying means we are weak, ungrateful, etc. The frequency of crying that much of society believes in is epitomized in one of my favorite movie lines from *A League of Their Own*—"There's no crying in baseball." Hopefully, this line makes you burst out laughing as I do when I hear it because it's the truth, so ridiculous that it is funny.

Our tears are meant to help us release emotions. They are the energy of the divine. Tears help us understand that the obstacles or miracles that truly remind us how beautiful, powerful, connected, and worthy our soul is cause us to generate the life-sustaining element of water.

We have all cried tears of sadness and despair that have helped lighten the dark within. Many have cried tears of anger to help extinguish the destructive yet transmutative fire the anger created. The tears of grief could be used to gain clarity on the new adventure that a death can offer you by changing the direction of exploration your soul is meant to meander into. The tears of frustration just feel good to release and can give you clarity on a new way to resolve the issue frustrating you.

The tears we cry when we feel connected in a positive way, like the tears of laughter and joy, are so precious and heart-opening that they create an infinity loop, guiding you open to even greater love if you see them that way. Tears remind us to ground ourselves in this 3D reality so that we can access the bandwidth of the power of love in this 3D dimension and create not only in this dimension but also in others.

Last, my favorite tears are the tears of humility. I invite you to start looking for the daily blessings that tears of humility will offer you. You may need to turn off the fear porn and the programmed hatred your television feeds you daily to do this. When you turn off the TV, your reality will change. Read an opening spiritual book or go for a walk in nature instead of sitting in front of the TV. When you do, a new reality will be revealed. You will start to open to the copious blessings gracing you with their presence in the immediate environment around you in nature or through the realities that a spiritual book can offer you. Your heart will soften and open, and the path to the vibration of humility will be revealed. You may find yourself being grateful for the smile or kind word of a stranger, the beauty of a tree or flower, the love of a pet or fellow human, or the anticipation of what version of our magnificent soul you may be graced to be in the presence of today. Once you learn to vibrate in humility, you will even be humbled by experiences you may have initially interpreted as offensive. Those tears of anger, grief, sadness, despair, frustration, and joy can all end in the tears of humility when you discover gratitude for being allowed to experience the entire bandwidth of emotions on this planet in a way that we cannot in any other dimension.

I find the tears of humility help me surrender to the energy that is our collective soul. When you find this indescribable vibration, you will want to give your attention to the beautiful symphony we are all of the time. You will walk the Earth looking through the lens of compassion, understanding, wisdom, kindness, patience, and love that we all are. You will find the God particle you have within and look for every opportunity to play with the God particles of all of those around you.

So, will you shed some transmutative tears with me today so we can all open and connect as one soul in this dimension and create a world of love we can only imagine together, united by our God particles through the vibration of the tears of humility? Don't try to understand this vibration; just surrender and embody its indescribable magnificence. I love you all. We got this.

Your star

Did you know all souls are stars?

I want to tell you one of the most moving stories I have been graced to experience in my lifetime. In the past, I was honored to care for a beautiful, healing soul I will call Grace. Grace and I crossed paths because she wanted to try acupuncture to feel better. She had a history of a family member molesting her as a child and had not healed from this trauma; thus, she was manifesting symptoms of low energy levels and trouble sleeping.

Grace had started a kundalini yoga practice and had started to have visions beyond the typical 3D spectrum. She was on my table and I was putting needles in when she said with fear that the family member who had molested her was in the room with us. He had already left this dimension and was on the other side of the veil, but he was in the room with us as a spirit. His presence provoked fear in her. I believe that souls are all light beings. Drawing on ideas from Michael Newton's *Journey of Souls* and Dr. Sue Morter's *The Energy Codes*, I was able to explain to Grace that it was possible the molestation was a pre-life contract to help her embody the vibration of a 10/10 forgiveness.[2, 3] She calmed down, and we proceeded with her biodynamic craniosacral energy treatment. At that time, as a healer, I was channeling the energy of the void through my heart chakra so I would feel the energies of the void pass through my chest into the patient in front of me. During the healing Grace saw the offending family member turn into a star. As she witnessed this, I had such a strong yet tender and passionate loving energy flow through my chest into her that I cried for three days. That day, she healed in ways she had never before healed. Likewise, I healed in ways I had never healed because every time the tenderness of a loved one beyond the veil appears in the space you inhabit, the ability of your heart to love and house more compassion grows.

I know this may be a new way for many of you to look at a horrible act that humans commit. However, this belief system helped Grace heal from her trauma. If you have been stuck in a similar trauma, you may consider using it to shift your perception. What if it is true that we are all bright, loving stars? What if another's light is perceived as dim in this dimension because of a pre-life plan to hide their light for your benefit? Will you give this opening to healing a chance to help you forgive someone today and allow yourself to heal in the process? Will you find a way to see and speak through your loving heart so that you vibrate with and stimulate another's light instead of communicating through your pain body, which usually pokes their pain body, causing both of you to suffer unnecessarily?

Please take a deep breath through your heart or belly, find your star, and communicate and connect by radiating the energy of your loving star today. You will not be disappointed and will start seeing "miracles" appear all around you. For fun, visualize yourself without a pain body so that when someone tries to poke you, they are only poking holes in the sun within you. Hopefully, this thought makes you giggle as you imagine your light getting even more beautiful and shining brighter and infusing the world with your brilliance because there is no limit to the capacity of y/our sun's ability to generate loving light. We got this. I see and feel the light in *all of you* with the third eye in my belly and the eyes of my human suit. Our light is so beautiful. I love you.

Peace

How do we find peace?

We all would like to see more of the state of peace in both our inner and outer worlds. How do we get to this place of calm and contentment? This is an age-old question that I am going to postulate an answer to. I think it starts by allowing unconditional love for ourselves and others to run the generator of our energy field. How do we allow unconditional love to be our energy generator? We love our mind and the human suit it is projecting unconditionally. We work on accepting that all the past steps of our journey are not "good" or "bad" but are simply information we gather for Source. We work on taking all future steps solely on the pathway of kindness, compassion, understanding, forgiveness, and connection. When we stray from the steps of our path created through an open and flowing heart consciousness, and we dance the steps of the duality through Ego, we need to forgive ourselves and allow ourselves to be grateful for the information we gathered while off the kindness pathway and return to it as soon as we can. There is no right or wrong; it is just more information on how we can allow unconditional love to run our energy generator as much of the time as possible. The great Maya Angelou said, "When you know better, you do better." Forgive yourself and the Ego that drives your "undesirable" behaviors for getting stuck in the vibration of your limbic system. Please do this. The world is in an energy shift, and it is lovingly asking you to fuel your human suit with unconditional love as much as possible.

When we forgive ourselves, our Ego/human energy can release the burden of always trying to be better. When the Ego surrenders to just being, it feels our soul and remembers how good the connection with this source of unconditional love is. Our soul has always desired to merge fully with our Ego/human, but it does not resonate with the harshness of the human emotions we feel as pain. Since there is no time and we only have one soul, it seems possible that our soul can sense the pain and trauma our collective mind has been exposed to in the many dimensions our consciousness resides in. This can create a multidimensional PTSD reality that adds to the difficulty of our mind and soul achieving the resonance of singularity. However, if we love the mind in this dimension, we love it in all dimensions. Thus, when we heal current traumas, we can heal the traumas of past and future lives, and when we heal past-life traumas, we heal in our current dimension of consciousness. In all dimensions where the mind dominates, we experience fear because it is essential to playing duality. However, let's lovingly ask our multidimensional minds to surrender to our hearts and God particles. Our minds will release their attachment to fear, and we can experience the bandwidth of the light of our souls while wearing a human suit. This state is the definition and vibration of peace in this dimension.

When our soul and human suit combine to the fullest extent possible, Source runs our energy generator. This fully enabled capacity of the symbiosis of Ego/human/soul/Source that we are capable of achieving is how we and all the energy fields we are connected to will resonate in a state of peace we may have never imagined could exist. Source does not know how to judge and thus understands the beauty of every step of our collective journeys. You will forget how to judge when God is running your energy generator. When you are awake, you vibrate in the peace of realms of singularity and emit through embodiment that frequency to share in realms of duality.

I believe there is no soul on the planet that is not in resonance with unconditional love. I have seen souls from the other side of the veil whose humans committed horrible acts while they were gathering information from the suit/mind of the human they were giving life to. Many of these souls have come back into my acupuncture treatment room devoid of the human Ego, and their purpose is to heal the human they wounded. I am pretty sure our souls just want us to understand the unconditional love we can share while wearing a human suit if we allow the divine to fuel our energy generator through them. Trust me, you want to allow yourself to feel the love y/our soul has to share with your mind/Ego. This love will grace your mind with peace and gratitude that will not only nourish you in a way that you have never been nourished but also nourish all other energies on this planet and all forms of energy that have been or ever will be.

Will you allow yourself to open new doors that offer an opening to remembering the light of your soul to strengthen our collective pathway of kindness and compassion? Will you allow yourself to be fluid enough to let your and others' "missteps" melt away into the ethers? Will you allow yourself to dive into the empty within and let the light of your soul that resides there guide you in discovering new ways to love, and then incorporate them into your energy field generator? Will you love yourself enough to be present in the now to fully connect and share your love with others?

You will realize you are creating more love and compassion for all when you share your love and compassion with others. How many steps will you take on the path of kindness, compassion, understanding, forgiveness, and connection today?

Thank you, Jenniffer Weigel, for asking me, "How do you find peace?"

Forgiveness

The frequency of peace is embodied through acts of service to the collective.

I help people heal by guiding them in letting go of the energies in them that are causing dis-ease. I feel their blockages in my body as pain or an uncomfortable sensation. I understand that these uncomfortable energy frequencies are a gift to the person feeling them and to myself because they allow both of us to heal and embrace a stronger connection to our collective soul/God/Source.

I recently was helping another healer with a very similar energy composition to my own, and during the session, I started to feel pain in my left hand. I tried to guide her to release the pain, but it was challenging. The wound I felt went entirely through my hand, and it was more painful than the usual pain I feel when I help others heal. The pain was black with a ring of fire and surrounded by another black ring. It was different from any other pain I have ever felt. After a while, I mentioned to the person I was working on that I thought it was a crucifixion wound. She agreed. Eventually, her pain disappeared, and mine lessened through the idea of sending peace through the wound. I even asked her to send peace through her left hand to clear her hand and mine, which helped.

However, the pain returned in the next few days as I worked on others. I reached out to several people to ask if they had experience with wounds like this, and I got some ideas on how to transmute this "heavy" frequency. One friend told me to embrace forgiveness. Jenniffer Weigel suggested that I honor the wound. I liked this suggestion because honoring means we accept our steps with pride. As light workers, we have died so many times in our previous lives at the hands of judgment, anger, greed, and other vibrations we call "lower" frequencies. If we die in the resonance of any of these vibrations or with sadness, despair, injustice, or fear, we will carry those vibrations into all dimensions that our consciousness inhabits. These vibrations will show up as pain and dis-ease to remind us to create new energy from them by accepting that they offered us an opening path to create more love.

So, I decided to honor the wound and forgive. However, when I tried to forgive, I realized that to heal this wound, I had to become a bridge and connect with a dimension where forgiveness does not exist. Our multidimensional consciousness wounds are collected with the agreement that we choose to experience the vibrations of injustice, judgment, grief, sadness, etc., for our benefit. Our wounds should be honored for gracing us with the energetic opportunity to grow our compassion and love bandwidths. We should honor our souls for experiencing the pain of collecting them. However, to embody these "higher" bandwidths, we need to incorporate the frequencies of realms where forgiveness and judgment do not exist. In these dimensions, there is just experience and energy. The concepts of judgment, injustice, and forgiveness are not understood. Every experience is accepted; thus, peace is the resonance in which they vibrate. So, if you have old, heavier energies in you, creating separation from the dimensions where these energetic frequencies do not exist, will you consider letting them dissolve today by honoring them and embracing acceptance? Will you surrender to the dimensions inside of you that only comprehend peace, love, and compassion and emit those frequencies for you and others to heal? It was a river of golden peace I let flow from my heart through my crucifixion wound (and many more since) that was the frequency required to heal it. Let's play together and transmute the heaviness in all of us collectively. I love you all. We got this.

Joy

I did not fully understand the emotion we call joy until recently.

Many of you reading this would call yourself an empath. This likely means that being with large or even sometimes small groups of people is not fun for you. We can find joy in solidarity and small groups, but joy's true power and magnificence are found in larger groups that share heart coherence. Let me explain. I can find gratitude that melts me open with a flower or tree or catching air on my skis or mountain bike. These events can show me a short-lived glimpse of joy. Gigglegasms and cuddles with my family and friends open my heart and give me slightly longer episodes of joy. However, while in Egypt in spring 2023, I witnessed what joy looks and feels like with a group of about 125 people. One of the dinners we had was at a restaurant where we ate outside overlooking the Nile, and we traveled there by boat. Before we sat down, there was uninhibited dancing and singing, and you could sense that many group members were vibrating in the same heart coherence. My heart was in a protective mode at the time, so I could see what joy looked like and begin to understand how to welcome it into my energy field, but I could not feel or be part of it. So, since that time, I have been trying to remove the self-imposed prisons around my heart so I could know joy in a way I have not in this lifetime.

So, how do you open your heart walls? Your heart opens when you choose to honor and love all energies you have vibrated in. Let me explain. Recently, I was asked if I could help someone heal a glioblastoma. I know that my gift to share with humanity and beyond is my ability to offer the loving wisdom and healing capabilities of entities that have spent millennia embodying light and dark so that our soul could have an opportunity to understand that we create light by loving the dark. By offering a wavelength of wisdom and opening love to the souls that ask me to help them heal, the God particle in me helps them find a way to accept and then love the dark in them that is the cause of their disease. If they choose to receive and embody that loving wisdom, they heal. Healing is as simple as "God heals God." The God particle in me finds the God particle in you, and they share the wisdom and love needed to open the box of darkness that has created "disease," and the disease resolves if it is in the cosmic cards for it to resolve. As long as the lid to the disease box does not get closed again, there is no reason for it to return. The darkness inside that created the disease has done its job of awakening the soul it graced into opening their heart so they could love more.

I know I can offer any wavelength of love someone may need. But it was a completely different ballgame getting this science-based mind of mine—which was asleep and brainwashed into believing the limiting boxes Western medicine had taught me for the last thirty-plus years—to open to what is possible in helping someone heal a glioblastoma. So, faced with helping someone heal in a way I know is possible, I decided to open the box and change my ingrained limitations of imagination by choosing to believe a glioblastoma can heal with the vibration of love. I chose to open instead of remain stuck in that box of darkness that my Western medicine teaching placed me in.

How did I do this? I did a guided healing meditation of Dr. Sue Morter's, in which I heard that joy is found when you find your "note." My note is embodied and emitted through finding so much gratitude for every experience ("good" or "bad") in my life that I transcend into a profound state of humility that makes me weep. With these tears, the energetic field I call a human suit melts into oneness and has no boundaries. Without boundaries, my energetic field has the capacity to bring in any energy from any time needed to be in service to the whole of our soul. I realized that this frequency of service is my new definition of *joy*. When in this vibration, my heart is open to all hearts and sharing an infinite loop of creative love. This is one of my definitions of joy, for why would we limit this beautiful state to a tiny energetic resonance? Emitting my note at its maximum capacity is a joy. Sharing my symphony note with another who is also emitting their note at maximal capacity is indescribable joy.

If you get quiet and go within, you can honor and love our magnificent soul by honoring and loving open your energetic field. Then once you find the unique note only you can play, will you contribute its magnificence at maximum capacity to the superb symphony we are creating? If you need help with this rediscovery of you, ask for it; it will be provided by an energy source in your field or one wearing a human suit. I can't wait to hear and feel your note. I love you. We got this.

Liquid light

Our thoughts create our reality; our emotions solidify it.

Many of us are in the process of remembering that we are souls inhabiting human suits and playing the game of Earth. When we have opened to this reality, we start to feel our souls in our bodies. Knowing we are a soul in a body helps us expand the definition of what a body is and how its matter can be expressed. My understanding of matter is that matter is "anything that takes up space and can be weighed." Matter has volume and mass. We are told in science class that mass is created by particles resonating within the Higgs field.[4] Another concept of *matter* is the verb form: Things that are important or of significance in our lives *matter* to us.

My interpretation of these current scientific theories is what we consider to be important, the ways in which our thoughts and emotions vibrate, therefore interact with the Higgs field and give our thoughts and emotions mass. We create our reality with our emotions. Our thoughts are fleeting and many, but our emotions are more persistent, and they are the energy our body resonates in and thus the source of the solidification of the light of our soul.

I was just in a Spiritual Social Club online meeting, which is a sacred place Jen Weigel creates for humanity to heal by feeling safe enough to open their hearts in such a way that we heal each other. It also serves as a place for our souls to remember how special each of our soul's gifts are when we share them. Jen was discussing how she had recently realized she had moved so often in the last few years so that she could heal all the parts of her past that had her trapped in PTSD energetic triggers. These triggers had led her to places of painful emotions through visiting the physical environments they were first felt in. By choosing to relive the attachments to her old painful realities that were no longer serving her and love into old triggers through the cultivation of self-love, these painful emotions are no longer resurfacing. Jen recently moved to a new location that brings back joyful memories and where there is more nature surrounding her to remind her how fleeting yet beautiful life can be if you choose to appreciate the now. Her soul and mind are now using more joy-filled emotions to create her reality, and new beauty is solidifying in it.

I do think we are also changing how our human body solidifies. We have been living in collective pain for a long time. Thus, our bodies have been living in painful densities that manifest dis-ease to get our attention so that we can explore and create a more peaceful way of living. Our souls are light bodies. As we explore the opening of our hearts and rediscover that we are the liquid light of our soul, our bodies will shift into a higher frequency of vibration. This higher frequency will be free of disease because we will be in the state of solidity in which our souls were meant to vibrate in while in a human suit. In other words, our human suits are about to get an upgrade if we choose to love more.

We can choose the emotions that matter to us and vibrate in those energetic frequencies. If you are depressed, you feel heavy because that emotion is a heavy and slow vibration. When your energy is not fluid, you will manifest disease because the body cannot repair itself as well. When you giggle and feel joy, you embody a faster vibration, and your body becomes self-healing as the atoms are free to rearrange and repair your human suit. When your soul remembers it is liquid crystal light in a human suit, and your mind chooses to explore that frequency of existence, a whole new reality based on the frequency of light opens to you. This is why some see auras, others hear their guides, some heal with the light of their open hearts, some smell other dimensions, others feel the energetic net that connects us, and some just know that their light connects with all light and thus all thought and all energy. We have created a reality where many of us have remembered we are liquid light. Will you breathe open the densities within you through the light of divine acceptance of self-love so your soul and human suit can play in this magical reality with me and my friends? Let's let go of the densities of our "past" by shifting what "matters" to us. Let's start playing with the liquid light of our souls connected as one without any densities limiting us as we create the symphony that is the magnificent, unified light we see as our "future." I love you. We got this.

Human suits

I was doing yoga the other day and had an amazing time incorporating and weaving the knowledge and wisdom from the many dimensions of my consciousness into my current auric field, the Earth, and then back out of me again into the cosmos. Playing yoga like this can be a very enlightening experience. I also know that I am the cosmos, always whole, and have all of its information and wisdom in my auric field right now. Still, my human mind likes to be entertained. Thus, it enjoys the illusion and the light show that is the perception of culling our universal loving consciousness into this tiny human suit I am adorning myself in called Julie Foster.

Yoga is also a good way to laugh at myself, as I tend to fall over a lot when I am trying to hold poses that make me laugh out loud just thinking about getting into them. Laughing at myself is a frequency of energy I never want to not have in my field because it is so healing and freeing. However, I noticed I was angry at the end of this yoga session in Savasana. Of course, my mind immediately asked why I was angry, and the immediate answer was, "You are pissed that you are in a human suit."

When we awaken and realize the scope of our cosmic totality, we can become frustrated when we think we are limited to a human body. Once you know you are more than one human lifetime, many want to leave this dimension of our consciousness and return to "better" dimensions. However, once you realize there is no such thing as time as we know it, you understand your consciousness is never leaving this dimension. So you may be mad about being human, but you will always have a consciousness that is the human with the current name you call yourself. Also, your consciousness chose to come to this dimension to collect energy for our universal soul and the cosmos to play the game of creation with. So we must get over ourselves and make peace with being "here" at this "time."

How did I do this? Two years ago, in my first energy class, not long after I woke up from the ignorant (but at times peaceful) slumber that I am more than the human named Julie, I imagined that my soul and my human mind were holding hands and combining as one. To me, our mind is the masculine part of the energy of our consciousness that leads us away from our oneness. The mind is the tool that is used to experience duality and is needed to participate in the evolution of our one soul. Our minds allow us to translate the realities that our soul plays in. I see my/our soul as the tether to universal consciousness and God/Source/the divine/the universe. Our soul is the feminine that wants us to feel, be, and remember that loving bond that connects us to the bliss of unified consciousness. That day, after my mind and soul played nice together, held hands, and embraced, they merged into one, creating a linear tether to Source. This tether, for me, was a bright white light with all colors of pastel crystals infused in it.

The next day, we had a sound ceremony in which everyone played an instrument, and during that ceremony, what I perceived as Source (the white light with the pastel crystals) entered my belly. At that time, it was so much energy and such a foreign sensation that I freaked out. It was then time for a group healing, and I was asked to get on the table. After some protesting, I did. When you play with healers, they feel your energy. One woman could not get closer than three feet to me because the energy was too powerful for her field to be in it. I released the energy through my feet into the Earth that day, and the healer sitting at my feet sure felt it. I now have an additional two years of playing with energy and thus have increased comfort with its beauty and power in the toolbox I use to connect with, embody, and share it.

So, while in Savasana, I went back in time and went to the place where this source of energy was in my belly, and instead of releasing it into the planet, I incorporated it into my body to "upgrade" my human suit. I figured since we are never leaving this dimension of consciousness, one way of making peace with this is to continue to nourish my body with the love that is the consciousness of God. Our human suit does not seem so restrictive when we allow ourselves to receive this nourishment. I have surrendered and allowed this/our bond of love to strengthen in me most days since January 2022, when I chose to start actively receiving the love of the field of our consciousness when I needed it to heal an ouchy in my body. In this vulnerability of allowing ourselves to be one with the universe/God/ the divine, we become God. We may even get to the point where we are grateful we are in a human suit because we will get to a point where the human suit is so beautiful and connected in love that we want to be in it here in this time and dimension, creating as God with other human suits that are also one with God.

So, will you surrender and let the universal intelligence of energy that is your human suit play with receiving and remembering your divinity today? Will you open your heart to our universal heart and feel the heart coherence pulse of God today? Will you surrender to the embodiment of all the colors, light, and love our soul wishes to bestow on you today so that we can know oneness in this dimension of duality? I love you. We got this.

Love of self

As a doctor and healer who lives in a very sacred place, I am blessed to meet the most amazing souls. After my hands turned on (aka I began to feel pain in others' bodies with them) in 2021, I began to open to understanding how to help my patients heal in a different way than applying the prescription Band-Aids that my training in Western medicine taught me to do. Instead of a blood pressure medication, I ask that patients turn off the news and embody love and hope instead of fear and anger. I guided a patient to release their anger and heal an acute, extremely painful shingles attack in under an hour. The cure to IBS is found in the release of fear and frustration. However, through my exploration of the energetic realm, I have come to understand that the most common ingredient of our essence that helps us to heal is the vibration of self-love.

From the second we are born and our light body projects a human suit in this realm, we are brainwashed into believing we are not worthy of love. It is time to create an Earth where this limitation is no longer in the bandwidth of our loving vibration. Here are some ways to do this:

- Turn off the TV and limit screen time on your phone. I had a patient who was in her early twenties and came in to be treated for severe anxiety. She was in a loving relationship, was in college, and had a job. In her free time, she was playing a violent video game where she was killing people. I postulate that our soul does not know the difference between a video game, a TV show, and the hologram we call reality. Thus, if you are a human killing someone in a video game, your soul cannot differentiate that you are not doing this in "real life." If you watch a violent movie or TV show, your soul thinks this is what is happening in its "real" environment. Engaging in the game of life through these windows will cause the soul and your limbic system to vibrate in fear and sadness. Thus, your body creates the diseases of depression and anxiety. She stopped playing the video game, and her anxiety dramatically improved.

- Understand you are loved by everyone and every energy that crosses your path. A harsh comment is an opportunity to love an angry person and thus love the parts of you that are angry. A depressed loved one is an invitation to call back the parts of your energy field that you have abandoned and love them so much you relight them and all energy connected to them. A death is a necessary event that lets you explore a new path your soul begged to explore in this lifetime. A harsh judgment you or another makes about you or someone else is an exploration of where you can go and what energy you can understand when cast into separation and hate. You can transmute it and create a vibration of love that matches it to create a new step of your path for your light to grow brighter with.

- Start playing with the idea of no "time." Reread chapter 5's section "Listening in time."

- Ask your guides and angels to help you embody and become love. Even if this sensation lasts for only a few seconds, you will crave to never be far away from this feeling. You will know you can always find it with a few deep breaths and use it to open your heart and create the steps of your reality at any time.

- Laugh at yourself because this vibration is the ultimate alchemy of healing love.

- Understand that those you call an "energy vampire" or "narcissist" are guiding you to pull your energy back onto yourself with voracity and temporary shields. You do this so you can be guided deep within your energy field and find the dark cavern within that you will not regret exploring with your light and love. Find these caverns through the understanding that they are the painful parts of your body and energy field. Hug them until they melt open and you remember the energy that your human suit is composed of is love. The tangles we place our suits in are just an illusion of 3D reality we use to get our attention and help us remember we choose consciousness in this dimension so that we can create by harvesting the energy of emotion. Quietly withdrawing into these caverns allows you to open another prison you have created around the light that is y/our heart so you can embody another frequency of y/our love. Our dark is a frequency of our love. We just don't recognize it as this. When you open the prisons of your mind, you dissolve the veil that keeps you from blissfully understanding all energy is love.

I hope the list above helps you find a way to play with self-love and healing. You will discover your unique way to play self-love as you play healing and share it with all of the cosmos when you do. Thank you for playing remembering awake with me through discovering new ways of self-love.

8

Remembering the Joy of Embodying Oneness

Gigglegasms

Gigglegasm is my favorite word because laughter is the best medicine. When we laugh alone or with others, we enter an energetic state of healing and manufacture the chemicals and frequencies that allow healing to occur. When your body shakes with laughter, healing hormones and vibrations can be delivered to places they cannot reach without the fluidity that comes from the opening vibration of your laughter. Laughter opens your chakras in a way that allows divine love to flow more freely through your fascia and light body. When not in flow, our fascia becomes restricted and boxes old beliefs, fear, anger, grief, etc. These boxes are recognized in the form of pain and other diseases. When these boxes remain unopened, we become imprisoned in a veil of limitation and sickness because our soul yearns for connection, not isolation.

When we laugh, we open. We expand our awareness, and the veil surrounding us becomes thinner. The veil might become so thin you temporarily forget you are not one with those around you. You may feel a soul-to-soul connection with another you are laughing with. Or you may go beyond that and remember we all share the same soul and feel the bliss of knowing in the felt sense that beyond this realm, we are one magnificent energy playing the game of creation as one loving heart and mind. You may find that you are so humbled and grateful for getting a glimpse of knowing that our soul can connect in this way. Your goal in this dimension will become playing the game of transmutation through the vibration of gigglegasms felt with a soul-to-soul connection as often as possible.

I am reading the book *Earth, the Cosmos, and You* by Virginia Essene, and in it, Archangel Michael talks about the Ha, Ha, Ha meditation.[1] He recommends sitting alone or in a group, repeating "ha, ha, ha," and keeping it going for as long as possible. Michael explains that *H* carries the geometry of the four *L*s and the vibration of the number eight. The four *L*s represent:

- Law: balance, the marriage of mind and soul
- Life: the power of being in the now (past and present at once)
- Light: unified consciousness flowing through you
- Love: creation through our shared heart

To embody and fully know the wisdom and bliss of the vibration of the four *L*s, imagine becoming a bridge from this dimension into all dimensions of the frequency of the consciousness they emit. So, you would link the definition of the *L* on this side of the veil with the totality of the wisdom and understanding of that concept on the other side. So you would have to add four plus four, which equals eight. The number eight represents the infinity symbol and reminds you that you are energy in motion that is constantly recycling itself, exploring dark, light, and then back to dark again.

If you coax your mind into sailing the seas of your totality, your energy is always exploring duality here on Earth and in at least some of the 144,000 dimensions of y/our consciousness. The dimensions of y/our consciousness can be felt in your human suit as unified consciousness through playing engineer, and creating infinity symbol bridges into the 144,000 dimensions of you. I use this symbol to dissolve the concept of karma by loving into any energy that a brainwashed 3D human mind attaches to the idea of karma. We have created the limiting vibration of karma by being taught to judge so that we can play the game of duality. When you no longer judge, there is no need to be stuck in the limiting belief of time or the painful lower vibrational states in which self-judgment or judgment of others will leave your fascia boxed in. When your fascia is free to explore all dimensions of y/our consciousness, you will discover there is no longer a veil around you. When there is no veil around you, there is no time. When you are in no time, you are the center of the infinity symbol, and the direction you choose to travel from that point is up to you. You can go forward or backward into all 144,000 dimensions of your essence or be in all time and all dimensions simultaneously. Or just hang out and enjoy the bliss of letting your mind rest on the photon, your God particle, which is the center of all your energy found in the center of your human suit.

Michael's Ha, Ha, Ha meditation is one of the ways to find your God particle. I did have the opportunity to ask Michael through Heather Sprigg if the purpose of this meditation was to have collective gigglegasms for ascension purposes. He said, "When you say 'ha, ha, ha,' you laugh, and when you laugh, you raise your vibration." Thankfully, my friends and patients help me raise my vibration daily. I also find laughing at myself extremely helpful in opening up new areas to love myself. I picture myself laughing with Maya, Māra, or Lucifer (the "gods" of duality, which are just part of our minds that allow us to gather emotions to explore and create with). I tell these gods of duality, "Wow, we really got stuck in that experience for a while. We must have wanted to understand and embody that vibration very well so that we could take the intricacies of that vibration and create many new pathways to love from it." I then laugh (transmute) that creation of love into existence.

It is time to feel our oneness again, so let's laugh ourselves open. I had a patient on the table recently whose higher power was the universe. When I feel a patient's mind racing everywhere, I usually ask them to put it in the hands of whatever they call their higher power. For some reason, I asked this patient to put her mind in the giggle bubbles of the universe instead of the hands of the universe. Immediately, we could feel all sorts of giggle bubbles all over her body. And we could feel her mind playing with and surrendering to the giggle bubbles. She then thought of a scene in *Mary Poppins* where Bert the chimney sweep starts laughing, and he floats.

So I said, "Let's see how high you can float while your mind has become the universe's giggle bubbles." Within thirty seconds, she had floated so high that we could see the Earth below us. It was a beautiful experience to surrender your mind to the universe's giggle bubbles; you may want to try it.

Another patient put her mind in the joy bubbles of God. These bubbles came out of the ocean and the volcanoes of the Earth and traveled to what felt like other galaxies. We find God when we play with a child whose mind has not yet absorbed the frequency of limiting rules. I invite you to play with your imagination. Become whatever form of a happy bubble you can imagine and see where you float off to while traveling, embodied in the safe vibration of giggles.

So, who will you play the Ha, Ha, Ha game with today? The sound and vibration of our collective giggles may create the mass ascension some people are looking for. We should explore this sound and vibration as often as possible and share its opening and loving frequency with as many people as possible. Let's thin our veil with giggles as frequently as we can. We got this. I love you all.

How to heal as one

At Christmas dinner in 2023, I was asked, "What do you do that makes you happy"? My answer was to heal the planet. When I thought about this more, my answer should have been to spend time healing myself because this is how we heal the planet and all dimensions of our consciousness. In the sacred human suit we are blessed with in this dimension, we are graced with the ability to feel pain. Through pain (emotional and physical), our bodies reveal pathways to our multidimensionality that awaken if we choose to explore our webs of pain instead of ignoring or avoiding them. When we explore our pain, we understand that it is an invitation to create a new way or strengthen our ability to radiate unconditional love. With this increased radiance of unconditional love within, we heal ourselves and the planet (and all the planets we inhabit if your imagination and ability to surrender are created with the mind and heart of a child). We can then share the steps required to transmute our healed wounds with others and help them find the pathways to healing their/our soul.

I bet over a past holiday, there was a time that a place in your body ached after an interaction with someone. Every perceived negative interaction is an opportunity to love ourselves more. We do this by going within and offering the love that emanates from Source/your God particle inside you to that ouchy place you feel and hugging it, or asking for help from the guides or gods of your belief system, or allowing yourself to receive healing from the gods, angels, or guides incarnated with you in the form of another human suit (your friends, masseuse, meditation coach, etc.) that are crossing your paths with you daily. Take time to tenderly love your ouchy spots by holding and hugging them with your newborn soul that does not understand any emotion other than unconditional love, or hug it with the love of our collective consciousness. Suppose you do not know what that love feels like yet. In that case, I invite you to take a few deep breaths in your belly or heart and ask to open, surrender to your God particle, and allow yourself to feel this eternal infinity love because it is always in the ethers for you to heal with. I infused that energy into these words, so reread them with an open heart and solar plexus and ask to know in the felt sense what our collective love feels like, and you will know. Picture the love in these words surrounding you or the painful part within you. Hold the space of and around that area with so much loving light that the tangles of Earth's duality within it dissolve. With this dissolution, the remembrance of the connection and bliss of embodying our collective soul is a vibration that is no longer forgotten by the awe-inspiring energy that your note plays in the symphony of our soul.

While doing BodyAwake Yoga with Dr. Sue Morter and the collective consciousness she gathers in this and other dimensions, I had an epiphany of another way to play the game of transmutation. I learned how to play with an infinity symbol in my sacral chakra to heal the "wounds" of our consciousness in all dimensions. Many believe our "past" lives are stored in this chakra. While doing yoga, I felt the "pain" of other lifetimes and then realized what an honor it is to be chosen to experience a "pain" vibration for our collective soul. Through this pride, my energy rose to the outside of this chakra. My light reached into the web of ethers to touch and connect with the vibrations of "pain" of my past and future lives (other dimensions of my consciousness) to harvest the energy I had experienced as pain. Through the pride and humility of being chosen for such a grace, I was then able to cry tears of humility, which always lead me to the God particle within. I used those tears, which flowed in the form of an infinity river of connection, to transmute the energy of these perceived wounds into loving energy for Source/God/our soul to create with. This river of tears then brings the love you just created back to your God particle to nurture and increase the brilliance of its light. With its light you will remember awake and you are free to take new exploratory steps into new directions and dimensions. Nurturing love is the catalyst that creates our new paths and gives us the confidence to walk them.

Tears of humility transmute all energies you embody on your path by helping you dissolve the lens of duality. Without the lens of duality, we return to the peace of embodying God in every particle of our human suit and with all the dimensions our consciousness inhabits. When we are starring in our Earth movie while emitting this vibration, we create a more peaceful Earth by being and emitting peace.

As we star in the Earth movie we create from within daily, it seems at times that we and the others we interact with are winning an Oscar for diving deep into the energies of anger, jealousy, withdrawal, fear, guilt, grief, judgment, etc., that we let play leading roles. We must remember that we are this movie's director and plot writer, not just an actor. When we do remember this, we can see and feel the painful interactions of this incarnation as brilliant lights, helping us focus on areas within the vast dimensions of our consciousness that need nurturing. We can then be grateful and humbled by the characters in our Oscar-winning movie instead of being incited or wounded by them in ways that cause withdrawal and deviance from the energetic steps we were meant to coddle, plant, grow, radiate, and share with our collective soul.

Past lives

When you awaken to the idea that your energy encompasses more than this current lifetime and the exchanges with others that have transpired in your field since birth, you explore past lives. If you have read Dr. Brian Weiss's books, you have been exposed to the concept that if we heal trauma in our "past lives," we heal in this lifetime. I want to introduce the idea that we have energetic access to our past lives, and energy experiences that have been perceived as painful in those lives are for our benefit in this timeline if we see it as so.

Let me explain. I have a friend who remembers being chained to a tree in a past life and watching his whole tribe of peaceful, loving Druids be murdered in front of him before he was killed himself. When energetically assisting the souls on my healing table and remotely, I have felt crucifixion wounds, stonings, stab wounds, burnings at the stake, and the energy of being drawn and quartered. Why do we have access to past-life trauma like this? First, there is no such thing as time. Second, there is some sort of remembering of 3D energy when our souls enter human suits. Last, I think it is so that we can transmute these heavier energies for the purpose of creation. In this lifetime, when we awaken, we can choose to remember and embody all of the energetic exchanges we have had in all 144,000 dimensions of our consciousness. Why would we do this? It is the ultimate way to love open.

I'm not too fond of the describing our vibrations as higher or lower. In this 3D realm that exists because of judgment, putting yourself or others on a scale of worthiness is not ideal. So, I like the idea of constantly inviting myself to love open. In loving ourselves open, we drop all shields and boundaries that separate our one soul in this 3D realm, and we can reconnect and share in the bliss of oneness while still being separate notes in the grand symphony of consciousness and creation. So, I spend my days finding the boxes of perceived traumas in this lifetime and past lifetimes within myself and others to infuse them with love and peace and transmute them into the energy of openness and connection. Think about it. When we can access all the traumas of this and our past lives in what we perceive as a short amount of time, we have an amazing amount of energy we can transmute for creation. What will we use this big bang of energy for? Many say it is for mass ascension or creating a new Earth. Let's not label what we will do with this energy of love, bliss, connection, wisdom, and possibility because I have been told by Archangel Michael, "What you are here to do has not yet been spoken of." I don't believe there is a "me." I know there is only an "us." We are the world teacher, world student, and loving creator all in one energy of loving consciousness when we connect with our God particles because we all have chosen to love open in a way we never have. We may be choosing to play the game of duality in a new way that no entity has ever imagined possible.

So, will you play the game of loving yourself open with me today? Will you start exploring the 144,000 dimensions of your timeless consciousness with love? I can feel how magnificent you all are. I can feel our one soul joined in joyous union, playing the game of creation inside of me, and if you take a deep breath as you read these words and open your heart and belly, you can, too. I love you all. We got this.

Our soul's symphony

Every awe-inspiring step of your soul's journey since its birth has resulted in the fine-tuning and amplifying of the magical musical note that is the wondrous voice of the totality of the unique consciousness of your inspiring version of our soul. Please honor yourself for the courageous steps only you could have walked to collect wisdom and love and share it with all who choose to listen.

When our soul was born from its cosmic womb, it was created to discover its unique connection path with many different worlds and beings. Many souls have played in a plethora of different kinds of cosmic matter during their journey. With each experience in a different life form, your soul has added various notes to its unique musical chord. There have been many notes in the high range and many in the low range. None of these are good or wrong notes; all are just part of the fantastic journey your soul has been on since its birth. The frequency range of the chord of our collective symphony you create adds to the depth, understanding, and compassion of your soul and our collective soul we call Source/God/the divine.

When we only allow ourselves to recognize the high notes in our symphony because those are the comfortable ones, we deny ourselves and Source the beautiful music that opens us to a broader understanding and embodiment of the love that we have courageously gathered. When we immerse our human suit in the range of our unique symphony, we have many more notes through which we can connect to others.

I have asked many people what their bliss is; it is always a form of connection. The connection can be with other people, animals, or nature. The bliss connection is understood by resonating at the same frequency as a perceived outside source of energy. If we deny ourselves the low range of our notes, we lose an opportunity to connect with others experiencing those same notes. We may be losing an opportunity to heal ourselves and others by creating a moment of the bliss of connection between two people who temporarily resonate at the same frequency and thus become one, even if that frequency is an "uncomfortable" one. Often, the uncomfortable notes we connect on have the most power in the journey of remembering awake. The times you suffer and choose to reach out to find solace in the arms, words, or presence of another, you remember you are never alone. This could lead to your heart softening and opening, resulting in a connection to our collective consciousness in a new way. I ask that you remember a time when you were suffering and bonded with another for growth. The next time you are hurting, try to ease the pain by remembering how much growth can come from pain when we surrender to that pain and appreciate it for the chord of love that will be added to our symphony when we are done transmuting it. When you suffer and go within to heal, you may find God in the version of our collective soul walking with you to support you as you courageously take the new steps of your journey that create more harmony for your symphony.

I encourage you to understand that none of your notes should trigger shame or self-deprecation. All of your notes are part of your soul's beautiful, unique symphony, especially those created through hard work and suffering. Please recognize and appreciate all your notes, and try to do so during the creation process because it will ease the incorporation of the notes you perceive as more difficult. The more you allow yourself to feel the depth of your symphony, the more opportunities to connect in bliss with another soul or form of energy are available for you to play with. The more we collectively are in bliss as a human species, the faster the planet heals. How many other soul symphonies will you resonate with today? How many opportunities to feel bliss will you give yourself or another?

By the way, when I originally wrote this blog post in the fall of 2022, I thought I had come up with the idea that our souls are creating a symphony. I got the idea for this blog post at 3:30 a.m. and was told to get out of bed and write it. Since this time, I have heard and read about this idea from a few other sources. This has happened with a few other ideas of brilliance that I thought came only from my mind/Ego. We are one soul and stream of consciousness. When you have brilliant ideas, please communicate them to others and give yourself a pat on the back for being open to the stream of our collective consciousness and relaying the messages. However, if you want, when you find out the idea you thought was your unique creation has been around for eons, you can do what I did and laugh at or with your Ego for thinking it created the idea. That giggle will soften your Ego more so that you can channel more messages from our indescribable collective heart. It also takes the pressure off voicing a "new" idea into our reality because it is likely not new and you are not the only one who is, has, or will be communicating it. This book was translated through my human suit and mind but came from our collective heart. Thank you for helping me write this book by playing your soul's loving notes and holding a loving space for me to have the confidence to write about how magnificent our souls are. I love our soul, and the symphony we are constantly creating makes me cry every time I open and listen to it. We got this. Thank you.

Freedom

Freedom is contentment and power that is found only in the now.

I am writing this because I am angry. One might think that nothing good comes from anger, but I am choosing to play in a reality where wondrous, loving energies are birthed from anger. The emotion of anger is one of the sparks of love offered to us in abundance at times to access the energetic connection to the divine we need for creation. Let me explain. In the last forty-eight hours, three of my friends have said they have been so sad that they do not care if they live or die. When the ones you love say such things, it hurts. It causes my heart to break open because I can empathize with their sadness, despair, and isolation. The pain this heartbreak causes in my chest fuels the flame of anger within.

I am angry that they have been neurolinguistically programmed into the "I am not enough" belief system. I am angry that they look at others' joy and doctored Facebook posts and think, "Why am I not perfect like that?" I am angry that they see relationships that are failing or are just not wedded bliss as a defect within themselves. I am angry that we have allowed ourselves to be programmed into the fear box of the Ego that causes us to lose hope of happiness and contentment through our attachment to the reality where we are told that those places are found outside of us in vacations, loved ones, and external atomic solidifications. I am angry that so many souls believe they are only worthy of love if the gifts of X, Y, and Z have been bestowed upon them to prove they are worthy of being loved. The amount of sadness and detachment that this limiting belief system is causing is pissing me off and breaking my heart open. Breaking open is a choice you make, by the way. You can add a prison wall to your heart and continue to suffer in isolation, or you can tear one down and let light in and out of your heart so it can breathe with the cosmos with greater ease, peace, and grace.

So, how is anger going to help? It inspired me to write this when I would otherwise be reading a book. The first lesson in solving this problem is that we are not responsible for and cannot control another's behavior. However, how we react to their pain and fear will determine how content we are in our human suits. If you see a post on Facebook (or another social media platform), read a news story, or have an interaction with a fellow human that makes you feel sad, angry, or "not enough," look within and go to the place of the physical symptom that fear is creating. Breathe with the love of our collective soul supporting you and be held in the loving light that will help your mind soften. Realize you are only limiting yourself when you are trapped in feelings of "I am hurt," "This is not fair," "I am not enough," or even "I should know better." Decide with self-love that you no longer want your energy field to be attached to these painful, limiting thoughts that are solidifying as pain and disease in your body to such an extent you don't want to have the opportunity to experience a human suit anymore. Find within you the source of the feeling, thought, or physical symptom your Ego is attaching you to. Send the transmutative flame of anger to it until you have the epiphany that without your anger, you would not have been able to find the prison that has been trapping you from experiencing forward movement in the game of Earth. You may even want to try fueling and directing the anger flame by screaming, stomping, or punching a pillow to help laser focus its powerful energy of transmutation on the box within that is begging to be opened. That way, the energetic trauma of the past that is creating the box will no longer cloak the loving light inside it.

When you have burned open the prison with your anger flame, find the tender love that you had trapped within it and let it merge with the flame of anger. Create a stronger connection to our collective consciousness with the new wavelength of loving wisdom you acquired by transmuting another fear box. Sit and absorb the grace of this stronger and easier connection to Source you just created. With this more expansive connection, understand that you can breathe love into every fear prison in every cell in your body that your light has been trapped in. Realize that you can breathe open your prisons with light found in the energy of every atom in all creation if you believe you can. Realize you are every atom in all of creation, and the essence of that energy always breathes with you. Our one breath breathes you, and you breathe it with every breath you take.

To get to where you can experience this sensation, ask to be shown and then be aided in surrendering to this magnificent, energetic breath of life. You can also try a rebirthing session; this is where I first felt the universe breathe me. My friend Dr. Asha Swaroop blessed me with this experience in one of her guided rebirthing breathwork sessions.[2] She is another MD who wants to give her patients and society an opportunity to heal their disease and not stop them from healing it with a medication that tricks them into thinking they have healed. Medications are useful, and I prescribe lots of them, but I see them as a Band-Aid that temporarily masks the symptoms disease gifts us with so we can play remember awake.

I postulate it is time to allow yourself to be angry and have an angergasm so that you can release the self-induced limits of your potential through understanding that you are controlled by the emotions that distract you from being in the peace and contentment of "now." You are beautiful right now, and you are on the step of your journey you are supposed to be on. Accept this fact with gratitude, please. A human being/soul combination is a miracle and always deserves your unconditional love. When you allow and indulge in thoughts that trap you in pain, anger, sadness, grief, detachment, etc., you allow your mind to keep you from your potential and your purpose on the planet by replaying scenes that keep you from unconditional love. Please consider releasing yourself from your traps by using your emotions as fuel to burn open the boxes in which your soul/human suit's journey has become stagnant. I also believe people who choose to remain stuck in a thought loop are the people who get dementia because they are stuck in one part of their brain, and the rest of the brain withers from lack of use.

You chose to come to this planet and create the human suit you emit because you love the game of Earth and its magnificent creative capacity. Please, love the human suit you are creating and the environment you are creating around it. Please realize that the boxes of fear we create with our limbic system are part of the game of Earth we came to experience. However, staying trapped in these energetic frequencies is not fun, and many of us will ask for an exit strategy when we feel we cannot open them. Please choose to open them and move on to a more present/pleasant version of the game of Earth.

I love every human suit on the planet and the lesson and love its soul came to teach me. When I wrote this as a blog post in 2022, I wrote the following sentence: "I may not love the behaviors their pain bodies and shadow figures create, but I respect and love their human beings and their souls." I now see all the frequencies of energy we emit as a form of love I can use to create more love. I lose my light if I don't stay in a state of unconditional love. If I lose my light, I lose my hope (creations of the future through love), my laughter (the best medicine and most people's bliss), and my ability to channel the divine. If I am not resonating in the frequency of unconditional love, I cannot offer a spark of its light to the humans I cross paths with to heal themselves and then pass that healing on to others without even knowing they have done so. If I am not in unconditional love, I will miss the valuable lessons that cross my path so that I may grow and remember how beautiful I am and, through doing so, channel divine love to heal more of my boxes and share with others a higher percentage of the time.

Our reality is linked to our ability to perceive the wavelengths of light surrounding us. If our light is trapped in boxes of fear, it cannot perceive the unconditional loving light we are surrounded by, and our reality is "dark." Will you please play remembering oneness by using the energy of your angergasms, sadgasms, despairgasms, and gigglegasms to burn open your prison doors and embody your divine light today? I see a reality where we will greet each other soul to soul instead of Ego to Ego. This will happen when we see, hear, taste, touch, and smell with light. We will be able to do this when we have gone within and remember we are made of light and shift the perception of reality through this remembrance. I am sending you the vision of a beautiful reality in which our human suits greet each other soul to soul. Will you find the particle of light inside you that desires to create this freeing reality with me today? Pretty please.

Play

What would life feel like if we got out of bed every day asking, "Who am I going to cross paths with and share the joy of playing the magic of creation with today?"

As a child of the '70s, we were told to go outside and play. (Thankfully, I am old enough to have grown up in a time when outside was perceived as safe.) We were not told what to play or how to play, just to play. Sometimes, we played in the confines of the rules of the games society had created for us, and sometimes, we changed those rules and created a slightly different game because the old rules were not fun to play with. Sometimes, we made up new games. Sometimes, I just played by enjoying being outside in the company of others during all seasons of life in New England. My "play" was often climbing an apple tree in solitude and surrendering to the freedom and peace I could find sitting in the safe place I called home in its branches. When playing the games with rules, many of us enjoyed exploring through trial and "error" how we could play them better by allowing inspiration to guide us in mastering that game.

Now, we are adults and have the power of an adult to birth individual guidelines and rules to follow. How often do you allow the freedom of play and games to be part of the birthing of the rules you feel will keep you safe during our Earth experience? If the answer is not often, take a moment to reassess that you are likely missing the ingredient of innocence when you birth the rules you play Earth with from the cauldron of thoughts you call your mind. This cauldron births y/our reality. Will you consider adding the vibration of innocent, loving play back into our collective pot?

Can you imagine getting out of bed every day and getting excited that you have been blessed with another day on the planet to play? Imagine going to work, spending time with your loved ones, or spending time in self-discovery and thinking, "How am I going to imagine beauty in the world around me? How am I going to create feeling blessed, refreshed, and energetic today?" If you view any activities as work, mundane, necessary, frustrating, imprisoning, etc., you likely won't experience or emerge from them with any satisfaction. With this view, you get trapped in a stagnant thought cauldron and create an Earth prison (hell) for yourself, not a world full of opportunities to play open (heaven). However, suppose you approach your daily life as a game that you have been blessed with another day to play, one that offers you a path to transformation and connection. In that case, you may never be disappointed with the game of Earth again because you will find and remain in a dimension of the game known as heaven on Earth.

I encourage you to play the game of being present when you look into someone's eyes. See if you can sense their soul and what unique part of heaven on Earth you will share and create together. Invite yourself to play the game of walking in another's shoes, even if it is only for a few seconds. Invite yourself to play the game of shedding tears with another or laughing so hard with them that your stomach will hurt the next day. These steps of our journey—where we are joined with one another in a way that we share the creation of tears—reside in the heaven-Earth dimension. If you are sharing tears with someone now and cannot feel it as a heaven-Earth vibration, I encourage you to try new, less restrictive guidelines on how to play Earth.

Consider getting out of bed today while asking, "How can I embellish the frequency of play in everything I do today?" We are here on the planet to experience with fascination the wide range of emotions that human existence brings us. We may not get stuck in the experience of heavy ones as long if we no longer feel the Earth as a game with ups and downs and "wins" and "losses," but instead as a game in which every experience is a birthright we appreciate and use to play creation. There is no such thing as a loss; every time you perceive you have lost, it is an opportunity for growth through playing a new way to discover heaven-Earth by creating a new lens through which to see. The harder the perception of loss is, the more profound and opening the growth can be if you choose to play the game of transmutation.

How will you play your version of the Earth game today? How will you participate in someone else's game? How many people will you connect with to play the game together? How many moments of bliss will you create by playing with someone else? How many new aspects of the heaven-Earth dimension will you reveal to yourself by playing new loving rules into existence? Better yet, will you consider playing Earth without any rules or even a template and create a new game of Earth with me where we perceive all dimensions within it to be an aspect of heaven-Earth?

I can't wait to sense the ideas you add to the cauldron of creation to create this new game with me. You are so loved and appreciated for the wisdom and love you add to the cauldron with each step of your journey. Thank you. Let's play in the vibrations of love we create through our collective journeys of remembering awake together today. Thank you, Dr. Sue Morter, for the term heaven-Earth. The play you experienced to birth this term into creation birthed it into creation for us all.

Vulnerability

> "Wholeness doesn't mean perfection. It means acceptance."
> —Dr. Shefali Tsabary, *A Radical Awakening*[3]

From 2021 to 2023, I, like many of the souls I met and called new friends over these two years, experienced a dramatic shift in my reality. I remembered awake my abilities to help people heal, and they were dramatically empowered. These "new" abilities caused me to feel doubt and fear because it was overwhelming to me at times to be gifted with such "power." As I sit and rewrite this blog post for my book in 2024, I now see the channels of loving consciousness not as "power" but as a gift of grace that I no longer want to fear but to play with every time I am offered a chance to do so. I have also learned that this "power" is not solely mine because I can only help those who are willing to cast aside their limiting belief systems and embrace the transformation to a more loving state to be homeostatic in. If my Ego tempts me into offering a healing vibration while vibrating in any other emotional state than love, I end up not feeling well afterward, and thus, this "power" is diminished. Thankfully, I learned this lesson of what vibration to offer healing in very soon after my hands turned on.

I was helping a patient heal an ankle he had broken thirty years before he met me. I wanted him to feel better and tried really hard to give him the vibration that would make him feel better. It worked. His ankle pain was better than it had been in thirty years after his first visit. However, my right arm was in pain for about six hours. Since that day, whenever my mind gets a little boisterous about how to offer love to heal, I shut it up by saying, "God is in me, I am in God, we combine as one." This state of surrender allows our collective essence of love to flow through me to the person I am sharing a vibration with. If they have surrendered similarly, we share an amazing, lasting healing together. If not, they usually feel better for a short period of time, but since they did not shift the frequency they spend homeostasis in, the disease does not dissolve. Thus, to share my gift with others most effectively, we both have to resonate in a frequency that is sourced from the womb of our collective consciousness, which is nourished and replenished from the energy I call God. This womb births its frequencies in realms of singularity; thus, the "power" I share when offering healing vibrations is an energetic essence created for the betterment of all. The message in this frequency is often known only in the felt sense of a vibration or the wisp of a color that temporarily permeates the patient's field.

How did I uncover these abilities that had previously been unrecognized within me? Through the perception of suffering and the deep desire to help as many people as my uninhibited capacity will allow. I learned to surrender, absorb, and become the frequencies of vulnerability and faith. Through this vulnerability and trust in what I initially thought was a power separate and outside of me, I asked for help healing the part of me that had difficulty receiving love because I knew this lack of being able to understand love by refusing to receive and embody it was preventing me from sharing love with others. I asked for help transmuting the belief that love is conditional, which is a belief that we have all incorporated into our limbic systems lifetime after lifetime. Through this surrender, I was able to understand that we need to be able to receive love in order to have love to share. Through receiving, we can rediscover how to love ourselves in such a way that we remember a state of wholeness where the womb of creation can be found within our energy field.

With this surrender and trust, you will also be able to fully embody and fulfill your soul's purpose with supreme confidence and then share that vibration with all who are ready to receive it. You will be connected to the Dao/Source/God for direction and guidance and enjoy the wildest ride of your life. You will also realize that Source is not separate from you but part of you and dwelling within you, ready to be accessed for guidance and power at any time through surrender and an open heart chakra.

This magical surrender requires trust, faith, and so much vulnerability, but you can choose this path. Put aside the Ego part of you that thinks you are even remotely capable of understanding the perpetual transformation of the energies of the universe or multiverse. Just reconnect with the part of you that is tethered to Source and can understand and appreciate your at times seemingly insignificant role in that energy transformation. I can assure you your existence is not insignificant, or at least it will not feel that way when you surrender and allow yourself to feel the gift of performing your specific purpose with the guidance, support, and love of Source that resides within you.

I am now embracing and reveling instead of fearing and obsessing about my growth into this new reality most of the time. I am human and play one vibrating in fear very well at times, at least temporarily. The alchemy of this transformation and the limitless possibilities ahead I can now sense have me in wonder, awe, and the most gratitude I have ever felt. I shed tears of the humility of connection when I think of what can be loved, healed, and created with the surrender to the symbiotic relationship of human/ soul and Source within me. How will you surrender to the essence that is the womb of creation inside you today? What entanglement of fear lying in your subconscious energy field will you be vulnerable with today so that you can surrender and receive the unconditional love of Source to aid in the healing needed to unlearn the ridiculous rule that love is conditional?

Understanding

Why do many desire to be understood by another?

The dance of interacting with fellow humans often involves the desire to be understood. We desire others to understand our point of view and often want them to align with it. So why do we do this to ourselves and others? We do this because we desire another to connect with us in what we perceive to be a comforting way. If we are correct and agreeable, we are good. If we are good, we are worthy of receiving love, and it is easier to open the felt sense of connection by feeling safe enough to be vulnerable through the illusion of being "right." We also want others to understand us because when we behave in a nonloving way, we crave another's aligned justification of our actions. This desire to bring another soul into your pain and justify your anger, rage, sadness, depression, judgment, guilt, etc., by blaming another for it is just hurting you and the soul holding compassion for you.

So the next time you desire to be understood by another, how about taking the time to go within to understand yourself first? Please take a deep breath and feel where the desire to be understood emanates from in your body. Then, go into that area with your unique, loving soul and ask to witness what emotion your isolation is seated in. It may take a bit to comprehend the complexity of the emotion that isolates you from others, so be patient with yourself. Ask for help and a loving embrace from your guides as you go on this journey of self-discovery. You may ask a human guide to be present with you. However, ask that human guide not to agree with you so that you can have your actions justified, but to simply sit with you and hold space for you to find what part of you aches to be reembodied by loving it back into your wholeness. Ask them to join you in healing the separateness you feel within and heal it in themselves simultaneously.

We are a fantastically connected matrix of beautiful beings. We understand each other without words much better than we do with them. When you are upset, the field around you projects that vibration. Others in your field feel it, and their pain body can react by mirroring your pain back at you. This energetic exchange is uncomfortable for both souls involved, but that is how we set up this game of life. When this happens, consider playing the game without words that limit and harm and instead shift to playing the game with just vibration. Take a deep breath and ask for help to bring the vibration of love into the field you are embodying. When love is the vibration we communicate through, we are in tune with the note of our soul and all souls. Love is a bliss vibration; once you discover how to interact while vibrating in it, you will no longer want to spend time in other emotional vibrations.

You can connect to yourself by looking deep into another's eyes or removing yourself from the situation, breathing into your heart or belly, and asking to feel where your soul is linked to all souls and is witnessed and loved. Once you connect to others in this way, you will be understood by all and drift into the paradox that it no longer matters if another understands you. You will know you are a light body that is understood by the universe, and the more you listen with your light, you will understand the universe and emit its wise vibrations to share with others. Once you find the unimaginable beauty in you, it will not matter if others understand you because you will realize you have another opportunity inside of you to hear another whisper of the loving wisdom of our universal consciousness. Will you play the game of life with me like this today? Let's create a planet full of our combined loving bliss. We got this. I love you all.

Veils

> "The purpose of your life is to discover your creatorship" —Dr. Sue Morter, *The Energy Codes*[4]

> "Concentrate the energy and make it flexible; can you be like an infant? People live through flexibility and yielding; they die through obstinacy and forcefulness." —Laozi, *Daodejing*[5]

When we think of the word *veil* in a spiritual context, we think of the wall or gap in time and space that prevents us from making contact with those on the "other side" in non-Earth realms. I encourage you to understand that the veils that keep you from sensing realms outside of the dimension of the Earth are created within you. You choose to dissolve the energetic curtains that keep your soul from remembering awake. Behind these veils are gifts unique to your human/soul that lie dormant, waiting for you to discover them. How do you dissolve them? You feel instead of think.

I spent the first fifty years of my life as more of a thinker than a feeler. If you are like me, learning to feel may take some time, but if I can do it, you can also. If you are a feeler, ask not to get overwhelmed by what you are feeling but to be able to laser focus all that energy and follow it to the source of the overflow. Feel when someone is poking your pain body and react with quiet and calm introspection. Feel where you are hurting within— that is where a veil is begging to be lifted with tender, loving compassion. I sometimes send love to my veils with Joe Vitale's fifth Ho'oponopono phrase, "I forgives myself." The "I" is you and the divine, and the "self" is your Ego or pain body that makes the "unloving" decisions that created the energetic entanglement box that is a veil. We are supposed to make "unloving" decisions as humans. They are part of the Earth game. However, once we choose to play the Earth game on the level remembering awake, we can only move to the next level, awake, by dissolving all the veils we created when playing the other levels.

You achieve "awake" and find peace by accepting and loving the energy cysts that have created your veils. When these blockages in your energy body have been appreciated and transmuted, you remember you have a hara line. The hara line is a vertical line of light that runs up and down your body. It connects you to all light. I am discovering the art of dropping into my hara line and using this place to communicate with collective consciousness. One cannot ever understand collective consciousness by thinking with a human mind, but its expansiveness, oneness, and magical creativity can be sensed through your hara line and the God particle in the center of it. When you dissolve your veils with love and then surrender to the connection to the divine that this power line within you offers, time does not exist; anything is possible, and tears of joy and gratitude will flow from your eyes. Your hara line is a light frequency within you where your mind, soul, and Source are one. The hara is an energy vortex that your God particle can connect with to receive and then transform the cosmos's energy into a vibration that Earth and its inhabitants can heal and create with. It is where your and our soul's desire and purpose will be revealed to you as you dissolve your veils.

For the planet to thrive in peace and prosperity, we all need to resonate with thoughts generated from the nonjudgemental space of unconditional love and kindness to all. This frequency where we see and feel ourselves as one with all lies in our hara line. Cherish, honor, and embrace parts of you that you consider ugly but God considers essential information. When you can see the parts of you that you once saw as ugly as beautiful and share with others how you were able to change your perspective, our planet will thrive. We are all on the right path right now. It is time for you to appreciate the beauty and information your unique pathway is blessing us with. You dissolve another veil whenever you soften and honor yourself for the energy you have collected for us all. How many veils will you lift today so you can start to be one with your hara line? Will you play remember awake with me and experience the joy of dissolving your veils? Will you feel the magnificence of your hara line and the bliss of connecting it to another human hara line or, better yet, all hara lines in all time?

Yin and yang

Yin and yang represent the eternal dance of light and dark, connection and separation, hot and cold, male and female. When we respect and honor both for the magnificence and wisdom they create through nourishment within us, we embody the vibration of freedom. When we choose to flow back and forth with the ebb and flow of yin and yang, we become the energy of creation.

The eclipse in 2024 was a reminder of the power of yin and yang. The sun represents our yang. It can be understood as our drive to create the unique note we are destined to play in the creation symphony. We do this by separating ourselves from the oneness we are all part of and embarking on an individual journey to find the frequencies of love that open our hearts to the greatest extent so that we can find a unique, loving vibration to share with all. The moon represents our yin. It is a frequency of rest, observation, contemplation, and it is an opportunity to remember we are all one.

During the recent eclipse, our yin (the moon) reminded us of the beauty that can be found in the dark. Our energies were focused on a shared experience in our darkness that day. One could argue that the 7.95 billion different realities that occur daily (each human has a different reality when interacting with another) were a little more cohesive that day. It reminded us that in our perceived periods of darkness, we often surrender and ask for help from God/Source and other humans. In the vulnerability of surrender, we search for and often find an energetic connection of bliss that we may never have found otherwise. When we are vulnerable, we can go so deep within that we find the unique rays of light we are made of and remember how to share them as one light. This is how we will create beauty beyond imagination together while in this 3D dimension, donning our human suits. We will coalesce into a shared yang (sun) that is so bright and powerful with unified love that the idea brings me to tears.

The picture above, which I chose to represent this original blog post, was drawn by Gail Alexander. I am blessed to call her a friend. The mandalas she draws often open portals of wisdom for me. This particular one took me to this dimension where great sadness was present, which was very painful for my heart because the beings there had lost the ability to have compassion for each other. The situation there, one might say, is identical to the reality many perceive this planet to be in. However, the sadness was so profound for so many that the beings there came together as a unified light and created hope from the depths of the darkness of their collective sadness. We can find hope here again. There are many souls emitting the vibration of hope on this planet right now. They are ready to hold space for you so you may also remember the bliss of embodying this vibration.

Will you use what you perceive as a "dark" time in your life to be vulnerable and connect your soul with a beacon of hope and unconditional love? Will you hold the hands of God/Source or another human today, or stand in the sun to find the connective power of the light frequency that is hope again? Will you play with the alchemy of love that transmutes the tears of our collective sadness to the light of hope? By relighting the torch of the power of hope, we will be guided to remember and relight the torches of our other sacred gifts: unity, the power to forgive the unforgivable, and healing. Will you remember awake these sacred lights within you by opting to receive the nourishment that your unique yin and yang dance provides for you and us all? It may help to view the ebb and flow of your dance through the lens of the dance we call creation. That lens will let you see that every step of the cosmos, whether it is "dark" or "light," is beautiful, and you are creating that beauty with your courageous dance steps. Thank you. You and your dance are so loved.

Division

Why do we continue to cultivate division from other souls?

When COVID-19 crossed paths with the planet in 2020, I, like many, thought it was a wonderful opportunity for our world to start taking synchronous global breaths, remember our oneness, and start healing as a cohesive unit. It saddens me that just the opposite happened. In 2022, when I originally wrote this, we were seemingly more divided than ever. Why did we allow this division? Why would we rather fuel our Ego with the smugness of believing we are superior because we stand with the crowd that is "right" than be kind to all? Why do we not see the beauty of the intricate and wonderfully different pathways we all take as we explore the potential of our human/soul combo? Do you realize the pain you create for yourself when you would rather be correct than kind and empathetic? I am not asking you to give up your belief system—just the idea that it is the only correct one.

When I started healing with my hands in 2021, I came to work one day, stuck in judgment. I was sad because I thought that harm was being caused to others because of a belief I was choosing to carry. The patient I was working on that morning asked me, "Doc, where is your juju today?"

I told her I was sad and could not tap into the love I needed to help her heal. Thankfully, I released enough of the judgment causing my sadness that I was able to get some of my juju back that morning to help her. That day, I realized I could not help people heal if my energy field vibrates in judgment. I chose that day to try very hard not to judge as I walk the remainder of my steps in this realm. I realized that when I was playing the human Ego's version of God that day, I could not be a channel of the energy of God because that energy does not have the capacity to judge. The energy I know as "God" has no Ego, so it has no right or wrong side to attach to. That day, I made a choice to no longer carry the egocentric weight of sadness, grief, and anger that accompanies one who acts like a two-year-old with an entitlement that demands they always get their way. I surrendered and put my faith into the bigger picture, in which Source makes no mistakes and always gives us an opportunity for growth if we choose to receive it.

My juju has continued to strengthen since that day. I did go to a Reiki healer for the first time after this epiphany and set my intention to release my attachment to judgment. I understood in that session that this state of freedom is found through releasing your heart from the prisons of hurt you have built through time. There is not a week that goes by that I am not trying to open another prison I have created in the energy field of cosmic love that resides where my heart lies in my human suit. As you dissolve these veils, you will weep at the profound capacity you have to share the love you were born to share with all energies that cross your path and with all energies in all dimensions of time if you remove the shackles that bind your capacity to love.

I ask you to consider whether you really want to carry the burden of being right any longer. Proving you are right is a vortex of energetic entanglement that consumes energy that could be spent opening your heart to feel oneness with the profound love of the cosmos. Why would you rather be right and isolated to the restricted energy of a group that only thinks as you do instead of being kind, loving, and open to understanding all viewpoints and connecting with all energy? Why do you think your limited human mind can understand the cosmos's plan of what is happening in the world right now? Why are we allowing the media to divide us into red and blue, or black, white, and brown? Why can we not see ourselves as human, struggling, and in need of giving and receiving love and support from all who cross our paths? Why do we need to act like two-year-olds throwing temper tantrums when we don't get our way?

I challenge you to release your red or blue belief system and embrace and allow your pink, green, purple, white, yellow, or orange source of unlimited, unconditional love and connection within you to guide your actions. When I am one with God inside of me, that energy is felt as white with all colors of pastel fractals swirling in an endless sea of peaceful and passionate play. I did not consider myself creative before I saw this energy because I lived in a scientific-based human suit with a strong black-and-white Ego guiding its journey. My ability to create changed when I asked to release judgment so I could know and be one with God instead of playing God through a limited human mind. When you are surrendered to the energy of all creation, you become a creator. What I have created when surrendered is beyond anything my tiny human mind could ever have imagined possible. The souls I see and feel when surrendering to the energy of God are always fluid and changing. This is how we need to walk our steps to find the freedom of being one with God and creating with that energy together. Judging stops you from being liquid light and solidifies y/our energy field.

Will you let go of your rigidity and enjoy the freedom and bliss of becoming whatever fluid color your soul and Source choose to grace you with today? Pretty please. I promise you will not regret the decision to remove the frequency of judgment from your energy field.

9

Godding Up

Godding up

You and the Divine/God/Source are one, whether you like it, realize it, accept it, or not!

So many are "awake" while playing in this dimension of Earth that it is hard for me to comprehend that we choose to be here and not embrace our full potential. What is our full potential? I think we will endlessly re-member and reinvent it at the same time. How do we enter the fountain of creation to discover what our potential is today? You surrender your mind to y/our higher power and let it discover its unique path as a tool to aid our soul in playing cocreator. You love your mind and soul open so there is more ease and fun as you walk, run, skip, or bounce on your path. Or you don't and have epiphanies that smack you in the back of the head and remind you that you are God with a smirk of dumbass attached. FYI, most people who channel archangels and other divine energies will tell you they are very snarky beings who love to laugh with you and at themselves (you). There are many who channel messages from deities we have labeled as gods or angels, but only a few channel God's energy and can put it into words. All energy is God, so deities and angels are God. I consider them forms of God that we are able to find easier because so many have put their thoughts and emotions into creating this energetic form of God that they are easier to access. Those who know God in the felt sense describe this energy as peace because that is the best verbal description of the state of resonance you are in when you know you are all energy ever created and are just waiting to offer a loving vibration to you and those around you. Occasionally, that loving vibration guides you to give instructions on how to best guide it to be received into a human suit.

Let me explain how you are God even when you don't realize it. Jenniffer Weigel, a hilarious and amazing human I am honored to call a friend, discussed in a Spiritual Social Club meeting how she was on stage doing her one-woman show recently and could not find the clicker to control her slideshow. She had placed angels all over the room before the show to help the show go smoothly and with love, and she was sure the clicker was on the stage before the show started. Nonetheless, it was not there when she went to grab it during her show. (I am pretty sure one of the angels she placed in the auditorium hid it from her for the purpose of understanding God in a greater capacity.) She asked the staff for help, but for some reason, they weren't able to help, so she had to run to her dressing room to retrieve it. She found it in a spot where she never would have placed it. She then came back on stage very angry for about fifteen minutes. She stated she did not remember anything she said during this time period but was able to deliver her monologue with such grace that she was told after the show how great her performance was. People were laughing hard when she awoke from her dissociative angergasm, so it was not her anger she was speaking with. Most people I know who are good at channeling deities and angels will tell you they do not remember what they say when they are in the flow of channeling. Leave it to Jen Weigel to teach me you can channel God in pure form—the form of one of the deities we have labeled as God or one of the snarky angels she asked to make her show great—to deliver a monologue on how to find God when you are upset and not fully present. Thank you, Jen, for this beautiful example of how when we are called and willing, God will flow through us to deliver loving messages to others, whether we are aware of this or not.

So we are God, whether or not we want to be or even if we are stuck in an emotion that blocks us from this truth. It may be time to have some fun playing a new game called "What percentage of my 'time' on Earth can I be resonating in grace?" so that when God flows through you, you are aware of it. Every time I feel I am one with God, I am amazed at the wisdom and love of the words that come out of my mouth, the geometric light that my closed eyes see, the cadence and vibration of the voice that comes from me that is so loving it relaxes the hearts and energy fields of others so they can receive and heal. I love being aware I am God, so I don't waste time playing God, trying to control everything and everyone around me, or judging right and wrong. (By the way, you are still God when you are playing God, but this version of God emitting from you makes the game of life harder.)

In the last few weeks, I have had several patients contact me to help them find a way to heal their cancer. I only awakened about four years ago and have been known to freak out about the new expansive reality I am now part of. I am tired of the tool I call my mind thinking that something new is going to be harmful or telling me I have not yet learned how to play this part of the game. News flash: There is no such thing as time, so I/we have already played this part of the game. Also, all energy is God. Thus, no matter how I have played the game in the past, now, or in the future, I have played it in the frequency of God. This time, instead of freaking out for days or weeks, I freaked out for a few hours and then had my mind say, "Who I am now is a healer that cancer patients are calling to help them find the frequency of love they can heal with, so how do I do that best?" The answer was to go within and heal the places in me that were boxed in old cortisol reactions of doubt and fear.

How did I do this? I like to talk to myself, so I said, "Time to woman up and heal." However, all energy ever created is not a woman or a man, so my answer changed to, "Time to God up." How do you God up? Breathe. Melt. Open. Close your eyes and ask your guides or angels what your version of God looks and feels like. Then ask for help being that. Know that you have always been God and always will be, and you don't have to try to be God. You just are. Once these words have sunk in, breathe some more. I find God through breathing into the photon, which I call the God particle, under my xiphoid process. My mind will soften and focus on finding that place when it is surrendered to the energy of humility. As I am writing this, my eyes are tearing up because the emotion of humility is so loving it can transmute any fear I have of surrendering my mind/Ego. Humility holds me lovingly as I anticipate the grace that my mind, soul, and human energy field will witness today as God flows through me so that another can be taught to know God by loving themselves open. After surrendering to my God particle, I imagine opening the already established connections to all energy everywhere and remembering I am one with this energy. I direct my mind to play and explore the endless loving connections and wisdom of the energy of all consciousness. My mind will agree and willingly perform this task if it is not hung up in an old cortisol reaction somewhere in my energy field. So, for me, Godding up means releasing attachments to emotions that keep my mind from knowing the joy of exploring all energy that I/we/the cosmos have always been and always will be. You choose what your mind pays attention to because it is a tool you are in charge of using. Be kind and loving to this tool; it will soften and open to explore new dimensions of wisdom and love.

There is no wrong way to use your mind, but there are definitely playgrounds with different vibrations you can direct it to explore. Sometimes, the playgrounds need to be heavier emotions so you can lovingly show your mind that all energy is love and God. These are the playgrounds in your energy field that have created cortisol prisons that make your veil dense and keep you from knowing God. As we look into these boxes, they open and show us the present that is "now." In "now," we know God as our energy is not hung up in our past or worried about our future. How do we open boxes we have feared opening? Find a way to giggle your way through that fear. I was talking with a beautiful version of God in a human suit named Susan yesterday. She has been channeling Mother Mary and trying to release herself from her fear prisons that keep her mind from fully embodying the vibration we call Mother Mary. Susan has been one with Mother Mary's energy in multiple lifetimes, and because this loving essence has been deemed threatening to entities on this planet, she and her loved ones have been brutally murdered and tortured for trying to share this version of God with the Earth in the past. Together, we decided Susan could imagine Mother Mary dancing the Hokey Pokey on all of her prisons of fear so that they would open and no longer keep her from the bliss of fully symbiosing with this version of God into her current human suit. We were on the phone for over three hours, so this is not the only prison-obliterating scenario we gigglegasmed into possibility for her. I think we even told her to let the minds of her previous human suits alleviate their fear by having Mother Mary ride a waterslide. Conquering a fear prison can be seen as that first plunge down a giant slide at a water park. You are so afraid when surrendering to the flow the first time, but your fear is transmuted into the effervescence of embodied joy during the first ride. Then you keep climbing the steps over and over again to relive that sensation in a new way each time you choose to surrender to the flow of the water on the slide.

So, for me, Godding up means loving my fear boxes open so I can know God by being an active channel of this amazing energy as often and with the greatest capacity possible. The version of God I am graced to emit through this human suit is here to teach you how to love your mind, soul, and human suit so that your unique version of God's love can be shared with all. I believe we can become a more powerful version of God's energetic essence capable of generating a greater "share" of it with humanity if we do not have any cortisol prisons creating veils that keep us from embodying this energy. So, I will be Godding up by gigglegasming my cortisol prisons open as often as possible. Will you please join me in this version of how to play Earth? I love you. We totally got this.

The bliss of creation

The bliss of creation is felt when you know oneness with the sparkling light of bioelectric love discovered in universal heart coherence and when you marvel as this entity shapes into form whatever it can imagine as it pulses loving light into the biomagnetic black hole we were all created from. We find this womb of life where we create as one when we resonate in the symphony of light that is the oneness of our soul.

We are all blessed to be sentient beings with the power to create. The secret I will let you in on is to manifest a creation in which we weep in awe afterward; we need to play creation with another part or, even better, multiple parts of our soul. We can create all sorts of energies that keep us weighted in separation, like fear, despair, grief, sadness, guilt, anger, etc., by ourselves or with others, but the creations of light are tenderly manifested only through loving connections to other souls. When we surrender to the particle of lighted peace and tranquility within that is our unique particle of God through the trust and love of ourselves and the tears of compassion, kindness, connection, love, joy, or humility, we can connect to the womb of all of creation. In this realm, together as our one soul connected in an indescribable beauty and power, we can play the game of life in this dimension as we were truly meant to play it.

We are all lost and starving to find and then embody the peace of our wholeness that we so graciously surrendered to experience the heavy and light emotions of this dimension so that we can collect the yin and yang energies necessary for creation. Because of the five senses of this dimension, we can understand and feel the oneness of our soul through energetic explosions of bioelectricity and biomagnetism in a way we cannot in other dimensions. When you surrender your Ego and rediscover that there is only one soul experiencing this dimension, you will never again want to navigate this realm in the hologram of separation we have created here. You will always strive to relax into the vibration of your energy field that resonates in the frequency of the womb of creation because this is the frequency that remembers awake our oneness in an unimaginable way. The beautiful people, animals, and substances that create Earth are y/our soul. Please remember this and open yourself to the photon of light within that will unify you with all energy.

When you play the game flowing in photon coherence, you will be playing it in a bliss you may have never dreamed possible. You will experience interactions with the fractals of our soul, which you perceive as separate energies (other humans, trees, oceans, sand, etc.), in a new way. You will understand that these energies we perceive as separate are amazing mirrors that are lovingly placed on the steps of our path to guide us to the places in our energy field that need to be loved open so that our connection to the womb of creation can strengthen. You may begin to see and feel that your interactions with "others" create the most magnificent mandala of flowing geometry. This mandala represents the infinite, ever-changing flow of the chi of creation. Once you remember you are part of and creating this mandala, you can use it to link your energy field to any aspect of the energy of creation. Watching this mandala recreate itself over and over again with the energy of our linked bioelectric heart coherence is a show you will never want to miss.

Once you play the game of life walking and flowing in this magical felt sense oneness of your soul, you will never want to play it in any other way. Please try to feel the vibration of the womb of creation I describe here so that your mind has a path to remember it awake in your energy field. I felt the vibration of the womb of creation as a dense pit of biomagnetic energy within my center, and then I watched the green bioelectricity of the infinity net of our love offer it a lightning bolt of energy to create with. What gets created is beyond my mind/Ego's imagination spectrum. However, I can feel that whatever is created, there is a form of love. When my patients travel to the empty of this womb, they are always offered loving light to heal with. So, will you surrender and find the resonance of the womb of creation today to play the game of life in this awe-inspiring frequency of reality with me? It is time to play life as the collective symphony of creators we are. I/we need your note to be boisterously authentic and share its unique beauty with the symphony of our soul. We continually create and enjoy this symphony by becoming one with the dance steps of the never-ending flow of the chi of loving creation we call God, the divine, Source.

I love you. You are beautiful. We got this.

God giggles

Gigglegasm is my favorite word because laughter connects our God particles.

I am so blessed to know so many souls in this dimension that bring joy to my life. One of these souls is a patient who is 101 years old. When she comes in to heal and play on my acupuncture table, she opens up and shares the loving wisdom she has collected over this and other lifetimes with our collective soul. When I am in the presence of someone over eighty who does not have dementia, I shut up and listen to the love they have cultivated within so that they can age gracefully and try to absorb the wisdom that love has to teach me. You might also want to shut up and listen when these souls grace your path. One time, we were playing healing together, and I shared with her the frequency of the amazing experience of having a collective gigglegasm with over one hundred people who were in the opening and mind/Ego-diminishing yoga pose of Happy Baby. She called this experience "God giggles."

I see God as our collective soul and all energy ever created. Please feel free to call this energy whatever resonates with you the best. Many call it the universe, the divine, the creator, my higher self, the Earth. One person I know calls it geometry, which works very well for her because she sees math as an energy that always has an answer. Another calls it boobs. I know this is a hard-to-swallow synonym for God for many of you, but I had asked this person, who did not have a name for a higher power because he was not sure he believed in one, to do some "homework" and come up with a name. I asked him to find a name for the energy that would coax his mind into a state of quiet surrender. He came back in laughing and told me his higher power was "boobs." I hope you are enjoying some God giggles reading this because I sure am having them writing it. For this kind, creative soul who is very open to the collective consciousness, boobs are the energy that gets his mind to shut up. His energy surrenders to external femininity because it craves surrender to the feminine womb of creation within. (Yes, men have womb chakras.)

Another patient recently wanted to play with the Hathors as her higher power. These are the "gods" that adorn some of the temples of Egypt. Some think they are the aliens that created the human race and maybe even Earth. She feared opening her solar plexus. Her healing was fascinating because it involved coaxing her fear to be released by imagining flower petals opening in the form of a Fibonacci spiral. Once her solar plexus was open, loving Hathor energy entered back into her belly on Fibonacci spiral slides. Then, she went to a dimension that she felt was under the Great Sphinx of Giza and received healing from the timeless beings residing in one of the dimensions found there.

If you have a name for your higher power but cannot get your mind to shut up, try putting a binky (pacifier) in its mouth, wrapping it in a blanket, and tucking it into the place in your body it finds the most comfortable. This place is likely in the chakra with which your God energy identifies the most. For example, a person who is here to share peace would put it in their solar plexus; joy would be their sacral chakra, and healers may find their heart chakra the most comfortable place to tell a binkied mind to take a siesta.

When we laugh, we transcend into a vibration of connection and surrender that allows us to be present with those we are laughing with in a way that we can't while resonating in heavier emotions. The effervescence of laughter dissolves the walls of division we have created to "protect" ourselves. It is time for these walls to be eliminated so that our collective ability to love and be loved can be felt in a way we have forgotten was possible due to the brainwashing and vibration of fear we have embodied in this dimension. You cannot vibrate in love and fear simultaneously; if you are laughing, you embody the energy of love and connection. If you embody love and connection, you can access the God particle within your center and connect to other people's God particles. The bliss of this level of connection in this dimension is why we decided to have consciousness in this dimension. We can float in endless bliss in dimensions above 3D. However, remembering awake and resonating in the heart coherence of creation while in a human suit is a delight we could not pass up, so we eagerly agreed to come and play Earth to experience this sensation. I do feel that both the dark and the light of our emotional spectrum in human suits are so much more powerful than in many other suits. We are blessed to experience this power. Our God giggles are one of the tools we have available to sway back and forth between heavy and dense, masculine and feminine, so that wearing a human suit does not become mundane by getting stuck on one side of the spectrum of energy we are meant to experience all sides and all facets of.

So, the next time you start giggling, will you please see it as a way to remember you have a piece of God within you that can't wait for you to remember it is there so it can connect with other pieces of God in this dimension? When you giggle and feel the champagne bubbles of creation inside of you, understand that those around you and distant from you can feel them and will have a better day because of your laughter. They may not know why they are having a good day, but they will have one. It might be fun to play with the idea of asking when you have a gigglegasm, what part of y/our soul in what timeline will spontaneously start giggling with you? Can you imagine if all souls/our soul had a collective Earth gigglegasm? What do you think you/we could create from that inevitability of energetic love if we all imagine that resonance has already happened and collectively embodied its magnificence?

I invite you to play with the idea of a collective gigglegasm today. Don't forget to include all the elements of the Earth in the God giggles you experience today. Your giggles are the glue of creation and love that binds us all. Will you play/create more robust pathways of connection to each other with y/our God giggles today? We got this. You are never alone. I love you all.

God's soul

The energy we define as our "souls" was birthed from a singular cosmic womb. That singularity of energy, all its creations, and the energy of the space between other cosmic wombs is the energy I define as God; thus, with my heart, I believe we all share the "soul" of God.

I was raised Catholic and in church I learned that my soul was the immortal part of me but not me, and that all humans had a separate and individual soul. This definition of soul can result in the creation of an internal crater of isolation and loneliness. I would like you to start to comprehend that although we perceive ourselves as separate souls in this human/Earth realm, we are not. We all are one soul in that we all have the soul of God/Source/the creator/the divine intricately woven into the core of our being. When you remember awake that common frequency thread, the isolation and fear you often feel will transmute into heart coherence. Can you imagine what work of art or artistic performance will be revealed through the power, wisdom, and love of our collective soul if we all choose to unite in this common thread of creative capacity?

In a monthly global healing session I participated in with Dr. Sue Morter, I was able to go back to the birth of my soul and realize my soul was not born alone. It was born with all of you. We all were created from the heart of God/Source/the divine, which lies in an androgynous, unconditionally loving womb. We are brought to life when the energy of God/Source expands into more and more pieces and places as it desires to love and create the geometric playground we call the multiverse. We were created with a tenacity to explore, which gifts us with the passion for playing with the illusion of separation from the whole. However, within us, we have an umbilical cord that calls us home and reminds us that we have never left the tethers to God's/Source's safety, patience, wisdom, nurturing, and unconditional love. Our creator gifts us the perception of separateness to ignite the individual creator in all of us. However, we were also gifted the ability to remember to share our unique creative energy with the one soul we are part of so we never feel separate.

We find our bliss, potential, power, and purpose by remembering and allowing ourselves to unite with our collective soul. You are where you are supposed to be for the benefit of the collective. If you are struggling, you are gathering the energy resonance of whatever you are struggling with for our one soul to increase its compassion and thus its ability to create more unconditional love and more versions of our soul to play creation with. If you are healing and releasing or transmuting, you are also doing this for our collective soul.

Regardless of where you are at, remember you are never alone. You are part of the amazing soul of Source/God. If you have forgotten this, imagine a light deep in your belly (the light of your pure, just born soul), and then surrender with opening breaths to knowing the truth that your soul is part of a collective giant soul. Continue to take deep, opening, liquid light breaths so that you melt into the frequency of uniting your soul with this collective soul. Surrender to the expansion of the sun or even the galaxy of light in your belly. Remember awake that the guidance of the power, wisdom, compassion, patience, and love of our soul and the soul of God are always in the center of your human suit, waiting to support you on your infinite journey. Please remember you are *never alone* and are *always loved* and appreciated for exactly who you are at all times. Sometimes, to feel this light, it helps to say Joe Vitale's fifth Ho'oponopono phrase, "I forgives myself." This phrase helps dissolve all illusions of the "not enoughs" that keep you from feeling worthy of the love inside you. With each breath you take, release all of the "not enoughs" and the fear you carry within you until you feel the galaxy of energy you/we are meant to be glowing bright from within, lighting your path and, at times, all our paths.

It is time for us to remember we are one soul by resonating in the frequencies of unconditional love (found in the pure center of our heart chakra) and bliss (found through energetic connection with our collective soul in our solar plexus). So please choose to discover and live in this vibration of Source/God so that we all understand that we are all one unimaginably beautiful soul. Will you end the feelings of loneliness and isolation on this planet by choosing to connect to the God/Source soul we share in everyone you meet? Will you choose to do this by smiling with a stranger or loved one today? Will you choose to connect in your unique way to the essence of all energy in existence through the God particle found within you? Will you use your God particle, which was created from this all-encompassing essence, as a beacon that lovingly guides your mind home and reunites it with the totality of our loving energy? Will you let your thoughts offer ideas of new loving ways to play creation with our collective soul today?

Our team of ONE

Whether you realize it or not, you are part of a team of one.

This dimension has brainwashed us into thinking we are not OK if we are not part of a group that mirrors who we are. Although there are many on the planet with like-minded thoughts and feelings, there is no one else on this planet who possesses your unique and beautiful gifts. The blessing we embody by discovering our particular soul resonance causes many of us to feel isolated and alone often. We think and feel that others do not understand us and that we may never fit in. Please know that we are not meant to have a mirror that reflects who we think we are in this dimension because that mirror would limit our capacity. The mirrors that will reveal our true selves will be in the form of people, phrases, experiences, etc., in which we will glimpse fragments of possibilities, hear whispers of reassurance, smell openings to new paths, touch light frequencies of remembering connection, and taste the flavors of the essence of the capacity of our love. These subtle mirrors that reflect our totality are offered as blessings to show us the path we can use to cultivate an energy that is unique within us so that we can share it with the "team of one" we are all part of.

Over many years, I have been blessed to coach hundreds of beautiful girls and young women on many softball fields. I have also been part of many high school and college athletic teams, two of which were good enough to be inducted into my high school and college hall of fame (yes, my life has been incredibly blessed). Of all the athletes I have crossed paths within my lifetime, no two have been the same. Every athlete is unique and contributes their remarkable and essential gift to that team. The team would not be as powerful and blessed without each athlete's gift. If an athlete does not have confidence in their gift, the team may suffer. This is OK because there is much growth in suffering. I would tell the teams I coached that I loved the "mistakes" they would make in the regular season because it guided me on what we needed to practice more so their confidence and skills would grow as the season progressed. I only made them run laps if I heard the word "can't" come out of their mouths. The teams I coached won many titles because no one was left out, and everyone's unique gift was cultivated with loving encouragement. Everyone plays and bats in rec ball, so everyone on the team needs to believe they can contribute.

If the athletes on a team are encouraged to embody and emit their gifts with confidence, that team of ONE becomes a beautiful entity. This team not only wins titles but wins when all the team's athletes know what it feels like to be *one* together. I have witnessed and felt the power of a team of one on athletic fields and courts. I have felt the enmeshment of the energy of many becoming one and the vastness and connection that is embodied when the isolation of the individual human Ego experiences surrender to the Ego of the team of one. Our collective soul is always amazed at the power of love and creativity we become if we allow ourselves to submit to the unimaginable symphony we are creating with the power and love of the combined resonance of our unique soul notes.

Many feel isolated lately as we have tried to figure out our energetic spiritual gifts. Unfortunately, there is no instruction manual for embodying the unique vibration you are meant to become. This journey of discovery can create fear, anger, loneliness, frustration, etc. Trust me; I have felt all of these as I continue to discover the resonance of my gift. I have cried while trying to wrap my head around the rapid shifts my body has gone through to allow me to help others find a healing vibration that works for them while we are playing together in time zones sixteen hours apart. My limbic system has freaked out several times over the shift in the human identity I have portrayed in the movie of my life day to day. For many like me, this journey of rediscovering the depth and beauty of your soul is perceived as difficult. I even turned the fear of my gifts into a state of victimhood at one time. I was so afraid of my gifts that I went into a "why me" pity party. Thankfully, a soul I respect very much pointed this out to me, and I will forever appreciate that loving smack in the back of my head to shift my perspective from fear to gratitude. Without that smack, I may have remained in fear of remembering awake and would not have written this book. So be grateful for the teammates who are wise and strong enough to see how your gifts are going to be a unique contribution to the team. They have so much confidence created from the love in their heart that it helps you manifest your gifts when you are ready. Just realize if you are getting nudges to step into your power from these loving and wise versions of our soul, please do so so that they can concentrate their energy on others who need space for their gifts to be remembered awake.

I received this advice from another wise and loving teammate: "It is harder to run away from who you are meant to be than to be that person." I am very grateful to Gretchen Oehler Hogg for telling me this. She called me out on my fear of transition, and I am now stepping into each new discovery of who I am with more confidence and purpose. I am embracing the miracles that can be created when I play with others and spreading the joy, awe, and laughter I find in sharing my gift with others.

You are never alone on this journey. Please believe me regarding this. Just take a deep breath from the center of your belly and open the bright sun, galaxy, or multiverse you have inside you. When you feel the power of this light, feel how connected you are to all the energies standing with you and holding you from within. Feel how you are eternally immersed, loved, supported, and held by the team of one composed of all our souls combined within you. Let this unimaginably vast oneness whisper to you what the next step in your journey may be. Receive the peace of love that the oneness emits to heal any part of your body that is not in peace. (I play this game by sending a two-year-old version of my soul that is so young and tender it has not learned the version of love that is conditional and just wants to hug every part of my body until it feels peace.) Let our oneness teach you the power of unconditional love. Connect with others through our shared connection in the solar plexus and feel the light of their/our soul. If you want to have fun, connect your solar plexus to your heart or all your chakras and connect to others and the planet with the light you will find in this connection. Thank you, Dr. Sue Morter, for teaching me the power of an open solar plexus. I will forever be grateful to you.

You are on a journey of finding the beautiful talents you possess to help support your team of one. This journey can be very intimidating, but you got this. We are all creating a new reality based on more love, and I ask you to be patient with yourself as you find the love you have within. You are never alone. You have human guides and the collective within to support you. They can both be felt with one deep breath into your solar plexus. You are all so beautiful and so loved. I am blessed to share this dimension with you. Have fun playing the game of Earth with your teammates. I can't wait to see and feel all you can do as you play your necessary position in the team of one that we are. I love our team.

The "I AM"

Many recommend the mantra "I AM." It is only recently that I have begun to understand its power.

When a mind living in duality speaks the words "I am," the "I" is based on a lens of extremely limited perception, and the mouth of the Ego then follows the "I am" with an endless list of descriptive words to describe the perception of how important that mind thinks it is as an individual entity. These descriptors of individuality are cages we create that keep us from opening and remembering who we truly are. For example, I am a mother, doctor, teacher, coach, healer; a pain in the ass; a "grandmother" who makes an amazing meal and tries to force everyone to eat it; sad, happy, loving, fearful, judgmental, and angry. You get the idea. I am also time and essence, but to know in the felt sense I am time and essence, I have to drop the limited definition of the cages I describe my human lifetime with. The cages are the adjectives, nouns, and verbs the Ego needs to feel important.

When we are something other than "I AM," we are not fully connected to Source's purity and atoms. We are the descriptions our human mind needs to make us feel important and the descriptions that divide and prevent us from being one with Source, but we are also Source. I have had the descriptor of MD after my name since 1996. Within this box, I have attached the descriptors of success, financial safety, and someone who could offer advice to humans with medical issues and help them heal. If I had stayed in that comfortable MD box of the limited version of "I am," I would not be writing this book. As I was called to remember awake over the last few years, the walls of my idea of what an MD box should function like have crumbled. I have been able to create a unique medical practice where I see patients who adhere only to Western medical beliefs, as well as patients who have found me to help heal disease energetically and get mad at me when I recommend Western medicine advice. If I was not surrendered to a true "I AM," I would describe myself as an MD and a healer named Julie Foster. Through loving my mind and heart open, I have allowed those energies to remember and connect with the totality of who we are. I now feel that the closest descriptor of a name I have is essence or time. I feel that my soul does not really have a name anymore because it has been combined with so many other "souls" and energies that a name is unfathomable to it. I also like to feel our souls as one in this dimension of duality by saying, "We are, I AM." Knowing you are all part of me when I say this helps me connect into the common frequency our soul shares, where we have no name and all names and no cages and all cages. This helps me feel the totality of time and essence within me, and it helps me receive whatever energy that is creating awareness in my field at the time as a grace here to share creation in some way with "me." When we have dropped all descriptors of who we are, we are free to know and be all energy. In this vibration, there is no descriptor for "I AM."

Our descriptions provide us with the path to the purpose of this human and soul lifetime, but they also create boxes that limit our potential. The small area within the box can give us the illusion of control and superiority, and thus, we may never want exposure to the vastness outside the box. Boxes can also make us feel trapped and limited. We may be trapped and limited in a box someone else has created about us with the energy they have used to describe our human suit. It is up to you to have the courage to choose to ditch your boxes any time you want by simply dissolving their sides with a simple "I AM." You can find this courage through the energy of anger, sadness, grief, depression, etc. When you feel these emotions, use them to find the gift they offer you by softening into your center and saying, "I am Source, the divine, God, essence" until you find that energy deep in your core and know the energy you sense there is the true you. Then, breathe your center open so that you become that energy. When you say, "I AM," you will feel "who" you truly are and never want to be boxed into the human mind's idea of who you are again. With this opening and remembering of the vibration of love you are, love your mind so it will surrender and become one with the awe of the "I AM." Then imagine with each inhalation and expansion of your lungs/auric field that you can expand the breadth of "I AM" within you to reach every corner and every atom in the universe and remember you are one with their love, energy, patience, connection, and wisdom. With each exhalation, remember that energy has always been part of you. Then, for fun, see if you can feel the atoms of the universe breathing in you. Or even better yet, allow the universe to breathe you as you breathe it simultaneously. (Donna Eden and Master Chunyi Lin inspired the breath techniques here.[1] Also, James Nestor's book *Breath* is worth reading to understand the power of breath.[2])

The "I AM" or the Ohm are sounds many say can help you embody the vibration of God/the divine/Source. I propose that when you make these sounds, you let them melt you open so that you can listen to the energetic, loving knowing of God. Start by allowing them to melt your heart area open and dissolve any "prison" walls of protection you have created to keep you "safe." That safety your subconscious and Ego have created is the cause of all suffering because when you shield yourself from the energy of the oneness that we all are, you are plunged into the game of duality, and that is where we suffer. Suffering is purposeful because we use it to gather the energy of the emotions we feel and create with them. Still, once you have incorporated that vibration into your toolbox, there is no need to continue to inhabit the realm of duality. You can then open your heart and swim into the singularity of consciousness we all have access to that we call God.

How do we find the path out of duality? We listen. We listen with our ears to the subtle vibrations of another's words that we can understand because we have voiced those tones before. We listen with our eyes (open and closed) to the cues of body language that we can identify with and the colors of emotions and dimensions of consciousness we can see with our eyes closed. We listen with our sense of smell to the fragrances of energy that remind us to be open to love more significantly than we have ever known in the felt sense. We hear with our touch, which tells the stories of the energy our human suit emits through the incredible amplifying ability that a human nervous system can grace us with. We listen with our ability to taste because we can taste fear and love. We achieve the maximum capacity to listen with our heart, whose spiderweb of connection (our fascia) is eternally in tune with all that is, was, and ever will be. You sense all with an open heart that is unhindered by fear and allowed to breathe with the one breath of love we were all created from. This is how you melt into and merge with the energy that is the "I AM."

Once you understand the "I AM," you will realize it is never the same and will never want it to be. You will appreciate and crave change because you can't wait for the next epiphany of love and connection to cross your path. When I have been listening for ways for God to come through me and connect with the God particle in the patients I am blessed to cross paths with so that we can both experience the vibrations of God in healing ways, we have felt the following: Hundreds of angels came to play and heal a person with cancer. I have felt a green dimension of loving wisdom I can only describe as the vibration of all the souls we have called God combined as one emitting from me to offer healing to someone who could also feel, and then receive this frequency to heal with it. I have felt the violet flame of St. Germain's transmutative, freeing abilities burn away the energetic entanglements of fear and hurt to help me and others heal with. I have felt the peace needed to heal a crucifixion wound and many other versions of the love that can be embodied and emitted when you tap into the energy of all time and space and become it.

This is my understanding of the "I AM." So, will you melt into your heart and open and play with me soul to soul and God to God today? Will you venture outside your boxes and experience a new form of freedom, connection, and healing? Will you remember you are not the limited definition of what your or another's human mind thinks you are? You are "I AM." I can't wait to play creation with our hearts and minds surrendered to the vibration "I AM" collectively.

In the collective "I AM," we can play the game of creation and manifest a more loving Earth. Please play with me in the "I AM" today. I love you. We got this.

The divine plan

We plan, and God laughs. Will you choose to laugh with that energy of oneness to open your mind and heart today?

At least a few of my close friends have been shedding tears in the last week because life on this planet can sometimes be perceived as very painful. We did not ask to reincarnate in these human bodies for a joyride only. We came here to experience "pain" in a body/mind that thinks time is linear. Your soul created your body and mind to feel a depth of emotions a soul cannot understand without it. Think about that. We came here to immerse ourselves in the entire spectrum of energies we call emotions. We came to feel tears of joy and the rawness and pain of all our uncomfortable emotions. Pain can be used to fracture the boxes our minds trap us in. Once we are free of these cages, we are free to explore the depths of loving consciousness found in the vastness of our hearts. Yet when we feel pain and discomfort, we want to rid ourselves of them as fast as possible. We want someone to take our pain, someone to blame for it, to bury it, and to run away from it. As a result, we find ourselves absorbed in behaviors that help us dissociate from our discomfort, sometimes for very prolonged periods. We need to stop this.

Rarely do we have the insight or the courage to face our discomforts and inquisitively ask, "OK, pain, what information and healing am I supposed to absorb and transmute this time?" and "How can absorbing this information you are gifting me by 'hurting' me so deeply help me and others?" I ask you to take a few deep, gentle, loving breaths and allow yourself to feel your pain. Then if it resonates with you, tell your fear of exploring this pain to fuck off, or just be tired of avoiding the wisdom you will embody by exploring your pain. Surrender your desire to control this step and other steps of your journey, and laugh at the idea of your tiny human brain understanding the grand plan based in love that Source has to benefit you and others when you explore the wisdom and love that can be found in your "pain." Joy is found in acceptance. Surrender your mind to your heart and trust in the fact that everything is going according to God's plan, and your pain is a grace that opens you to knowing God's plan while in a human suit. It is time to surrender to this frequency and "heal" y/our pain.

It is time to heal in a way we may have never healed. I believe that the symbiotic balance of dark and light creates more energy. The veil is thin right now because so many souls in human suits are choosing to play remember awake and are thinning it for our collective consciousness. So, we have access to more love, light, wisdom, and compassion than we have had in a long time. It seems ideal not to waste this opportunity to heal with greater ease. Consider the idea of exchanging the word *sin* for information or opportunity. Release all judgment and see the possibility of creating new energy and understanding from the energy of "pain" that can only be experienced when one inflicts pain on another. Feel deep into the connection between you and another who is causing you pain. Feel that their soul is suffering when they hurt you. (If their hurt is abusive or toxic, please consider these actions from a safe distance and only when you have enough light within you to share because you have understood how to reveal the light that is in the "pain" in you.)

Embrace and embody the power of the light of love and acceptance you find through the path of suffering. Once you discover the light in your pain, you can feel the light in others' pain. This knowing is the key that opens the box that traps you in the idea it is hard to be empathic. Once this box is opened, you will see your empathy as a grace necessary to play singularity in a realm of duality. When you feel another part of your soul as part of yours, you are able to feel the love that lies deep in their pain by finding the love in the frequency of your pain that matches theirs. When you have played this game of finding love in your or another's pain over and over, you will begin to embody a vibration of peace that will remove the old definition of "pain" from the understanding of your mind. Your heart will now define pain for your mind, and with your heart defining pain instead of your mind, your mind will no longer be able to differentiate between pain and love. Your heart will guide you to the bliss of singularity in this dimension of duality, and you will always desire to surrender to this vibration because it is heaven-Earth.

So, will you cast off the judgment that your Ego loves to feel superior with through the word *sin*? See the "sins" of others as Christ did. See "sins" as actions derived from your pain body, which is created when one is lost in the human Ego and separated from Source. See your pain and others' pain as intelligence and energy gathered by brave souls that choose to experience anger, hatred, loneliness, sadness, etc., by taking a trip to this planet and willingly forgetting they are part of an unconditionally loving oneness. Will you choose to experience the essence of "Christ" and "cleanse people of their sins" by gifting them with your love and light to penetrate and merge with their "dark" and create new energy to dispel the lens of separation from God? When you help others find love for themselves through their dark, you understand that the love of God is part of you. This love is so profound that you weep and never want to be in a vibration where you lose connection to its peace and acceptance.

So today, will you embark on the journey of changing the definition your mind has for pain? Will you take a deep breath through your heart chakra when you are suffering and feel our light to help yourself and then others heal y/our collective pain body? The story of Christ teaches us how one can heal another's pain for them. That "one" is found through the connections of an endless heart chakra that defines pain as love. Please consider that you have this same energy within you waiting to be acknowledged and used to heal yourself, others, the planet, and even the essence of the cosmos or the "I AM." Will you find bliss by spreading your beautiful, unique, healing light frequency to as many souls as possible today? You are so loved. Please dive into your pain to discover the bliss of knowing how loved you are.

The dance

I invite you to view your soul's earthly experience as a dance. It is a dance that will always have new steps for you to experience and incorporate into the vibrations of love you can share so that your toolbox of connection is ever-expanding. It is a dance appreciated through the powerful tears of transmutation; it gives the mind a job that aligns with y/our collective soul's purpose.

When our consciousness lands in the awareness of a human suit in this dimension, it acquires the assistance of a human mind and Ego. Many say for spiritual enlightenment, we need to detach from the mind or let it surrender to the energy of our soul. I propose we use it as a tool. Without a mind, we would not understand the vibrations of this dimension. Our consciousness has landed here to collect the powerful energies of human emotions that can only be absorbed and shared with our collective essence through the vibrational translator we call a human mind. We need to dance with our mind, not dismiss it.

What do I mean by this? The next time you are stuck in anger, grief, frustration, anxiety, fear, or any other ouchy emotion, thank your mind and the energy of duality your mind is allowing your soul to experience. Say thank you to your mind for letting you feel pain and collect its powerful energy to create with. Then use that gratitude to feel into the area of your body that is tight or in pain and bring the energy of love into it to transmute this amazing energy that your mind creates for you. I encourage you to surrender to and marvel at the energy of the unique dance we call the game of Earth 2024. Allow one of your legs to be a dance step in "pain" as the other one is in the energy of the collective love and peace of our soul/the divine/God/Source and then picture your legs becoming one as you create a new wavelength of peace for all to dance with you in.

With this dance, the sum of pain and peace equals creation. When we share the pain and peace of our unique dance steps, the power of creation explodes. Believe it or not, we came to play the game of Earth to feel pain and then create with it. In other dimensions, there is just bliss, and we cannot create as well without the power of polarity. We tell ourselves we have gotten stuck in pain for longer periods of time than may be necessary, but those are just steps of the dance that we want to understand fully. We need the time to absorb the full power of that emotion to create something genuinely magnificent with its energy for our toolbox.

So, will you play the game of Earth like you are dancing a never-ending waltz of creation? Will you appreciate your mind and soul for coming together in this dimension to feel pain and honor your soul for doing so? Will you connect with others whose minds are collecting a similar vibration of pain and dance together so that the game of Earth becomes more fun and the capacity to create becomes more powerful? May I have the honor of having you as my divine partner in this magical dance? I love you. We got this.

Connect and feel our oneness

We choose consciousness in this dimension to feel separation, but you are never alone.

Sometime in 2020 or 2021, my body decided to pay attention to and gather information from a reality I had no idea existed. Before 2020, I was using my hands to palpate acupuncture points and asking my patients which one hurt more so I could put the needle in the more painful point. For some reason, this changed in 2020 or 2021. I went from palpating acupuncture points to "knowing" them. In knowing them, I could feel the pain they stored inside by connecting to my patients' energy fields in a way I never had before.

I shared the story of this energy shift with my Rolfer, who is a very old soul, and she guided me into reading books that would help me remember awake the gifts involved in the magic that this dimension labels "biodynamic craniosacral therapy." I also took some classes with Donna Eden of Eden Energy Medicine and read Barbara Brennan's books on healing. I took some more classes with Master Chunyi Lin of Spring Forest Qigong and with Dr. Sue Morter. I could feel energy surges in my body that were so powerful there was nowhere for them to go but out into the world, and sometimes with such force I felt as if I were being ripped open because my chakras were not big enough to handle the amount of energy flow. Through these and many other books and the wisdom of all the amazing teachers that Source guided me to find, I began to understand that by becoming one with the energy entanglements of my patients through the vehicle of pain, I was blessed with remembering awake that there is no separation of my energy from theirs. With this wisdom, the definition of "healing" that Western medicine had taught me dissolved, and the beliefs that my Eastern medicine or acupuncture training had taught me expanded. I have since shifted into a frequency where all the boxes are dissolved at times, and I am free to play healing in a frequency I will call the magic of love.

The process of remembering and incorporating our combined soul's energy into my 3D physical body was very fear-provoking. Trust me when I tell you I have had a lot of fear, especially in the last four years, and splattered that energy on many people. Thankfully, these souls had already loved themselves awake and had the capacity to help me love into my fears. I feel so blessed and eternally grateful that so many kind souls walked with me in the last four years and throughout this lifetime and that they have held space for and taught me how to love my fear so I could walk my steps with greater ease. These are the souls responsible for this book that will hopefully ease your journey of remembering awake. Take a breath with me, and let's send some gratitude to them together now. I have shifted into a new reality by allowing myself to remember that the pain of the patient on the table—or even the pain of humanity and beyond—is my pain. This is a beautiful reality but so different from the one I had lived in for over fifty years. I had difficulty accepting this new magnificent version of oneness reality because we have incorporated a vibration of fear of change into our nervous systems on this planet. I learned to become grateful every time my nervous system began to vibrate in the fear/pain of one of the beautiful souls (reflections of me/us) that sought my assistance in their/our healing because I realized every time I had had an opportunity to explore pain, it gifted me more wisdom and peace.

Peace is found in the flow of change. Exploring energy meridians for blockages caused by fear reveals lakes of pain (tight muscles, neuropathy, lipomas, osteoporosis, arthritis, cancer, etc.). Fear of change creates attachments that solidify as energy dams which prevent our energy rivers (the chi in our meridians) from flowing. When you love the dam for the wisdom of love that it gathers by creating the lake, the dam dissolves and releases the lake so that it can create new rivers, streams, and creeks of flowing energy exploration. The patient's lakes of pain and disease dissolve, and everyone heals because the energy of that particular dam has been loved into universal consciousness for all to heal with when they choose to play remember awake.

Once you are free of your dams, you can choose to remain free by immersing your mind in the flow of the excitement of what you will find around the next bend. Or you may find freedom in the idea of creating a new lake to stop and explore in, knowing you can set that lake of information, wisdom, and love free again anytime you choose to do so. Since I am fortunate enough to play "Love your dams open" with other souls/human suits, I get to experience the rivers they create. Their unique rivers, streams, and creeks always expand me into dimensions where occasionally I get an amazing story to share with you, but at other times are described only through the tears of awe, wonder, gratitude, humility, and connection my heart creates as I witness them.

As I began to accept that there is an energy of magical love we can play with to heal, I felt very alone at times because I thought I was experiencing many of the energy surges alone. I was told by a few, "You are not alone." I heard them say this but was so afraid I could not incorporate the vibration of "you are not alone" into my system. I now know these souls had achieved the state of oneness where my energy was theirs and were vibrating in that frequency but fear and ego kept me from being able to find that frequency in me. Please take a deep breath right now with the image of every fragment of our soul being a sparkling gold star within you. Know when you are breathing, all of our soul is breathing with you while loving you and marveling at how amazingly beautiful you and each step of your journey are. Breathe open your heart and solar plexus so that you can be one with this magnificent reunification of the fractals of our loving soul. You have never been and never will be alone. Please reread this when you feel alone and know that you are loved and cherished more than you can possibly imagine. The fact that you feel someone else's (our collective) energy is the ultimate definition of being not alone. Your mind will keep you in fear by thinking you are the only one who has remembered to open up and feel energy in a way that no one else does. You do have a unique energy signature, but you are not alone. Please feel my/our oneness energy holding space for you right now with a tender cosmic hug so you no longer feel this way.

There is a particle in your center that I call your God particle. This particle is all of our souls living in peace and harmony, connected in the bliss of acceptance. When you find this place by loving yourself and opening your solar plexus so that you get deep into the center where this particle is located and where "the one" of us loves, supports, and creates you, you will never want to take your attention off this divine connection. You will feel the connection of our soul within and then have the light, love, and perceptive abilities to find it in others you come across "outside" of you. This is the place I discovered through exploring the pain of others. Thank you to all the souls I have played healing with. You have gifted me the grace of writing this book.

I spent time playing in person with Dr. Sue Morter in the fall of 2023, and she playfully kept repeating, "There is only one of us here." We are one soul, and we are longing to remember the bliss of this. A loving vibration in this dimension will let you find and feel that bliss. You find this vibration when you surrender your mind to the God particle (love) inside of you from which you were created and will continue to create with. The surrender comes from trusting that you are perfect as is and are an essential piece of the magnificence of our soul. Please surrender your mind to the bliss of knowing we are one and you have never been alone. When you remember awake that connection to oneness, you immerse yourself in a reality where our collective soul is playing the most divine game of creation with the energies of love, humility, and endless giggles. We are blessed to be an essential part of the evolution of the beauty of our soul and the cosmos. Will you feel this bliss of being blessed with me? I love you. We got this.

God

My consciousness expanded in 2022 and reminded my Ego that we are one soul. With this awakening, I discovered in the felt sense that this was not my first lifetime. I have surrendered into my consciousness in many realms and feel I have lived (am living because there is no time) in many places besides this planet. I feel I may have also spent time on this planet in a nonhuman form.

I am a very blessed soul, so to help me stand a little more firmly in this reality that many cannot imagine is possible, I have met many amazing souls living in the same reality. I have met beautiful people who remember they are angels, Pleiadians, Arcturians, Lemurians, and Atlanteans in another dimension. I may have even met St. Germain wearing a human suit while visiting Shasta with a friend in the summer of 2023.

If you believe this reality story is possible, then you can see that some of the souls I call friends may have been or are being perceived as gods in other dimensions. Our souls may have been or are intrinsically linked with Hathor, Isis, Buddha, Shiva, Krishna, and Kali energies, to name a few. When our souls have played "God," they have likely done this through the lens of duality. When we have played God with the emotions of guilt, anger, injustice, frustration, fear, sadness, etc., we have played God through the illusion that the lens of duality creates. When we review our lifetimes in other dimensions, we feel we have made mistakes and thus feel and embody the vibrations of regret and guilt. This regret keeps us in fear of the power of remembering awake that we are creator beings in that we all have a piece of God within us. This God particle resides in the center of our human suit. If we fear this particle, we cannot know and embody the grace of God because we will be too afraid to surrender and merge with that amazing energy.

It is time that we forgive the Ego that played God in this and other dimensions and dissolve all regret that keeps us from becoming one with God. Forgive yourself and allow yourself to tap into the photon inside of you that connects you to all energy. Understand that regret is a concept that the energy of God cannot grasp because it is a lower vibrational energy. The energy of God is love. That is the only vibration it understands. I ask that you take a deep breath or a few while saying, "I am in God, God is in me, we combine as one," and surrender your Ego/mind to your God particle. Please substitute any other name you have for "God" that is more comfortable for you. With this surrender, there is a peace and tranquility that cannot be described. You become one with God by merging with all existing energy and remembering your energy is essential to the creation puzzle. "Miracles" occur when you share this God vibration with another residing in the same place. When we share it with as many souls as possible, think of the reality we could create through a vibration that only understands peace, unity, and love.

So, will you breathe with me and become one with God together today instead of playing God in a game of multidimensional duality? Will you forgive your Ego in this and other dimensions for playing the duality game the way it was meant to be played before you remembered to be one with God instead of playing God? You are, have always been, and will be perfect in the vibration you choose to embody. Choosing to be God while playing with another who desires the same is a fantastic way to play the game of life. Will you join me in creating through the photon-to-photon connected vibration of love responsible for creation today to create a new, more peaceful reality? I look forward to connecting my God particle with your God particle as often as possible. I love you all. We got this.

One

"The true you is the observer, the observed, and the
constant act of observing." —Dr. Sue Morter

I invite you to feel the power of the definition of one in which "one" is you connected to all that is, has been, and ever will be.

When we hear the word *one* in Western culture, we think of individualism. However, many raised in an Eastern culture interpret the word *one* as the combination of all energy. How do you understand the vibration of the definition of *one* connected to all instead of just the Ego of the individual within you? You surrender and allow yourself to melt into the energy you are made of and know yourself as that energy.

As suggested by Dr. Sue Morter in the quote above, become the observer of you. Watch your beautiful soul and mind as they "struggle" to incorporate and understand the step of the path your human suit is discovering. Then, start to feel what it would be like to love your human/soul/merged energy field from afar as if you were its mother, father, creator, lover, bestie, etc. Give that soul the compassion and unconditional love it deserves and desires. Then, as you send that soul your loving energy, ditch the boxes of time and duality and be the soul receiving that love simultaneously. Last, breathe through your energy field with closed eyes and magically understand that you are all those fantastic energies simultaneously. Dissolve into the atoms of those energies. Let the love, patience, peace, compassion, and wisdom found there resonate in every atom you can feel in that space. You may be surprised at how big your energy field's "space" can be, and at the same time, realize the essence of your energy field does not need any "space" because it can be felt in its entirety through your God particle in your center.

I encourage you to always play Earth while remaining in resonance with this awareness of your field. Melt your liquid light into the liquid light of its awareness and become that awareness. In this melding, you meld with all the energy; thus, you are the energy of another's perception and reality. This means if you are angry, they will feel anger. If you are love, they will feel love. If you have described yourself as an empath, you are aware that you share the energy fields of others in this way. However, you may identify with and box your empathic gifts into a victim box, as I did at one time. You can open this box by allowing the "space" you occupy to become bigger instead of smaller. Instead of closing the drawbridges that connect your castle to other realms where frequencies of love and peace can be felt and brought in to add to your energy field, open the drawbridges. Open the conduits within that connect you to the energy state where you are the observer (God) and become that energy. Your castle will become so full of wisdom and new ways to love that you may never see empathy through the lens of victimhood again. Have fun with the idea that you set the tone for the type of world you want to live in. When you stand as an individual Ego, that is what you are, with a very limited lens and energy field through which you can view the world. When you are all energy at once, the lens you look through has a never-ending choice of "miracles" to offer you so you can create the world you desire. I think that we all desire a more peaceful and loving world, so we have to start playing with the vastness of our energy field.

What role will you choose to play today? Will you wear the lens of the observer or the observed? Or will you ditch those lenses and be all energy enjoying the ride of the frequencies of all the simultaneous roles it plays in the game of experience? Will you feel and interact with others with the one of your individual Ego, or will you expand your definition of "one" and emerge from the crippling isolation of the Ego into the indescribable bliss of connectedness to the one of all energy in all time?

The power of heart coherence

I invite you to play with the idea that you are gracing the Earth and beyond with your soul's gift. The volume you share your essence with is up to you.

I have been very fortunate to meet and coexist with some awe-inspiring, loving souls that have blessed me with their presence and guidance. In 2022, I participated in group healing sessions for the first time in my life. In my first group healing session, I could barely feel others' energies. However, as I did more of these, my awareness and understanding of energetic connection was awakened. Therefore, I would like to invite you to try a group healing session so that you also can feel this connection. Dr. Sue Morter guides a meditation on the last Wednesday of every month that is free and very powerful; sign up on her website.[3]

Recently, as I have embraced each step of my journey with a desire to understand, connect, heal, and love more, I have realized we all have very beautiful and unique gifts. When we reach a state of self-compassion and allow the melding of our "dark" and our "light" into one, we strengthen the awareness of our tether to Source (or we know we are Source and there is no separation of identity or energy). When we sense this tether, we can strengthen it to understand that Source is always within us. When you know this, you will feel the unique gift you are providing for Source. As you spend more time playing with your gift in the realm of unconditional love, you will feel more comfortable offering it to others.

I recently realized that when we are all connected in a group meditation and offering our unique gifts to the group, that group resonates with everyone's gift at once. I believe we get to this sacred place through heart coherence. This state is achieved when everyone's hearts are beating in tune with the hearts of others. We can also beat with Earth's energetic heart and the pulse of all energy ever created. When we are in the fluidity of the resonance of cosmic energy and surrender to this with an open heart that listens for and finds the frequency to beat as one with this love, there is no greater bliss. This is the frequency in which we will create a more loving existence for the Earth and all dimensions. When surrendered to this frequency, these are some of the gifts I have felt in others:

- Healing love emission
- People who are reflective rivers and will make sure the energy of the group reaches everyone in such a way that they know how beautiful they are
- Emitters of wisdom
- Emitters of peace
- Emitters of compassion
- Emitters of joy
- Emitters of connection
- People who carry a light that will reach the darkest recesses in anyone and offer them hope and transmutation
- Voices that have a resonance that heals and creates meditative travel
- Those who can bring in information from other dimensions that the group needs for healing and share it effectively
- People who allow you to be you and create a space for self-acceptance

- Engineers who are playing in the quantum realm to strengthen the love resonance of our morphogenic fields
- Those who have the ability to birth and share collective consciousness in this and other dimensions
- People who emit an energetic current you feel as electricity going through your body so that you know you are loved and not playing remembering awake alone

I invite you to imagine what we can do with all of our love-opened resonances combined as one in heart coherence. The bandwidth of this loving frequency is so wide and so diverse it can reach and awaken so many minds and souls so much faster and more powerfully than one heart alone. Will you join a meditative group session with your unique gift surrendered to the will and the power of one so that it can be fully manifested and shared for not only your benefit but for the benefit of all? I promise if you choose to do this, you will never want to be separated from the "one" you feel in the heart coherence of a loving group again. If you don't know what your gift is yet or require healing, join the group anyway because when our hearts are combined as one for the purpose of creating love, Source listens. The connection of those who have learned how to open their hearts and become one with God will be shared with you. You will heal, and your gift will be revealed to you when your mind is surrendered to your open heart and thus able to sense it. Also, remember there is no time in the one, so all of our fires or emotional hurts that keep us trapped in the pain bodies we create in all of our lifetimes can be soothed with the water of our collective soul, and we will heal.

In these groups, there are souls that can connect to realms that are playing a role in healing this dimension so the essence of the wood (the conviction of loving wisdom) in those dimensions will be exchanged for you. When you receive the strength of that multidimensional tree and choose to expand the branches it gives you, you will connect to realms of consciousness you have not remembered you are part of. Eventually, you will no longer perceive you are tethered to Source. Your energetic field and your mind, through surrender and exploration of that expanded field, will know you are Source/God/the divine and that you are sharing your beautiful note with a grand symphony of oneness. So, will you join a meditative or healing group and remember awake the bliss of one? It is time. Thank you for your beautiful gift and precious presence on this planet at this time.

"When we face our own darkness, we remove darkness
from the world." —Kyle Gray, *Light Warrior*[4]

When you are in a healing group, it is easier to love your darkness.

The God particle

What if you had a God particle within you?

The Higgs boson particle has been called the "God particle" in the
media. (Funnily enough, the origin of the popular term is Leon Lederman's
book titled *The God Particle*, which he wanted to call *The Goddamn Particle*
because of how frustrating it was to detect, but his publisher renamed it.[5])
It has been theorized that the related Higgs field may have started interacting with particles like quarks and electrons just after the Big Bang that
created the universe.[6] Particles' interactions with the Higgs field is what
gives these particles their mass.[7] I was not a physics major, but to me, this
means the "God particle" is an energy that creates mass from the thought
energy of collective consciousness. And it is the energy that connects all
energy. What if you had a God particle inside of the matter you are made
of and could learn to play with it?

We, as humans, are part of the energy of the Big Bang. We all were
created from that initial energetic explosion. What if we all had a remnant
of the God particle at the core of our being that was just waiting for us to
discover its presence? What if, when we discovered it, we allowed ourselves
to surrender to it to witness its creative capabilities, wisdom, peace, love,
and endless nurturing connection? What if we then surrendered to our
God particle within and allowed it to radiate from us to create a world we
never imagined could exist?

Is this possible? I think it is. Every healer I know helps others heal by
channeling the energy of love. I think this fantastic capacity to connect
and emit love is found in the center of your body and emerges from a
God particle within you that you just need to imagine is there to find it. It
is a vibration you can request to feel. For me, it is the vibration of peace.
Within you, this particle lies in a dimension where no other emotion is
understood but peace and the love that emanates from this eternal peace.
When I channel a healing vibration to share with humanity to help us heal,
I go to this tiny, extraordinary particle within and allow it to find a vibration
to emit that will be healing for the person/people/energy I am connecting

with at the time. I surrender to the energy of this particle's connection to and emission of collective consciousness and watch the miracle show of playing healing through my God particle. I am always humbled and in awe of the blessings I witness and how I am allowed to play the game of life on this trip to the planet by understanding how to access this photon in the center of me.

You can also play the game of life like this. You can play the game through the love of your God particle. Will you surrender to yours and communicate with others through this unexplainable humbling energy connection of the one of the universe? Will you play the game of life through the lens of the peace, love, connectivity, and creativity in this particle within you? Will you remember how we are one by connecting back to the one we came from and playing in this place of peace with others? Will you remember we are all one soul that chooses the illusion of separation so we can find different energies to experience and create with? Will you rejoice in the feeling of reconnecting our soul through our loving God particles? Will you share a connection and heal yourself and another through your God particle today? Please enjoy playing the Earth game in a way you never imagined possible by playing it surrendered to your God particle. I promise it will be fun. I love you all. We got this!

Our journeys

We all are on a unique journey that has been tailored to our specific needs and the pre-human incarnation planned soul contracts we imagined before we began this lifetime.

When we respect that each one of us is on a unique journey and that this is a miracle because there are so many different ways to approach the same goal, we can be left in awe. I have always been fascinated by the inner workings of others' journeys. As a doctor who practices both Western and Eastern medicine, I see many medical problems as blocked emotions. I have seen many medical issues cured by tenderly loving away the attachment to the trauma that is the source of the emotion that causes an energetic entanglement of a patient's fascia. This box that blocks energy flow and causes disease is loved open by changing the lens through which the patient views the original trauma and replacing it with the lens of love through which God sees. I am always eager to learn what "switch was flicked" in a patient that got them to love themselves open because I can then pass on the frequency of that switch (journey step) to another person who needs a new way to try to love open to heal. When love is the emotion that flows unhindered through our fascia, we will be disease-free because our thoughts (our fascia) create reality, but our emotions solidify it. If you are stuck in the heavy emotion of a trauma, your body will grace you with that knowledge. Suppose you have no idea what the "trauma" is because the information regarding it is stored in your subconscious, or it was not created in this lifetime. In that case, your body will still show you a place where duality has gifted you an opportunity to create with the light of love. There are many healers who can help you love these boxes open without you having to consciously remember what caused them.

Compassion for oneself and the steps of our journeys (which seem so slow and painful at times) will bring a light from within that heals. Caring for and feeding this light within you will help you dissolve the heavy and dimming energy cysts that block your energy field and keep you from being healthy. How will you have patience and compassion for your or another's journey today? What will you learn from another's journey? Who will you share or receive light from today? What wisdom, courage, or inspiration to love more will you gain from another's journey? You and every step of your journey are so loved and appreciated. Let's remember we are journeying together and make this trip to planet Earth way more fun. Let's play healing, connection, and creation while knowing our consciousness can be simultaneously singular and separate in this blessed dimension of Earth. I am so humbled that I get to play with such beautiful reflections of our soul on these magnificent steps of my/our journey. I love you all. We got this!

Acknowledgments

I hope you enjoyed this book, where I shared my thoughts and stories on my remembering awake journey over the last four years. I have been blessed by so many loving souls who made this possible and full of gigglegasms along the way. These souls have helped me embody and share the magnificent vibration of "I am blessed so that I can be a blessing."

I want to thank my daughters, Eden, Grace, and Lily, who always show me a new way to love them and the reality they see and feel through their eyes and hearts. I love their telepathic, at times amazingly sarcastic, witty humor, honesty, and conviction they have in making sure they will leave this world a better place than when they entered it. I would like to thank Guy, the man I was married to for twenty-eight years, for gracing me with the time I got to spend raising our children and finding my true path in life. I want to thank my mother, Marguerite; my brother, Robert; and sisters Patti and Tammy for being the family that graced me with the roots of strength to write this book. I can't forget the nieces and nephews who open my heart to love more when I am around them. Thank you, Bryce, Claire, Sarah, Lexie, Logan, Callie, and last but definitely not least, the ball of magic we call Adrie.

I would also like to thank Jenniffer Weigel, who graces the planet with her tireless efforts to get humanity to wake up and embrace their gifts with ease. Her Spiritual Social Club is the safe place where I meet new members of our awake spiritual family all the time and the place where I was held tenderly as I remembered awake who I truly am. Jen is also responsible for creating a space for me to teach about finding your God particle. Jen, I also want to thank you for the far too numerous to count gigglegasms (thankfully, only one made me pee my pants) and the space you held for my fear of this new reality by picking up the phone and crying and laughing with me when I needed an energetic hug. You are the best.

I want to thank Dr. Sue Morter. I have remembered so much of who I am because of her ability to hold loving space for me and all souls on the planet. The JourneyAwake trips I took to Egypt and France with her and the loving souls she attracts changed my life, and every time I get on the yoga mat and play BodyAwake Yoga with her, I remember another dimension of my/our consciousness. Her monthly healings have been extremely helpful in helping me believe in my gifts. You have helped my heart open in so many ways, Dr. Sue. I will always be eternally grateful to you.

I want to thank Gail Alexander, who created the mandalas for this book. I met Gail less than a year ago as a human, but our souls are timeless friends. Gail, I want to thank you for all the beautiful and powerful mandalas you share with me that help me connect to our consciousness everywhere, even if it feels like I am not very solid for a while after I play with them. Thank you for remembering who I am with your knowledge so I can remember also. I am so grateful to know you and be blessed to giggle with you.

I also want to thank Heather Sprigg, Pat Longo, Flo Magdalena, Gretchen Oehler Hogg, Therese Rowley, Robin Graber, Patti Dettori, Patricia Elliot, Erika A. Olivas and all the other healers who have held space for me to awaken on my journey.

I would like to thank Dr. John Ediss for being a chiropractor who is always available to help me release the stress that causes my muscle pain, and for being gifted enough that I passed a 7mm kidney stone after one of his amazing treatments.

I would also like to thank Karin Love-Ediss for greeting the patients of Flowing Chi Medical with warmth and kindness when they walk through the door, for being a human that can make me smile every time I enter the office we work in, and for being a friend that has supported my transition from MD to MD/healer.

I want to thank the tribe of friends who have supported me when I needed it for close to forty years. Thank you, Katie, Karen, Kim, Kristin, Carrie, Tammy, Dodie, Daniela, Patricia, Sue McGury, and all the others I have been blessed to call friends.

Thank you to the patients who have allowed me to play remember awake by learning about my gifts through playing healing with them. I have been so blessed that you all have supported my nonconventional Flowing Chi Medical practice in such a way. I am blessed to be an MD in 2024 who loves my job. Thank you all so much.

For Further Information

Gail Alexander

www.gail-alexander.com

I Don't Know How I Know . . . I Just Know

Sharing What I Know

The Great Awakening 2020: A Mandalic Journey

Suzanne Alexandria

www.suzannealexandria.com

Barbara Ann Brennan

Hands of Light: A Guide to Healing Through the Human Energy Field

Light Emerging: The Journey of Personal Healing

Deepak Chopra

> *Metahuman: Unleashing Your Infinite Potential*

Thomas Cleary

> *The Immortal Sisters: Secret Teachings of Taoist Women*
>
> *The Secret of the Golden Flower*

Donna Eden

> https://edenmethod.com
>
> *Energy Medicine: Balancing Your Body's Energies for Optimal Health, Joy, and Vitality*

Virginia Essene

> *Earth, the Cosmos, and You: Revelations by Archangel Michael*
>
> (with Irving Feurst) *Energy Blessings from the Stars: Seven Initiations*

Kyle Gray

> *Light Warrior: Connecting with the Spiritual Power of Fierce Love*

Gretchen Oehler Hogg

> www.souljourneys.coach

Jean Houston

> www.evolvingwisdom.com
>
> *The Possible Human: A Course in Enhancing Your Physical, Mental, and Creative Abilities*

Laura Lynne Jackson

> *The Light Between Us: Stories from Heaven. Lessons for the Living.*

Lonny Jarrett

> *Nourishing Destiny: The Inner Tradition of Chinese Medicine*

Pamela Kribbe

> *The Jeshua Channelings: Christ Consciousness in a New Era*
>
> *The Forbidden Female Speaks: Conversations with Mary Magdalene*

The Forbidden Male Speaks: Messages from Jeshua on Love, Relationships, and Heart-Based Masculinity

Vishen Lakhiani

The Code of the Extraordinary Mind: 10 Unconventional Laws to Redefine Your Life and Succeed On Your Own Terms

Laozi

Daodejing

Master Chunyi Lin

https://www.springforestqigong.com

Born A Healer: I Was Born a Healer. You Were Born a Healer, Too!

Dr. Bruce Lipton

The Biology of Belief: Unleashing the Power of Consciousness, Matter & Miracles

The Living Matrix (documentary)

Pat Longo

www.patlongo.net

The Gifts Beneath Your Anxiety: A Guide to Finding Inner Peace for Sensitive People

Flo Magdalena

https://www.soulsupportsystems.org

Sunlight on Water

I Remember Union: The Story of Mary Magdelena

Eva Marquez

www.evamarquez.org

Pleiadian Code I: The Great Soul Rescue

Pleiadian Code II: Cosmic Love

Pleiadian Code III: Alien Fragment

Activate Your Cosmic DNA: Discover Your Starseed Family from the Pleiades, Sirius, Andromeda, Centaurus, Epsilon Eridani, and Lyra

Lynne McTaggart

The Field: The Quest for the Secret Force of the Universe

Drunvalo Melchizedek

The Ancient Secret of the Flower of Life, Volume 2

Dan Millman

Way of the Peaceful Warrior: A Book That Changes Lives

Anita Moorjani

Dying to Be Me: My Journey from Cancer, to Near Death, to True Healing

Dr. Sue Morter

www.drsuemorter.com

The Energy Codes: The 7-Step System to Awaken Your Spirit, Heal Your Body, and Live Your Best Life

Angela Muñoz

www.expectlotus.com

Caroline Myss

Intimate Conversations with the Divine

James Nestor

Breath: The New Science of a Lost Art

Michael Newton

Journey of Souls: Case Studies of Life Between Lives

Erika A. Olivas

https://aurorahearthealing.com

Lori Rhodes

lori@biofieldtuning.com

Dr. Therese M. Rowley

> https://thereserowley.com
>
> *Mapping a New Reality: Discovering Intuitive Intelligence*

Michael J. Shea

> *Biodynamic Craniosacral Therapy, Volumes 1–3*

Heather Sprigg

> www.angelhealer111.com

Asha Swaroop

> www.ashaveda.org

Eckhart Tolle

> *A New Earth: Awakening to Your Life's Purpose*
>
> *The Power of Now: A Guide to Spiritual Enlightenment*

Dr. John Upledger

> *SomatoEmotional Release: Deciphering the Language of Life*
>
> *Your Inner Physician and You: CranoioSacral Therapy and SomatoEmotional Release*

Jennlffer Weigel

> www.jenweigel.com
>
> *I'm Spiritual, Dammit!: How to Keep Your Feet on the Ground and Your Head in the Stars*
>
> *Stay Tuned: Conversations with Dad from the Other Side*
>
> *This Isn't The Life I Ordered . . . : Setting Sail When Your Relationship Fails*

Dr. Brian L. Weiss

> *Many Lives, Many Masters: The True Story of a Prominent Psychiatrist, His Young Patient, and the Past-Life Therapy That Changed Both Their Lives*
>
> *Same Soul, Many Bodies: Discover the Healing Power of Future Lives through Progression Therapy*

Notes

Chapter 1. Playing Awake with Nature

1. Eva Marquez, Spiritual Consultant, Soul Healer and Author, https://evamarquez.org.

2. Lori Rhodes, email: lori@biofieldtuning.com

3. Gretchen Oehler Hogg, Soul Journeys Coach, http://www.souljourneys.coach.

4. Heather Sprigg, Angel Medium and Healer, https://www.angelhealer111.com.

5. Erika A. Olivas, Aurora Heart Healing, https://aurorahearthealing.com.

6. Angela Muñoz, Expect Lotus, https://www.expectlotus.com.

7. Dr. Sue Morter, Bridging Science, Spirit & Human Possibility, https://drsuemorter.com.

8. Jenniffer Weigel, I'm Spiritual, Dammit!, https://www.jenweigel.com.

9. Gail Alexander, Energy Mandalas, https://www.gail-alexander.com.

10. Pat Longo, Spiritual Healer, https://www.patlongo.net.

11. Flo Magdalena, Soul Support Systems, https://www.soulsupportsystems.org.

12. Jean Houston, Evolving Wisdom, https://evolvingwisdom.com.

13. Thomas Cleary, Editor and Translator, *Immortal Sisters: Secret Teachings of Taoist Women*, second edition (North Atlantic Books, 1996).

14. Thomas Cleary, Translator, *The Secret of the Golden Flower* (HarperOne, 1993).

15. Deepak Chopra, *Metahuman: Unleashing Your Infinite Potential* (Harmony, 2019).

Chapter 2. Exploring Ego

1. Flo Aeveia Magdalena, *Sunlight on Water: A Manual for Soul-Full Living* (De Agostini, 1996).

2. OWN, "The Best Advice Dr. Maya Angelou Has Ever Given—and Received | SuperSoul Sunday | OWN," May 19, 2013, 4 min. 1 sec., https://www.youtube.com/watch?v=aHvTWvKIPHo.

3. Caroline Myss *Intimate Conversations with the Divine* (Hay House, 2020), 119.

Chapter 3. Discovering the Power of Our Light

1. Pamela Kribbe, *The Jeshua Channelings: Christ Consciousness in a New Era* (Booklocker, 2008).

2. David G. Myers, C. Nathan DeWall, and June Gruber, *Psychology*, 14th edition (Worth Publishers, Macmillan Learning, 2024).

3. Rachel Yehuda and Amy Lehrner, "Intergenerational transmission of trauma effects: putative role of epigenetic mechanisms," *World Psychiatry*, 17 (2018): 243–257, https://doi.org/10.1002/wps.20568.

4. Caroline Myss, *Anatomy of the Spirit: The Seven Stages of Power and Healing* (Harmony, 1996), 5.

5. Laura Lynne Jackson, *The Light Between Us: Stories from Heaven. Lessons for the Living.* (The Dial Press, 2016).

6. Condolence letter to Norman Salit (March 4, 1950), Albert Einstein.

7. Perla Trevizo, "A year before Uvalde shooting, gunman had threatened women, carried around a dead cat and been nicknamed 'school shooter,'" *Texas Tribune* and *ProPublica*, July 17, 2022, https://www.texastribune.org/2022/07/17/uvalde-shooter-warnings-background.

8. Albert Einstein, *On Cosmic Religion and Other Opinions and Aphorism* (Covici-Friede, 1931).

9. "Conversations with Masters: Jean Houston," transcript, Stagen, accessed September 19, 2024, https://stagen.com/wisdom/jean-houston.

10. Drunvalo Melchizedek, *The Ancient Secret of the Flower of Life, Volume 2* (Light Technology Publishing, 2000).

11. "GVA – 10 Year Review," Gun Violence Archive, accessed September 19, 2024, https://www.gunviolencearchive.org.

12. Amy O'Kruk, Kenneth Uzquiano, and Anna Brand, "In the last decade, an estimated 40 million Americans lived within 1 mile of a mass shooting," CNN, August 30, 2023, accessed September 19, 2024, https://www.cnn.com/interactive/2023/08/us/americans-living-near-mass-shootings-statistics-dg.

13. The global peace index has decreased nearly every year since 2008, and both external and ongoing conflicts have increased significantly since then as well.

    "Global Peace Index 2024: Measuring Peace in a Complex World," Institute for Economics & Peace, June 2024, accessed September 19, 2024, https://www.visionofhumanity.org/resources.

Chapter 4. Hearing Awake

1. Vishen Lakhiani, *The Code of the Extraordinary Mind: 10 Unconventional Laws to Redefine Your Life and Succeed On Your Own Terms* (Rodale, 2016), 173.

2. Eckhart Tolle, *A New Earth: Awakening to Your Life's Purpose* (Penguin, 2016), 129–160.

3. *The Living Matrix*, Greg Becker (2009; United States; Emaginate).

4. Virginia Essene and Irving Feurst, *Energy Blessings from the Stars: Seven Initiations* (Spirtunfold, 1998).

Chapter 5. Playing Healing Open with Your Heart

1. Graham Lawrence, "Love," *Webster's Unabridged Dictionary* (C. & G. Merriam Co., 1913), accessed online October 2, 2024, https://www.gutenberg.org/ebooks/29765.

2. Virginia Essene, *Earth, the Cosmos, and You: Revelations by Archangel Michael* (S. E. E. Publishing Company, 1999).

3. "Guilt," *Merriam-Webster*, last updated September 14, 2024, accessed September 25, 2024, https://www.merriam-webster.com/dictionary/guilt.

Chapter 6. Remembering the Grace of Flow

1. Dr. Sue Morter, *The Energy Codes* (Atria Books, 2019), 16.

2. Dr. Sue Morter's Youtube channel, https://www.youtube.com/@DrSueMorter.

3. Ronelle Wood, "Fascia Magnified 25x (Subtitled)," February 1, 2013, 3 min., 10 sec., https://www.youtube.com/watch?v=uzy8-wQzQMY.

4. John E. Upledger, *Craniosacral Therapy* (Eastland Press, 1983).

5. Lonny S. Jarrett, *Nourishing Destiny: The Inner Tradition of Chinese Medicine* (Spirit Path Press, 2004), 87, 93.

6. Laozi, *Daodejing*, Verse 71.

7. Suzanne Alexandria, Healer's Healer, Angelic Channel, Spiritual Coach, http://www.suzannealexandria.com.

Chapter 7. The Frequencies We Play Healing In

1. Dr. Therese M. Rowley, Advanced Intuitive Insight, https://thereserowley.com/.

2. Michael Newton, *Journey of Souls: Case Studies of Life Between Lives* (Llewellyn Publications,1994).

3. Morter, *The Energy Codes.*

4. Matt Strassler, "How the Higgs Field (Actually) Gives Mass to Elementary Particles," *Quanta Magazine*, accessed October 2, 2024, https://www.quantamagazine.org/how-the-higgs-field-actually-gives-mass -to-elementary-particles-20240903/.

Chapter 8. Remembering the Joy of Embodying Oneness

1. Essene, *Earth, the Cosmos, and You.*

2. Asha Swaroop, Ashaveda Executive Life Coaching, https://www.ashaveda.org.

3. Dr. Shefali Tsabary, *A Radical Awakening: Turn Pain into Power, Embrace Your Truth, Live Free* (HarperOne, 2021).

4. Morter, *The Energy Codes,* 59.

5. Laozi, *Daodejing,* Verse 10.

Chapter 9. Godding Up

1. Donna Eden, Eden Energy Medicine, https://edenenergymedicine.com, and Master Chunyi Lin, Spring Forest Qigong, https://www.springforestqigong.com/master-chunyi-lin.

2. James Nestor, *Breath: The New Science of a Lost Art* (Riverhead Books, 2020).

3. Dr. Sue Morter, https://drsuemorter.com.

4. Kyle Gray, *Light Warrior: Connecting with the Spiritual Power of Fierce Love* (Hay House, 2017).

5. Leon M. Lederman with Dick Teresi, *The God Particle: If the Universe is the Answer, what is the Question?* (Houghton Mifflin, 2006), 22.

6. Heather Gray and Bruno Mansoulié, "The Higgs boson: the hunt, the discovery, the study and some future perspectives," ATLAS Experiment, CERN, accessed on September 27, 2024, https://atlas.cern/updates/feature/higgs-boson.

7. Department of Energy, https://www.energy.gov/science/doe-explainsthe-higgs-boson.

Julie Foster, MD, has been board-certified by the American Board of Family Medicine since 2000. She was trained in medical acupuncture by the Academy of Pain Research in 2015 and became an energy healer in 2021. Dr. Foster blends Western, Eastern, and energy medicine techniques to help you find a way to heal. She opened Flowing Chi Medical in 2017 to have more time with patients and explore the realm of medical acupuncture so that she could help them heal instead of offering them a pharmaceutical bandage during a five-minute visit. She realized that diseases can be cured by releasing the emotional blockages in the body's energy meridians that cause disease. When her hands "turned on" in 2021, she began to play with the techniques of energy medicine, and through this, she discovered that we all have a God particle in the center of our body and that when those photons connect through love, "God heals God," and miracles become an everyday occurrence.

You can learn more about Dr. Foster at www.flowingchimedical.com and www.brightenallsouls.com.